D1202157

INFANTRY

An Oral History of a World War II American Infantry Battalion

TWAYNE'S

ORAL HISTORY SERIES

Donald A. Ritchie, Series Editor

PREVIOUSLY PUBLISHED

Rosie the Riveter Revisited: Women, The War, and Social Change
Sherna Berger Gluck

Witnesses to the Holocaust: An Oral History
Rhoda Lewin

Hill Country Teacher: Oral Histories from the One-Room School and Beyond
Diane Manning

The Unknown Internment: An Oral History of the Relocation of Italian Americans during World War II
Stephen Fox

Peacework: Oral Histories of Women Peace Activists
Judith Porter Adams

Grandmothers, Mothers, and Daughters: Oral Histories of Three Generations of Ethnic American Women
Corinne Azen Krause

Homesteading Women: An Oral History of Colorado, 1890–1950
Julie Jones-Eddy

The Hispanic-American Entrepreneur: An Oral History of the American Dream
Beatrice Rodriguez Owsley

FORTHCOMING TITLES

Between Management and Labor: Oral Histories of Arbitration
Clara H. Friedman

Building Hoover Dam: An Oral History of the Great Depression
Dennis McBride and Andrew Dunar

RICHARD M. STANNARD

INFANTRY

An Oral History of a World War II American Infantry Battalion

TWAYNE PUBLISHERS • NEW YORK
Maxwell Macmillan Canada • Toronto
Maxwell Macmillan International • New York Oxford Singapore Sydney

To Elaine

Twayne's Oral History Series No. 9

Infantry: An Oral History of a World War II American Infantry Battalion
Richard M. Stannard

Twayne Publishers
Macmillan Publishing Company
866 Third Avenue
New York, New York 10022

Maxwell Macmillan Canada, Inc.
1200 Eglinton Avenue East
Suite 200
Don Mills, Ontario M3C 3N1

Library of Congress Cataloging-in-Publication Data

Stannard, Richard M.
Infantry : an oral history of World War II American Infantry Battalion / Richard M. Stannard.
p. cm. — (Twayne's oral history series ; no. 9)
Includes bibliographical references and index.
ISBN 0-8057-9112-4 (hc). — ISBN 0-8057-9117-5 (pbk.)
1. United States. Army. Division, 103d. Infantry Regiment, 410th. Battalion, 2nd—History. 2. World War, 1939-1945—Regimental histories—United States. 3. World War, 1939-1945—Personal narratives, American. 4. World War, 1939-1945—Campaigns—Europe. I. Title. II. Series.
D769.31 410th.S73 1992 92-30199
940.54'1273—dc20 CIP

The paper used in this publication meets the minimum requirements of American National Standard for Information Sciences—Permanence of Paper for Printed Library Materials. ANSI Z3948-1984.∞™

10 9 8 7 6 5 4 3 2 1 (hc)
10 9 8 7 6 5 4 3 2 1 (pb)

Printed in the United States of America

Contents

Foreword

"Everyone who remembers a war first-hand knows that its images remain in the memory with special vividness," Paul Fussell wrote in his classic study, *The Great War and Modern Memory*. All too often military history has focused on grand strategic planning and the lives of high-ranking officers, to the exclusion of the foot soldiers who retain their own vivid memories. The perspective of the infantryman differs greatly from the view from headquarters behind the lines, and perception similarly diverges according to location. Memory being largely dependent on perception, Richard Stannard collected the recollections of his own infantry battalion—including its second lieutenant, Paul Fussell — to recreate their combat experiences in Europe during the Second World War. Taken together they offer a gritty, realistic, soldier's eye-view of the battlefield, as well as the anxiety and anguish of their families back home. Their stories combine fear and courage, tactics and circumstance, survival and death. Regardless of technological changes in modern warfare, the emotions they summon back remain timeless. During the war's fiftieth anniversary, this oral history serves as a fitting tribute to those who fought on its front lines.

Oral history may well be the twentieth century's substitute for the written memoir. In exchange for the immediacy of diaries or correspondence, the retrospective interview offers a dialogue between the participant and the informed interviewer. Having prepared sufficient preliminary research, interviewers can direct the discussion into areas long since "forgotten," or no longer considered of consequence. "I haven't thought about that in years" is a common response, uttered just before an interviewee commences with a surprisingly detailed description of some past incident. The quality of the interview, its candidness and depth, generally will depend as much on the interviewer as the interviewee, and the confidence and rapport between the two adds a special dimension to the spoken memoir.

Interviewers represent a variety of disciplines and work either as part of a collective effort or individually. Regardless of their different interests or the variety of their subjects, all interviewers share a common imperative: to collect memories while they are still available. Most oral historians feel an additional responsibility to make their interviews accessible for use beyond their own research needs. Still, important collections of vital, vibrant interviews lie scattered in archives throughout every state, undiscovered or simply not used.

Twayne's Oral History Series seeks to identify those resources and to publish selections of the best materials. The series lets people speak for themselves, from their own unique perspectives on people, places, and events. But to be more than a babble of voices, each volume organizes its interviews around particular situations and events and ties them together with interpretive essays that place individuals into the larger historical context. The styles and format of individual volumes vary with the material from which they are drawn, demonstrating again the diversity of oral history and its methodology.

Whenever oral historians gather in conference, they enjoy retelling experiences about inspiring individuals they met, unexpected information they elicited, and unforgettable reminiscences that would otherwise have never been recorded. The result invariably reminds listeners of others who deserve to be interviewed, provides them with models of interviewing techniques, and inspires them to make their own contribution to the field. I trust that the oral historians in this series, as interviewers, editors, and interpreters, will have a similar effect on their readers.

DONALD A. RITCHIE
Series Editor, Senate Historical Office

Acknowledgments

First of all, my thanks to the veterans of the Second Battalion and their wives who spoke so frankly of their wartime memories. Without their cooperation, this book would never have happened. They provided leads, they dined and housed me, and they sat patiently through interviews that typically lasted two hours or more.

My thanks to my wife, Elaine, who was the first reader of the manuscript and provided many helpful suggestions.

And my thanks to my sister, Emily Stannard Levine, who doesn't know it, but who had a lot to do with this project. A wartime bride of 19, she packed up and traveled alone by train from Santa Barbara to Boston to be with her sailor husband at a time when she had never been east of Sacramento.

My thanks to the very professional staff of the Seattle City Library who led me to books and documents and patiently answered arcane questions over the telephone, and to the archivists of the National Archives and Records Administration in Suitland, Maryland, who provided essential documents from their incredible treasure trove.

And finally, to Carolyn Reeder, who guided me through at least some of the mysteries of word processing.

Most of the battalion's war was fought in the Vosges region of Alsace, France, but it ended with a fast trip through southern Germany and Austria. *Map by Karen Schober*

Introduction

The world thought the war in Europe was all but over when the Second Battalion of the 410th Infantry Regiment, 103d Division, went into combat on Armistice Day 1944.

The 900 men of the battalion arrived in Marseilles in late October and rode in jam-packed trucks for 350 miles north up the Rhône River Valley as fall turned toward winter.

The battalion was typical of the infantry combat units that fought the European war from D-day on 6 June 1944 until the German surrender on 7 May 1945. In that scant 11 months, American divisions in France increased from the 5 that made the Normandy invasion to 42 infantry divisions, 16 armored divisions, and 3 airborne divisions—nearly one million men. Over half of them arrived in the fall and winter of 1944, some as late as March 1945. All saw combat and suffered casualties. Overall, infantry and marine divisions accounted for 77 percent of American military deaths in World War II.

Ninety-one thousand men were killed in the fighting in France, Germany, and Austria—about 74 percent of the total army infantry deaths in World War II. Of these, 821 were suffered by the 103d. The Second Battalion of the 410th accounted for 66 killed.

The 103d was a typical "triangle" division, with three regiments: the 409th, 410th, and 411th, plus artillery, quartermaster, and other support units. Each of the regiments, in turn, had three battalions, and each battalion had three rifle companies. This story is about the three rifle companies of the Second Battalion:[1] E (Easy), F (Fox), and G (George), and its supporting heavy weapons unit, H Company.

The 103d Division was formed in 1942 of farmers, craftsmen, and laborers drafted from civilian life in the first months of the war. For two years, they trained in the swamps of Louisiana at Camp Claiborne, and then on the plains of northeast Texas at Camp Howze. Twice, the division was stripped of its trained men for replacements.

In the spring of 1944, with the massive D-day landings in France scheduled for that June, the 103d was rebuilt with thousands of students, primarily from the Army Specialized Training Program (ASTP), but also from the air force. These youths, intellectually the cream of the army's millions of draftees, had been students in uniform in colleges all over the country, looking forward to second lieutenant's commissions as meteorologists, engineers, and language specialists. Cancellation of their safe, prestigious programs came as a shock, but they soon blended into their new units.[2] Fast learners and ambitious, they were a pleasant surprise to the division's officers.

Along with the old-timers and the ASTPers, there was a third source of manpower in the division that finally went overseas: 18-year-olds like myself. Trained at infantry replacement training centers, 18-year-olds could be sent overseas only as members of divisions, not as replacements. The dubious theory was that our survival chances would be better that way.

A small fourth group of career soldiers (lifers) completed the makeup. Few in number, they proved to be the backbone of the battalion. Everyone was white. The army was totally segregated, although the all-black 614th Tank Destroyer Battalion was attached to the battalion from time to time.

Infantrymen did most of the dying, but little more than half of them routinely had their necks on the line. The rest were cooks, bakers, armorers, truck drivers, doctors, planners, generals. To the rifleman in the foxhole, they were as remote and safe and comfy as his own living room back in Paducah.

The rifle battalions, as they were sometimes called, had no independent identity except to the men who served in them. In each regiment, they were numbered, logically enough, as "1st," "2d," and "3d." Only with rare exceptions did they operate outside their own division. The best-known exception was the 100th Battalion, later incorporated into the 442d Regimental Combat Team. These were all-nisei outfits (except for a large number of white officers) who fought as independent units in the racially segregated army.

Most of the riflemen carried semiautomatic M-1 rifles (called "Garands" by civilians, after their inventor), which fired eight rounds a clip. Each squad also had a Browning Automatic Rifle (BAR), a cumbersome, powerful hangover from World War I. A fourth company, H (Howe), was equipped with heavy .30-caliber, water-cooled machine guns and 81-millimeter mortars.

There were three rifle platoons and a weapons platoon in each company. The latter had two .30-caliber light machine guns and three 60-millimeter mortars.[3] The machine gunners from the weapons platoon and from H Company were assigned to the platoons leading the attack.

Every company had an "FO" (artillery forward observer), whose job was to call in close support artillery fire. Finally, each platoon had a medical aid man assigned to give battlefield first aid. These aid men ran all the risks of other front line troops. Several riflemen tell how medics saved their lives, sometimes at the cost of their own.

Every rifleman was acutely aware of a hierarchy of hazard. The first scout, who was out in front of everybody else, envied the lieutenant, who might be 25 yards behind him. The lieutenant envied the company commander, who was 200 yards back. Viewed from the top down, division headquarters clerks considered the job of artilleryman dangerous. Mortarmen, who were right behind the lines, thought they lived in safety compared to the riflemen.

An astringent observer and recorder of this scene is Paul Fussell, distinguished professor of English at the University of Pennsylvania. Fussell was a second lieutenant in F Company, and nearly lost his life as a result.

Like every other man who fought in the infantry, he has been marked for life by the experience. Although professing little in common with the men with whom he served, he dedicated one of his best-known books, *The Great War and Modern Memory* (1975), to his platoon sergeant, Edward K. Hudson, who was killed by the same artillery blast that nearly killed Fussell.

"The war. I'm still in it," Fussell says.

As a consequence, Fussell has given up scholarly, arcane discussions of English literature to become this country's foremost commentator on the meaning and the realities of war. He shared some of his views for this book.

FUSSELL

I was young, I was athletic, I was stupid, I was very gung ho and I thought I would be a good small-unit infantry commander. I wouldn't think that now, but in those days I did. It never entered my mind that I was entering perhaps the most hazardous job in the whole army. And I assumed the war would be over before I got into combat. The Americans had taken Paris and reached the Rhine River before we got to Europe. I assumed the Germans were rational people, which proved not to be.

*

Fussell was wounded 15 March 1945, and spent three months in hospitals before returning to F Company, just as the 103d Division was breaking up, in July 1945. The European war was over, but Americans and Japanese were locked in a savage battle for Okinawa at that time. Fussell, along with many other members of the 103d, was transferred to the veteran 45th Division. Destination: Japan. Like everyone else in the European theater, he expected even more deadly fighting in the Pacific.

FUSSELL

We were bound for Japan, and I assumed I would be killed at some point.

If you assumed that, did you consider taking off for South America?

FUSSELL

Never. I would have disgraced my parents. Everybody was expected to act properly.

Isn't it amazing that thousands of men assumed they were going to die and yet went ahead and followed orders?

FUSSELL

That's what you did. Any other course of action would have been unthinkable. I assumed I was going to lead a rifle platoon up the beach at Kyushu and be machine-gunned to death. A Canadian interviewer a few years ago asked me how it is possible to order men into situations where you know they're going to be damaged: killed or wounded. I told him you just do it. You don't think about it because somebody's done this to you as well.

But that does not explain why a man goes ahead and does something irrational that he knows will probably get him killed, like staying with a division that was going to attack Japan.

FUSSELL

Yes, but there's no alternative. I recall what James Jones said. He and his son were at the Antietam battlefield when his son asked him, "Why did these young men do it?" Jones's answer, I think, is the answer to our question: "Because they didn't want to appear unmanly in front of their friends."

What was your mental attitude, anticipating all of that?

FUSSELL

I said, "I'm dead already. It doesn't matter. I'm going to be killed." I slept very soundly. Just a matter of waiting for it to pass, waiting for it to come. I hoped it wouldn't be painful. Fear didn't seem to enter. I'd overcome my fear the day I was wounded. "There isn't anything I can do about it anymore, so why think about it? Let's have some fun." [Fussell tells the rest of his story in chapter 11.]

*

As it turned out, the war in the Pacific ended before Fussell's new division left Europe. He and the other infantrymen in this book thus survived to tell of the extraordinary things that happened to ordinary men in a few short months in 1944 and 1945.

It was dangerous, unforgettable work. Churchill once said, "Nothing in life is so exhilarating as to be shot at without result." A corollary could be that nothing in life is so unforgettable as to be wounded and survive. During the two-day attack in March 1945 that led to the final breakthrough into Germany, 46 of G Copmpany's men were killed or wounded; F Company lost 55, including Fussell. Some of the wounded were permanently disabled.

There were few such days, fortunately, but the tension and anxiety were unremitting. Soldiers never knew when a wrong step would set off a mine or a careless nighttime cigarette would attract a sniper's bullet.

I was a rifleman in the Second Battalion, drafted a few months earlier from Southern California. Those brief six months of combat have been a powerful part of me ever since, but it was not until I attended a reunion of the battalion in 1985 that I discovered how true that was for all of us.

Some of these men have been attending reunions since 1948; four of them even have a minireunion of their machine gun squad. As I listened to the talk at that first meeting, I realized I was hearing stories that should be preserved. Eyewitness knowledge of the war is disappearing every year. Several men have died during preparation of this book.

Unlike rear-echelon soldiers for whom the war was an exotic vacation, these frontline veterans talked of life and death, and the luck that produced one or the other.

Armed with a microcassette tape recorder at the 1986 reunion in St. Louis, I set out to collect these stories. It was a project that stretched over six years.

The first step was the interviews. Seventy-seven veterans of the battalion and their wives were interviewed. Women as well as men were deeply influenced by these events, particularly those whose husbands were killed or disabled. Their memories were surprisingly consistent, considering the nearly half-century that has passed.

I supplemented the interviews with casualty reports, battle descriptions, and radio logs, all carefully preserved in the National Archives in Washington,

Then and now. The author at 19. Men and women of the 1990 reunion of the Second Battalion (author standing sixth from left).
Group photo courtesy of Reunion Photo

D.C. Top secret at the time, these documents have been declassified and are available to any interested person. I found occasional errors in casualty statistics and made the necessary corrections. These archives documents were the essential underpinning for this book.

Although officially "in combat" for 166 days, nearly all of the battalion's fighting was packed into 11 days, mostly for obscure villages in a few square miles of eastern Alsace, France. Only the last battle was in Germany. The "battle villages" in France were Nothalten-Itterswiller-Andlau, 30 November 1944; Offwiller-Rothbach-Bischholtz-Schillersdorf, 21–27 January 1945; and Gundershoffen-Engwiller, 15–16 March 1945. Finally, there was Erkenbrechtsweiler, Germany, 22–23 April 1945.

These names will not be familiar to most of the men who fought there. It will come as a surprise to most of them that the battalion fought as a unit much of the time. The soldiers walked and walked through the snowy mountains of the Vosges that winter without knowing where they were, following the man in front of them, never understanding the strategy. They fed on K rations and rumors and knew little about what was going on, even in the next foxhole or the next platoon. Many members of E Company, for example, believe one of their commanding officers was court-martialed and executed for giving secrets to the enemy. In fact, he was investigated but never prosecuted.

Until spring, they almost never got a ride unless they were wounded, but after the Seventh Army's breakthrough in March 1945, they joined the mad race through a collapsing Germany on tanks, trucks, jeeps, weapons carriers, and even horses.

In this book, they tell what happened to them in those six months, how most survived and some did not, until the Germans surrendered in Innsbruck, Austria, on 4 May 1945.

ONE

E Company

Kenneth Kopko.

I

THE FIRST

Kenneth Kopko of Queens, New York, was one of those young men who had everything: tall and handsome, intelligent, a member of a large and loving family, future West Point lieutenant.

Kenneth Kopko at the age of 19 was the first soldier in the Second Battalion to die in the war—not in combat, really, but from a random mortar shell, which came in as he sat on the edge of his foxhole. It was E Company's first day on the line, 11 November 1944.

Already accepted by West Point, he was waiting for orders to transfer back to the States and the safe life of a military cadet when the shell came in.

MARION KOPKO

He was my first cousin. Boy, you're whipping up a lot of memories. He was 18 when he joined the army, a very smart young man, and 19 when he died. Only two weeks before he left for overseas, he made out a will. We were all together that evening when he told us, "I'm never going to see you again." It was such a strong premonition. The family got very upset.

1st Lt. MARVIN SHELLEY
E Company

I knew him pretty well. An officer had to be present when he took the [West Point] test, and I happened to be the officer. He passed on the first try. What got me was he was one of the smartest, most intelligent, capable young men we had.

ELIZABETH BESENBECK
Kenneth Kopko's aunt

I never knew he won the appointment. We were all hoping, of course. It was my husband, Bernhard, who got him to apply. He was a smart, gifted boy, but very shy. He didn't think he had a chance, but my husband urged him to try.

ROBERT BRENNAN
mortarman

[Kopko] was a real clean-cut kid. He and another guy were outside their foxhole. There was a little sunlight coming through the pines, and they were sitting on the edge of their hole talking. A mortar burst came in and caught him right in the back. Just about split him open. We found out later he was going to be relieved and shipped back to America.

I was two foxholes away. We didn't fool with Kopko, but I helped carry the other kid out that was with him. He was hit in the arm and shoulder.[1] Kopko was almost a direct hit.

RAY MYSLIWIEC
mortarman

It was a tree burst from a mortar. The shell went through the top of his helmet and came out through his jaw. That was my baptism of fire. I had to erase what I'd seen from my mind and go on. I had to realize it was an individual that I wouldn't see again.

THE REVEREND WILLIAM KLEFFMAN
Catholic chaplain

His fiancée wrote to me. She could not believe he was killed, so I had to assure her that it was true. We had his dog tags.

MARION KOPKO

Kenny's sister, Doris, could not accept that he was dead. She went to mass every day for two years. She absolutely refused to believe her brother was gone. It was a terrible strain on the rest of the family. Finally, she accepted it. Then they brought his body back after the war. That was another horror.

JUNE BEST
Kopko's cousin

Kenny and his sister, Doris, were very close. I remember so well how intelligent and good-looking he was, about six feet two with sandy brown hair and grayish eyes. My memories go back to the summers we spent at the beach at Rockaway Point. He went to Sacred Heart Grammar School, but he went to public high school. I wrote little letters to him when he went in the service. I was ten when he died.

DR. RICHARD BARRY
widower of Doris Kopko Barry

Doris still wasn't over it when I came into the picture in the fifties. She didn't want her own son to go to war. She was very antiwar, very vocal about Vietnam. (Mrs. Barry died in 1984.)

MARION KOPKO

Kenneth was two years older than me. Our families had summer homes at Rockaway Point. All the girls would say, "He's your cousin?" He was a very handsome young man, but very shy.

ELIZABETH BESENBECK

Kenny was a wonderful person. His death was the downfall of my poor sister, Margaret, Kenny's mother. He was her only son. She was no good after that.

7852-84 St
Glendale N.Y.
Dec 10, 1944

My Dearest Kenneth,
How are you my dear Son
I have not heard from you in a long time what is wrong Dear Ken, Did you receive the letter with the pins for your watch in it.
also the letter with the medel in it or some of the packogs
Fred Cloer sent a letter home here to you that he received his wings. I will send it to you, his address is

Margaret Kopko's last letter to her son. She wrote to him 10 December 1944, unaware he was killed a month earlier. *Courtesy of Elizabeth Besenbeck and Beth Barry.*

-2-

is not on it, so I dond see how you are going to answer it.
How are things over there with you, have you met anyone you know yet or any of the boys from ~~here~~ the block
Margie has had a off for a rest. Margie got a new coat green with beaver fur or that is brown fur.
Doris got a red coat with brown fur on it. both are very pretty.
I wish you were with us. so you have some

-3-

mice cloes two ~~Keke~~ when dad was living. What a world to live in.

Ken Dear do you get enough food I hope so. I sent its ~~a~~ ~~box~~ of food you asked for also the pipe.

I hope you ~~enjoy~~ enjoy it my Dear Son. I love you very much God Bless you and perotect you to come home soon to us my Dear I miss you very much

I will close for now with all my love to you my Dearest Son Kenneth
xxxx Love, Mother x x x
x x x x x x x x x x x x x x

P.S. Send me some of your friends names and address

She was sick all the time and had no interest in anything. She was very angry at my husband. He was German and stayed in this country [in the air corps] when Kenny had to go over there.

JUNE BEST

Kenny's father died in 1942, and then two years later Margaret lost Kenny. She went into a depression, but she was a strong-willed Irish gal and she continued on. She kept hoping it was not true. When the remains came back, she said, "Maybe it's not him." You always hold a little bit of hope, I guess. Maybe the dog tags are mixed up, you know. I don't think she ever really accepted his death.

MARION KOPKO

He'd met a young lady when he was down in Texas in training. We heard he got engaged, but his mother didn't know where to find her. She felt bad because she could never talk to the girl.

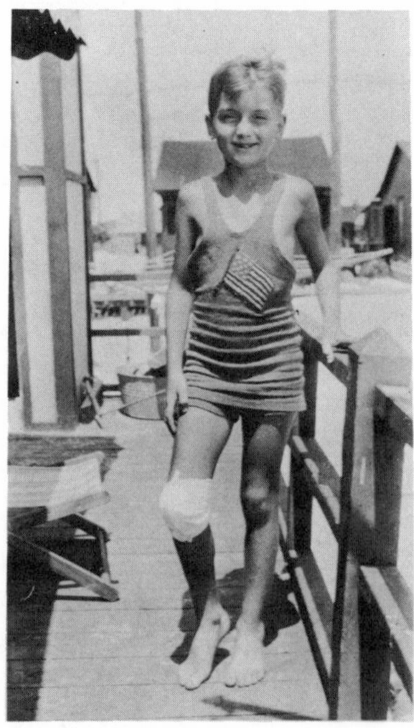

Kenny as a child.

2

OVERRUN

E Company made it through the first two months of combat without much trouble. Then, on 22 January 1945, 29 men were captured when the company was overrun by German mountain troops.

That it was not much worse was due in large part to the quiet leadership of 2d Lt. Hugh Chance.

Hugh Chance has lived all his life in the far western reaches of Appalachian Virginia. His farm is 12 miles out of Jonesville, the urban center of the region, with 874 people. This plainspoken, courageous little man started out in life as a country school teacher in Flatwood and was drafted in 1942 right out of his seventh-grade classroom. Teaching, apparently, was not considered an essential, draftproof occupation.

After earning an infantry commission, he transferred to the air corps for flight training, but he never got into a plane. He and 1,300 other student pilots in his unit were sent to the infantry in the spring of 1944 as the army built up its ground forces for the invasion of Europe.

Chance was made leader of the Third Platoon of E Company that July, and shortly became an outstanding combat officer.

CHANCE

It didn't bother me to go to a good infantry outfit, except I wanted to fly. There was a little image problem to overcome at first because they all thought I'd washed out of flight training, but we soon got beyond that.

We went on line November 11, 1944, to relieve the Third Division near La Bolle in the Vosges Mountains.

In those early days, there was all this talk about what we'd do if we got hold of a German. One time, my men and I were in the kitchen of a château cooking a hot meal when all of a sudden the guard hollered "Halt" and fired a couple of shots. We saw movement in the moonlight and called on them to surrender, but there wasn't any answer for a few minutes. Then somebody hollered "Verwundet, verwundet, verwundet" (wounded). It was a 19-year-old German soldier who had taken a shot through the thigh. His buddies had left him. And so now we had a German prisoner, and what did we do with him? Our medic dressed his wound, and a guy gave him hot chocolate. The men treated him like one of their brothers.

Our battalion did a lot of night mountain climbing. One time, we went over this mountain and then got word to dash back to where we'd been to help the 411th Regiment, which was getting pretty well beaten up. My platoon and the Second Platoon got orders to attack a high point called Hill 411, that was named after the 411th. There was quite a bit of German enfilade machine gun fire. If it had hit us . . . but it went over our heads.

During the night, our artillery opened up. I thought, "Well, I'll never be scared again." The shells were going right over our heads and down the slope on the other side.

We moved out from there, cleaning out machine gun nests as we went. A couple of our men were hit with mortar shells, Pvt. Steven Jancar from Michigan and another boy. The Germans were in a vineyard over a hill; G Company was ahead of us on the attack [30 November 1944].

My phone to G Company kept going out. Twice I went down and found the break and tied it back together. I was tired and worn out, and I thought, "I'm going to have a smoke before I go back up." When I sat down and struck a match, somebody fired at me from close by. I got out of there quick.

The next time the line was cut, two of our men went to fix it and found a fellow lying on the ground with a GI overcoat over his head. They thought he was a wounded GI and started to take a look when he lunged at them with a knife. German. They dispatched him, and we didn't have any more trouble with the wires. He had an empty machine pistol. I suppose he fired his last round at me.

We were going toward a town called Nothalten. The Germans were all around us, shooting at anything they could see or hear in the fog. G Company was getting most of the wounded. At nightfall, I was down where they were bringing them in when some big, tall fella walked in with a casualty over his shoulders. "Where do you want this man, Lieutenant?" he says. It was dark, but when I looked close, I saw he was a German. He had no accent at all. He'd been shanghaied off a merchant vessel while he was working in Brooklyn and sent back to Germany, where he was born. He was waiting for a chance to surrender.

The next morning, we entered Nothalten. The Germans had quit fighting and moved on. We learned that was what often happened. So we moved on too; E Company was in the lead of the battalion, up a foggy, rainy logging trail. It was pitch dark when we stopped for the night and put out security. You know what "security" means. Somebody goes out there and goes to sleep. Lieutenant [Marvin] Shelley [see chapter 4] wanted a cigarette, so we covered our heads with my raincoat and lay down in the trail and smoked. I can still smell the stink of that wet raincoat with the cigarette. We went to sleep right in the trail with water running under us.

The rains stopped when we got into December, but every little bit there'd be a real hard flurry of snow, and it was getting colder by the day. We were on the line in front of Selestat one night when I threw a couple of grenades at what I thought were patrols prowling around in front of us. Later, I heard a few shots. The next morning, we found two of our men had been killed in their foxhole by a German patrol, and two taken prisoner. That must have been the shots I heard.

JOHN SEWARD
rifleman

I had to pull a couple of our people out of their foxhole. We hadn't heard from them during the night. When we went out to their outpost to check on them, we found them both dead. The Germans had surprised them. I remember one of them had an Italian name. They were sitting in the hole with their sleeping bags halfway zipped up. I guess they were trying to keep warm.[1]

CHANCE

The next night, a couple of men got hurt pretty bad in their foxhole when one of them pulled the pin on a hand grenade. He must have fallen asleep and dropped it. I reckon he wanted to be ready to throw it in case somebody came around. I don't think they were killed.[2]

In January, we stopped in a mountain resort town called Niederbronn-les-Bains [on 18 January 1945]. Me and T. Sgt. Tom Young and my messenger, Bob Lyons, were on the second floor of a house. I was asleep with my head in my helmet when something hit me in the back. I thought it was machine gun fire coming through the window and tried to tell the boys to get under cover. Then a conk on the head dazed me.

I couldn't hear a thing. I just felt bricks and stones falling and covering me. My nose filled up with dirt and dust. I saw stars overhead. A German shell had come through the roof and exploded and took the whole top of the house off. Bob Lyons had a slab of that wall lying on top of him. We had been side by side on the floor. I thought he was probably done for till I heard him say, "Get me out of here, Slim. I'm smothering." I got ahold of one end of the slab and got a block under it. With some other men, I was able to get him uncovered, but his hips were crushed.

BOB LYONS
platoon messenger

When I came to, everyone else seemed to be up and around, but I was trapped, covered with stones and debris. I ended up with a fractured pelvis and a ruptured bladder, and got sent home on a hospital ship. For almost a year, I was a patient at Woodrow Wilson Army Hospital in Virginia. The aftereffects haven't been too bad. I lost a bit of motion in my hip, but I've always been able to work at the plumbing trade till just lately. My real problem now is I had a knee replacement from arthritis and I can't work.

CHANCE

Sergeant Young came crawling out of the debris, groaning and holding his back.

TOM YOUNG
sergeant, Third Platoon

The three of us had just laid down on the floor and were starting to go to sleep when all of a sudden we heard this loud bang. When I looked up, all I could see was sky. The whole roof was open. The beams fell on Lyons and me. My back was hurt, but they couldn't find anything serious. I wanted to get back to my outfit, so they let me go after two or three days. I never got a Purple Heart. There wasn't any blood.

CHANCE

At the aid station, they wanted to send me to the hospital, but I said no. You get away from your outfit and you never get back. All I had was some bruises and skinned places on my back and head. They gave me a Purple Heart.

It wasn't long after that we got word the Seventh Army was going to straighten the line.[3] We went back several miles to the town of Offwiller. It was snowing like everything. The CO told the second and third platoons to set up outposts a mile and a half or two miles ahead of the MLR. There might have been some machine gunners and mortarmen with us too. The 36th Engineers was supposed to be on line to our left, but I walked all along their sector and couldn't find anybody.

When I told company headquarters our left flank was wide open, we were ordered to stay out there anyway. A couple of days went by. We could hear firing once in a while, and on the night of the third day, we had contact with the enemy along the highway that ran through our position. They scattered when we fired on them, but then we heard machine guns behind us. They'd come over the mountain through that unprotected left flank.

I got a call from 1st Sgt. [Orland] Woodbeck: "The town's full of them. Battalion said to tell you fellas to get out of there the best way you can."

Three of us were in a house right close to the highway. I stayed till the rest of my platoon got going. It was night, but the moon was shining bright and the snow was knee deep. We went past Offwiller, where the Germans had overrun E Company headquarters, and there on the other side of town was a whole group waiting, Rhye's and Millek's men and my platoon.[4] Sixty or seventy men in that bright moonlight on the snow, standing there in the open. There was no panic, but it panicked me to find everybody waiting for me. Well, I didn't do anything but run and get ahead of them and beg them to get some distance between us and the town.

Dogs started barking. A big bald-headed fellow flung open a window. I hollered, "Don't shoot him." Nobody did. We covered that two miles back to the main line without a shot fired. I'm sure the enemy thought we were a column of Germans.

RAY MILLEK

technical sergeant, later a 2d lieutenant

There was this lieutenant, real nice fella. Yeah, Chance, that was his name. One of my men said, "Hugh Chance is leading us out. We're going across the snow, not down the road." I'd had a feeling something was wrong, so we all followed Chance and his people. It was dark, but one time we saw this bunch of krauts against the snow. We yelled, "Hey, are you GIs?" When they started talking German, we ran one way and they ran the other. All our people made it back safely to the MLR, Chance's boys and John Rhye's and mine. How Chance made the decision to take that route I don't know, but he saved us. He must have done it on instinct.

SAM NATTA
mortar sergeant

Lieutenant Chance took us over fences, through back alleys, and what have you to get us back to the main line. I was running with a case of mortar shells on my shoulder. Finally, I just dumped 'em.

CHANCE

None of the men on the outpost were lost or wounded, but the Germans captured the whole E Company headquarters group that was behind us in Offwiller, Captain [———], Lieutenant Shelley, Sergeant Woodbeck, and their men. I think there was a mortar outfit from H Company captured too, and one of my messengers, Timmons [see epilogue]. He died after the war, maybe from problems of being a prisoner. When we got back, I was so exhausted I fell asleep on the snow. I woke up to machine gun fire over my head the next morning. That's when they hit G Company at Rothbach, a mile to our right. I thought my feet were frozen, but after I walked around a little they were okay.

Things settled down for a few days. We were at a road junction called the Spider, where our battalion communications outfit had put a switchboard in a big, deep crater. E Company's new CP was in Schillersdorf, about four miles behind Offwiller. One night, [25 January 1945] I went in to Schillersdorf to get into my duffel and stayed there that night so I could sleep in a building. Low and behold, just before daybreak, here comes a bunch of Germans into town from K Company's area. The word we had later was that K Company left the line open and came in to Schillersdorf. Whether they did or not, here the Germans were. Some were riding captured E Company jeeps.

I was in the supply room. Some of the men and I ran out on the street and blocked them for awhile, but there were too many. Capt. Bruno Lambert, the battalion surgeon, hollered over at us, "Help me get these vehicles and the wounded out of town. You know what they'll do to me if they can." He was a German Jew.

We made it back to the high ground at the Spider, but the Germans had Schillersdorf. The artillery launched a strong counterattack the next day, and another outfit retook the town. I don't know who they were.[5] E Company was in reserve for that one.

February was quiet. We milled around Kindwiller, Schillersdorf, and Rothbach, and did some patrolling until March 15. That was the date of the Seventh Army's final offensive. E Company was in the lead when we jumped off under a smoke screen. We knew there were Germans to our right, but we were trying to get past them without a fight and get to Gundershoffen, where there was a bridge we were supposed to capture.

All at once, the smoke screen lifted and there we were, naked as newborn babes. I've always been thankful for one kraut who fired his rifle too soon and gave us warning. There's no telling what they'd have done to us if he'd waited. As it was, most of us got under cover before their machine gunners opened up. They shot the top off of the ditch we were in. While we were hunkered down there, a .50-caliber shell bounced off my helmet. Our own people were firing on us. Fifty caliber is American ordnance. It was a mistake, of course, but it made me sick.

After a while, we got ourselves together and cleaned out the woods where the Germans were firing from and spent the night there. We didn't get into Gundershoffen till the next day, even though we were supposed to have taken it in the first three hours of the attack. I don't know who ever figured out such an unreal schedule.

The war ended for me just before VE-day while we were crossing the Alps near Austria. I was the company's executive officer by this time. A jeep I was riding in wrecked. The trailer turned over on my legs and put me in the hospital for a few days.

They sent me to a replacement depot when I got out. I begged them to send me back to my company, but instead I went to the 45th Division. We were in a staging area at Le Havre getting ready to go to Japan when the A-bomb was dropped. Remember the roar that went up over that place when we got the news?

You ask why I was luckier than a lot of people. I don't know. It seemed to me that people who were too careful or too scared got hurt the most. It was the ones behind me who got in more trouble than I did. I don't say I wasn't scared all the time, but some of us did things, maybe, that others tried to avoid doing. I didn't stay behind my men. If I couldn't go and do it, I wouldn't ask them to.

EPILOGUE

Robert L. Timmons, one of Chance's messengers, died shortly after the war. Bob Lyons, the other messenger, said Timmons was the youngest man in the company.

RALPH TIMMONS

My brother was drafted in 1943 before he finished high shcool. The doctors told us he got tuberculosis from milk in a hospital in England after he was released from the POW camp, probably because he was run-down and undernourished. I don't think he had any injuries. He never talked about it much.

It seemed like he was always in bed till he went back to the VA hospital in West Allis [Wisconsin]. That's where he died, in 1948 or 1949.

I have another brother who was captured in the Bulge with the 106th Division. He made it okay. He's still alive.

CHANCE

After I came home, they put me in the Ninth Service Command at Ft. Lewis, Washington. That was enough to cure anybody of thinking about a military career, so I went back to teaching. I quit in 1950 and went to work for the Powell Valley Electric Cooperative and stayed 33 years. We've raised a son and three daughters, and now we have two grandchildren.

DOROTHY CHANCE

We were married in nineteen and forty two at Middlesboro, Kentucky. When he went in the army, I moved back with my parents. Once, I took the bus to Camp Croft, South Carolina, to visit him. It was scary. I was 18, and I hadn't been away from home before.

We wrote each other every day.[6] When he went to Camp Shelby, Mississippi, I went with him. We just had a bedroom till we found a small apartment. Other people probably turned down some of the places we took.

When the war ended, I was just tickled. I had a brother and lots of cousins in the service. They all made it home all right. Hugh came home on the bus in September 1945, and I drove our little Willys over to meet him to show him I had learned to drive.

F Company machine gunner during December advance to German border at Climbach. Maginot Line fortifications in background.
Courtesy of National Archives

Second Platoon, F Company, resting at Maginot Line, 15 December 1944. 2d Lt. Paul Fussell (upper right).
Courtesy of National Archives

3

"YOU GOING TO CUT OFF MY LEG?"

Ray Millek is a streetwise golf pro who started making his own way in the world when he was 16. He capped a checkered career when he became part owner and general manager of a suburban Detroit golf course. When he was drafted in 1942, he went straight to the infantry.

Leo Lowenberger is a Manhattan lawyer and onetime one-legged UCLA wrestler, who was drafted out of Brooklyn College. He went to UCLA after the war. They have nothing in common except a harrowing incident in the Vosges Mountains of France on 30 November 1944.

Lowenberger hardly knew Millek. He was a private and a mortarman. Millek was a sergeant leading a machine gun squad. They moved in two different worlds.

Millek had begun learning his craft two years earlier, when he was sent to Camp Claiborne, Louisiana, as part of the original makeup of the 103d Division.

MILLEK

It was a shock to be sent to the infantry, naturally. Nobody wants to be in the infantry. I'd been around when I went in, so I probably could have pulled strings to get another assignment, but I didn't try. I decided since I'm here, I'm going to do the best I can. I started studying and reading books. I took it seriously.

I decided to get as high as I could because the higher you were, the softer the job. But as far as being an officer, I really didn't want it. I wasn't educated to be an officer.

When we first went on line [on 11 November 1944], I went up two days early with an officer to reconnoiter our relief of the 3d Division. They had maybe 35 men where we were bringing 190 in. I said, "Oh, oh." We were supposed to take over their holes, but naturally there weren't enough to go around. We had a tough time getting the men in there. It was night, and every time we moved, we'd draw artillery fire.

We had a lot of people from the ASTP program, and some of them were very good. One I remember specially was Leo Lowenberger. This was on our first big attack [30 November 1944, at Nothalten, Alsace]. Naturally, men were getting hit in the machine gun sections, so I called for volunteers. Leo really surprised me. He came right over and was gung ho.

Leo and [Cpl.] Tim Morse and I were going into position to get a field of fire down a row of grapevines when shells started coming in. We all hit the ground. When the shelling stopped, I yelled for Leo and Tim; only Leo answered. I went over to Tim and turned him over. There was nothing left of his back. This shell hit him in the back and came out the front. He was killed instantly.

Leo, his leg was hanging by a thread and all he could say was, "I don't wanta lose my goddamn leg, I don't wanta lose my leg." I don't know how he could have felt it. I put on a tourniquet and started carrying him back, yelling for a stretcher. When we got him to the aid station, the first man I met was Father Kleffman.[1] Leo was saying, "I don't want to lose my fucking leg." I says, "Leo, be quiet. This is a priest," and Leo says, "I don't give a fuck who he is."

As bad as he was hurt, the leg was still attached, hanging by a thread. His right leg, I think. Father Kleffman said, "Leave him alone," and started praying over him. He told Leo, "I'm a Catholic priest, but I'll pray your way over you." Leo's a Jewish boy. Father Kleffman had some Jewish prayer he knew.

LOWENBERGER

I was the gunner on a mortar squad, but we weren't using the mortars in the mountains, so I'd been carrying the wounded out to keep busy. Millek asked for volunteers, and I came over.

We were advancing through a grape arbor. Timothy Morse was carrying the gun barrel, and I had the tripod. He was so tired he didn't want to sit down to rest. He was standing with the gun on his shoulder when a shell landed between us. He got it in the chest. I was lying down. The blast threw me in the air and turned me over.

A shudder went through [Morse] from head to foot, and I realized this kid was dead. Six feet from me. When I tried to get up, that's when I felt very warm and gushy in my right leg. A fragment had gone through one side of my leg and out the other.

Millek and a medic came up. I really didn't feel any pain, but I knew it was bad when the medic said, "Don't look." They got me back to the aid station, and there was Father Kleffman. I was mad as hell, swearing like a trooper. There was nothing much he could do except tell me I'd be evacuated. I never lost consciousness, but I must have been in extreme shock. I thought all I had was a broken leg. It was a tourniquet that stopped the bleeding.

In the hospital, I gave them my watch and wallet and never saw either one again. "Oh, shit," I told the doctor, "you going to cut off my leg? I run track. I need this leg." All he said was, "Lie down, Son, we're going to take care of you." Just the way he said it, so soothing, I went right out. When I woke up, I was in a body cast, and there was tremendous pain. I asked the attendant to straighten my leg, and he says, "They cut it off," just above the knee.

MILLEK

The krauts shelled us like clockwork. John Rhye and I were in a dugout when the shelling was so heavy dirt was coming in from the top. I was never religious till then, but John knew how to pray, and I said, "John, teach me."[2] It wasn't funny at the time.

Fear can make you do strange things. I was stringing wire in the Vosges one time when they started shelling me. I went straight up that mountain with a roll of wire on my back. When I got to the top, all my fingernails were pulled out. No one could believe a man could climb that cliff.

We had to retreat in January when they told us to straighten the front. E Company was told to set up an outpost line in front of Offwiller. Our job was to fire on 'em first and give warning to the rest of the battalion on the MLR. The country was a lot like my golf course, rolling and open with patches of woods, and deep snow.

The captain we had at this time was a son of a bitch. Scared to death. He'd whimper and lay in bed and ask me to do this, do that, do everything for him. "Go to Battalion. See what's what," things that he as captain should have been doing, and he'd be laying in bed drunker than hell. It was easy to get booze up there. I think he had a couple of runners who scrounged for him. A pack of cigarettes would get you anything you wanted. When the krauts hit us, he was worthless.

Before things heated up, we were in two houses straddling a road to block infiltrators. Along comes this real pretty girl, and she asked to go through our roadblock to the next town. Oh, God, she was making these eyes at me, and she spoke English. I told her the Germans were holding the town she wanted to go to, but she said, "That's my home. I want to go back." I let her through. I've often thought about that. When she got to the next village, she probably told the Germans there were only three or four of us on a roadblock.

It was maybe a night or two later that we heard firing to our rear. I called Woodbeck [1st Sgt. Orland Woodbeck] at the CP in Offwiller. "There's a few civilians coming into town," he says. "We'll handle them." What he didn't know and we didn't know was that krauts on skis in civilian clothes had gotten into Offwiller by coming over the mountain from behind.

The firing back there kept on for maybe an hour. When I called Woodbeck again, the line was dead. Woodbeck and the captain and the whole company headquarters had been captured. [See chapter 4.] I told my guys, "There's something wrong back there. We're getting out of here, but don't go back by the road." We met up with Lieutenant Chance, and he led us back to the main line. [See chapter 2.]

We went into reserve outside of Schillersdorf where Battalion had its headquarters. We were sleeping outside, and it was plenty cold, I tell you. We decided to rotate part of our guys into Schillersdorf so they could sleep in beds. This was maybe four days after we got chased off the outpost line. There was about six of us in a house, all asleep, when we heard firing. We ran outside. There was this one fellow, I won't mention his name, I put him up in a barn where he could see real good and told him, "You see anything move out there, shoot it."

The battalion medics were set up right across the street, and this doctor captain comes running over and grabs me and says, "Make sure they don't get me. I'm Jewish," and I said, "Don't worry. None of us is gonna get captured." I was getting them started out of town when somebody ran by me like a bullet. It was that son of a bitch I'd put up in the barn.

I asked him about it later. "I wasn't going to stay out there alone," he says. I don't blame him now, but it wasn't funny at the time.

The medics had at least one wounded man on a stretcher across the back of a jeep. They got out okay. Then the rest of us just dropped out of the town. As we moved back, we could hear firing, but my own group didn't fire a shot till we got to the high ground and set up our machine guns. By that time, the krauts had Schillersdorf and came on through town in some of our captured jeeps. We opened up and turned a couple of them over.

I remember this kid, a rifleman that I'd converted to a machine gunner. I don't think he'd ever fired a machine gun except in training. It was colder than hell, but here he was laying in the snow smiling and shooting. The cold made his nose run and the snot was froze on his face. He was all smiles when he hit those jeeps, but all I could think about was that frozen snot.

During February, I had to lead some patrols. I'd been commissioned as a second lieutenant by then. At first, they only sent enlisted men out, but it got ridiculous. They'd go out a ways, just stay there, and come back.

The big thing was the attack on March 15, when the whole Seventh Army moved into Germany. E Company was leading the Second Battalion that morning. Pretty soon, we got lost in a smoke barrage. Another officer and I were studying the map when I looked up and here was a big kraut coming out of the smoke not 10 feet away. I started pulling the trigger on my carbine and put all 15 shots into him before he fell.

To our great surprise, the smoke suddenly lifted, and we were caught in the open. We dived into a ditch full of ice-cold water and crawled through a culvert to the other side of the road, where we had some cover.

We attacked into a woods and lost a few men there. Then the Germans threw in artillery, and we lost some more. It was just a natural firefight, that's all I can say. Our job was to break through the German line and take Gundershoffen and hold a bridge, all by nine that morning. I don't know who figured out the timetable. We got there the next afternoon. E Company was in reserve by that time, so we just walked in.

After that, not much happened till we got to a little town in Germany that was up on top of a mountain. [See chapter 24.] When we finished up there, the war was nearly over. There was one other incident, when we were in the Alps. A man was shot by a sniper. We had the bürgermeister bring all the townspeople out and line them up in the snow and warn them that if any GI was ever hurt, we would burn the town down. We had to do something to stop it. They claimed an SS man who was hiding in the bürgermeister's house did it. We got the guy. [See chapter 29.]

That's about it. I always figured I'd make it through. I had some shrapnel wounds that never showed up till after the war, when my face started swelling up. They pulled a little sliver, smaller than a needle, out of my face, and found some more in my neck and my back. I don't know where I got them. I never got the Purple Heart, no. I didn't apply.

EPILOGUE

Millek was a Midwest snowbird, summering in Michigan and wintering in Florida. He suffered two heart attacks, and underwent open-heart surgery in 1987, but recovered and was in good health when I interviewed him in the summer of 1988. He died in the summer of 1992.

Like the other long-time attendees of battalion reunions (he has been coming since the early 1950s), his career in the infantry was the outstanding time of his life.

Lowenberger got a bachelor's degree at UCLA and returned to Brooklyn for law school. He lives in Port Washington, New York, and practices in Manhattan. He and his wife, a psychologist, have two children.

MILLEK

After the war ended, I expected I would command another rifle platoon, but I never did. I was discharged in April 1946 and got married that same year. We raised four kids before we got divorced. In 1969, I got into the golf course business.

LOWENBERGER

When my leg first came off, it was like someone was holding my toe and ankle. There was tremendous pain even though there was nothing there. I figured life was over. My first surgery was in a hospital in St. Die. I went home on a hospital ship from Marseilles. On the ship, I got jaundice from a blood transfusion. That was bad, throwing up and crapping at the same time.

There was one incident on the hospital ship that I don't like to think about. It was the only anti-Semitism I ever ran into in the army. Another Jewish guy was in a body cast, and that cast stunk. The crew asked us for comments about the ship, and somebody wrote that they should throw all the Jews and their stinking casts overboard. The guys were passing their comments around; they didn't realize I was Jewish.

From February till I was discharged in November, I was in Thomas England General Hospital in Atlantic City. I had to have another operation, and to toughen the stump, I swam a lot in the salt water. Then they fitted me with an artificial leg.

I'd been a football player and a wrestler in college. When I went west to UCLA after I got out of the army, a friend says, "Come out and wrestle with me." I had strong hands and upper body strength, and I made the team in the 120-pound class in 1947–48.

Thirty years after the war, I went to my first reunion, and there's my old mortar sergeant, Sammy Natta. He said to me, "Leo, I always felt it was my fault you got hit. If I hadn't been back of the lines, you wouldn't have volunteered." "You crazy SOB," I said, "I volunteered. Why are you taking it on yourself? It had nothing to do with you. Now tell me what happened to you." So he started from the time I got hit and told me in great detail everything that happened till the war was over.

I says, "Sam, that's only 1945. What's happened in your life since then?" He didn't want to talk about it. He had a lot of adventures, but the war was the big thing. He had nothing else to tell me.

So I says, "Let's go downstairs," and we see Millek, and he says, "I always felt bad that you got hit because I asked for volunteers." I said, "Everybody's looking for guilt to pick up in the world. Guilt all these years? Throw it away! I'm glad to be alive. Now tell me about you."

It was the same thing. He talked about the war from beginning to end, and that was it.

Millek nominated me for reunion altar boy this year [1989]. Father Kleffman says a memorial mass every year. It was just a gag, of course. Somebody else was picked.

4

THE PRISONERS OF WAR

Twenty-five men from E Company and eight more from H Company were lost on the night of 22 January 1945. E Company headquarters was overrun by Germany's Sixth Mountain Division, brought down from Norway in an effort to crack the American defense line in Alsace.

Two Americans were killed on that snowy outpost, one died of the effects of prison camp life, four were wounded, and the rest were captured. The Germans achieved their breakthrough, but did not have the strength to exploit it. Three days after overrunning E Company, they broke the American line again, and that time nearly captured Second Battalion headquarters in the village of Schillersdorf. The battalion commander, his staff, and the medical aid station barely escaped.

Battalion lore blames the commanders of E and K companies for the debacle. Many E Company veterans remember their commander as an incompetent alcoholic. His successor, 1st Lt. L. B. Doggett of Bethesda, Maryland, later wrote a letter of complaint to higher headquarters, which resulted in an investigation. The investigators cleared the captain.

The K Company commander remained in command. There is nothing in the record to indicate an investigation, only cryptic references in the regimental Journal of Operations and Narrative of Operations indicating he had appeared at regimental headquarters when he should have been with his men at the front and ordering him to return. (See chapter 14.)

Three E Company survivors who spent the rest of the war in prison camps were 1st Lt. Marvin E. Shelley, the executive officer; Pfc. John "Bubber" Seward, a rifleman; and 1st Sgt. Orland E. Woodbeck, the company's highest ranking noncommissioned officer.

Shelley was in the Indiana National Guard in 1941 completing one year of mandatory service when the Japanese bombed Pearl Harbor. The National Guard was called to federal service ("nationalized") and he didn't get out of the army for four more years. He was assigned to E Company in the summer of 1944.

Woody Woodbeck was a soldier on the fast track. Drafted early in the war, he was assigned to E Company just as the division was being formed. Within a year, he was first sergeant. At one point, he was scheduled for transfer overseas as a replacement. He and his wife, Edna, had a farewell tryst at Camp Claiborne before she went home to Ladysmith, Wisconsin, carrying his partial plate in her bag. The army wouldn't let Woodbeck face mortal danger without a full set of teeth, so he was taken off the replacement list and stayed another year in the U.S.

John "Bubber" Seward has always been a news maker. At Duke University, he was a star forward on a team that won two Southern Conference championships.

SEWARD

I'd been at Duke three seasons when the coach said, "We need to get you into a reserve." This was 1943, and the war was heating up. I went to see the marines, and they told me I had an overbite on my front teeth. Then the naval ROTC told me I had an overbite on my back teeth, and the air corps said I didn't have enough teeth. The only thing left was the Army Enlisted Reserve Corps, so I went there.

I was accepted for officer training at the field artillery school at Ft. Sill, Oklahoma, but about that time it closed down. There were already too many artillery officers. Then along came a program called ASTP, if I remember right. I'll have to brag a little bit. You had to have an IQ of 110 to get into Officer Candidate School, but you had to have 125 to get into ASTP. You couldn't have any rank, but I had none anyway.

I went to ASTP at Oklahoma A & M, which they now call Oklahoma State, for six months, till March 1944. It was about this time they were getting ready for the Normandy invasion, though of course we didn't know that. All of a sudden, they disbanded ASTP. I was sent to the 103d Division. It was a shock and a disappointment. I felt capable of being an officer, but there was no chance whatsoever of going to infantry OCS. Sometimes you're not at the right place at the right time, or you're at the wrong place at the wrong time.

I'll always remember my arrival at that camp. A body came flying through the barracks door. The next boy came after him. They fell down the steps and fought, and nobody tried to stop it, just let them fight till they quit.

I thought, "What have I got into now?"

ROBERT SCHROEDER
G Company

Yeah, there were a few teeth parted company when the boys got too much booze.

SEWARD

When we got overseas, I did a lot of combat reconnaissance behind the German lines. I enjoyed it. I was athletic, and sometimes we got to sleep in a farmhouse instead of a foxhole. I was young and didn't worry about being killed. I can understand why the army thinks 18-, 19-, 20-year-old soldiers are the best. They don't have any second thoughts.

But sometimes you wondered what the point was. Once, our assignment was to get some champagne that was hidden in a cave. We got shot at, and I don't even drink.

I only got hurt once, when a shell knocked the company radio into my ear, but I didn't go on sick call. After I was captured, my feet were frozen when I was locked in a boxcar, but not so bad that they didn't come back.

We were on an outpost [on 22 January 1945] when we were captured. Our leaders knew there was enemy activity in the area, but they left us out there till the Germans infiltrated and cut us off.

We fought for what seemed like an eternity, but it was only a matter of hours. Finally, SS troops in white camouflage came charging down like a bunch of Indians in a Wild West show. When we ran out of ammunition, we were at their mercy. If it weren't for a young German lieutenant that was out to capture prisoners, they would have killed us all. There's no doubt about it. One of them shot a person right beside me in his throat. We all expected to be killed. My mother's and father's faces flashed through my mind, and I thought, "I'll never see them again."

I laid my rifle down and threw my hands up. I'm not embarrassed about it. We gave it our best shot.

We were taken to a sort of wire barrier before they moved us on. This German put a Luger underneath my ribs. I thought, "Well, this is the end." But he thought we were coming out too fast. He was pushing me to motion me back in.

SHELLEY

We got a new captain during the winter, a strange man to be in the infantry. He'd only been an administrator. He told me to find him an orderly who could speak German because his job was going to be to keep him in schnapps. He didn't interfere, just stayed in his little room at the CP. When we got our whisky allowance, you wouldn't see him till the whisky was gone.

The night we got hit, there was gunfire all around the CP. We decided it was time to get out of there and back to the MLR. Our line of retreat was supposed to be through G Company in the next town [Rothbach], but when we got to where they were supposed to be, there were Germans there instead. Years later, I saw G Company's commander, Al Torrance, at a battalion reunion. I told him I was glad to see him because I'd been looking for him for a long time.

Our captain was in a drunken stupor, but I got him awake and told him the Germans were right across the street. "Call my jeep driver," he said, and he took off.

The rest of us ran for our prearranged retreat route up an old antitank ditch the Germans had dug. It was dark by then, 10 degrees below zero and lots of snow. Pfc. Joseph Kennedy was in the lead. I was right behind him when he saw these figures and called out the password. The answer was brrrrrrrrp from a German burp gun. He just did a flip-flop, hit right in the forehead. I'm sure he never knew what happened.

We backtracked and laid there in our little ditch real quiet. I told the men not to open fire till I gave the command. We didn't have to wait long, probably about midnight, when here came the Germans wearing white snow capes. We picked up one, then another one. Oh, oh, there's a whole line coming, very slowly. When they were 50 or 60 feet away, we opened fire and shot every round we had. The next thing we knew, they came yelling like Comanche Indians and jumped in the ditch.

All I had left was a hand grenade. I pulled the pin and thought about dropping it and being one of those kamikazes, but I also thought, "What is that gonna do in the winning of the war?" I'm standing there with this armed grenade in my hand when this big tall German guy comes up behind me and says, "Raus mit!" I took my watch off, tightened the band around the grenade, and let it drop in the snow. The time comes when you have to realize the jig is up.

Looking back, I don't think he'd have shot me. They were a very disciplined outfit. One of their privates took my two packs of Camels. His superior saw him and just chewed him. He gave 'em back.

I've often wondered what happened to that grenade. I hope some poor cuss didn't find it when the snow melted and say "Wow, there's a wristwatch."[1]

WOODBECK

When we heard gunfire up in front of us, we started to work our way back to the main line, but the Germans brought fire from two machine guns on us. They shot behind us, not into us. It wasn't long and another group came over the knoll and stuck guns in our faces. We had ammunition left. We were just overpowered. This was around eleven o'clock or midnight. They didn't get us right away. I don't know if they were playing cat and mouse or what.

It was kind of a consensus to give up. We talked it over and saw we were going to have to surrender sooner or alter. We took our weapons apart and threw the pieces away.

Of course, the Germans didn't know we were disarmed when they jumped in that ditch. It's a wonder nobody was hurt. Would the Germans have survived if the circumstances had been reversed? We-l-l-l-l, I don't know. They probably wouldn't have.

They made us clasp our hands behind our heads. The Germans, when they surrendered, had a tradition of throwing their helmets away and putting on field caps. We didn't do anything like that. How to surrender was not part of our training.

Before we broke up the weapons, one of the guys stripped down to his skin, put his uniform back on, and then put his long underwear over the uniform. He thought the light gray color against the snow wouldn't show up so much. But when he tried to work his way out of the trap, it wasn't long before we heard machine gun fire and figured he'd gotten it.

They put us under a building. Then, the next day, they took us to an old schoolhouse that was their CP. There was a lot of activity there with SS troops working around that area. A small American artillery plane was flying around, and it wasn't long before the Americans threw a round against the school. We took some of the tables and dumped them on end for cover just as the second round burst in amongst us. There was a guy by the name of Joe Reith who got a big chunk taken out of his shoulder from shrapnel.

SEWARD

They took us to a school building or a church, the tallest building in town. Well, you know the artillery always picked a high point to fire at, and an American artillery shell came in and took half the building. One of our soldiers was hit by shrapnel. The skin on his skull was slit down so all you could see was the bone. We decided to come out of the building. The Germans had set up machine guns and weren't going to let us out, but I said, "We don't have anything to lose. We'd just as well move out because the next shell has probably got our name coming in."

WOODBECK

When they interrogated me, all the questioning centered on our tanks, information that I didn't have. Maybe that's why they didn't kill us on the spot, so they could interrogate us. The SS troops who captured us were supposed to be the hottest there was. They took me to an old castle. The officer there, he had a German briefing booklet on the 103d Division. I learned more there than when I was on the line. The book even had our shoulder patch on the cover.

SEWARD

I was interrogated by a man from Chicago who spoke perfect English. He told me he left Chicago in 1934 to fight for the Fatherland. "Well," he said, "what does your captain look like?" I told him I was only required to give my name, rank, and serial number. "That's okay," he told me. "We've captured your captain. We got him drunk, and he's given us the overlays of all your positions, the number of men you have, and so forth." I heard later on the grapevine that the captain was court-martialed.[2]

WOODBECK

I was interviewed a year after the war by some investigators who wanted to know all about the night we were captured: about the captain's drinking, and how John Lucas, his jeep driver, got killed. Somebody turned him in, I don't know who, and I never heard any more. He should have gotten something for what he did.

He had only been with us a month or so. It seems like he was a man who liked his liquor. I went to the rear for a couple of days. When I came back, there were empty bottles lined up all around our CP. "Boy," he told me, "you sure missed a good party." I can't say I ever saw him drunk, but the night we were captured, he was not capable of walking back to the main line with us. That's why he took the jeep, and that's why his driver, Lucas, was killed.

We tried to get him to go back with us so that we'd all be together, but he wouldn't.

Talking to the other guys later, we put two and two together and figured the Germans didn't bother with us much because they got all they wanted from our captain. I might be prejudiced, but that's my feeling.

SHELLEY

They took us to an old house and ripped off the lattice work around the porch and told us to get in there. As I crawled under, the guard hit me with the butt of his gun. What I expected was, they were going to get us all under there and spray us with machine guns because that would have been much simpler. I had heard of the Malmedy Massacre[3] up at the Bulge, and I thought the same thing was going to happen here.

They kept us under there for a couple of hours. I can't remember any of us saying a word. I was silently bidding good-bye to my wife and son. But the worst that happened was we about froze to death. I got frostbite in my feet. Before daylight, they walked us back to Offwiller and put us in an old schoolhouse. It was a beautiful clear morning, and when we saw this American artillery spotter plane overhead, we knew we were in for it.

One shell went over, then one landed out in front, and the third one came right in the window. Our own people knocked that schoolhouse down, with us in it.

Both our guards were killed. Richard Gwisdala, one of our jeep drivers, and Joe Reith[4] were hit with shrapnel. Gwisdala's right eyeball was hanging out of the socket. The German medics took him, and I have heard he survived. Gwisdala was an avid reader. That was the first thing I thought about when I saw his eye hanging out. Sergeant Reith, my radio sergeant, got hit in the back. It took out a hunk of meat about the size of your fist, but he also survived.

Our shells were really falling by this time. We ran out to the street and found a storm cellar. The place was full of German soldiers. One of them noticed we were GIs and kicked us outside.

After the shelling stopped, we were gathered up for interrogation. I looked like just another GI. Our officers didn't wear insignia in combat. But when I went in for my interview, this German pulled out E Company's roster and said, "You're *Lieutenant* Shelley. Do you know we've captured your company commander and your company jeep?" He spoke excellent English. He looked at the picture of my wife in my billfold and said, "She looks Jewish." I said, "No, her maiden name was McGonigle." "Ah, non-Jew." Then, "You have Lieutenant Chance, you have Lieutenant Doggett. Where are they?" I said I had no idea. He showed me a map that had the positions of the Second Battalion, the Third Battalion, and the 410th Regiment, and said, "I'm a little rusty on my symbols. What does this symbol refer to here?" I said, "I'm only supposed to give you my name, rank, and serial number." "Okay," he said and pulled out a dictionary of American military symbols. "Ah, that's an artillery piece there." That map had symbols for each unit's location and artillery placements.[5]

Finally, this guy said, "To be honest, the infantry doesn't interest us that much. We want to know about your armor, air corps, and artillery." They were very careful of our artillery, and very bitter. They'd say things like, "If we had that kind of artillery, we would win the war."

The artillery observer we had with us, he got captured too. He was in solitary confinement for 36 hours. When they finally came to interrogate him, he started in saying nothing but his name, rank, and serial number. They made him strip and stood him for an hour in the snow till he was in agony and begging to come back in. They let him put his clothes back on and gave him some hot soup, and the old major said, "Now we will go ahead with our interrogation." I asked the FO what he told him. "Well, I didn't have to go stand in the snow again" is what he said.

WOODBECK

I was in several POW camps. Hammelburg was the main one. I was lucky. I had two pairs of wool pants, and they kept me warm. We got a Red Cross parcel every once in a while, never a full parcel. It was split up among five guys. Our food amounted to a cup of tea or coffee in the morning and a bowl of soup at noon, different kinds of soup. They had one that was kind of green and looked like tapioca pudding, with little seeds in it. You ate that, you'd have diarrhea for a week. They also had kind of a barley soup, and that was very good. They gave you a piece of German bread for supper, dark and very heavy. Wasn't too bad. If you ate the whole thing at supper time, you had nothing to go with your coffee at breakfast.

SHELLEY

By the time they moved us to our first prison camp, my toes were black from frostbite. I don't know why I didn't get gangrene. We had dirt floors in the camps and no heat. What saved me was I still had my fur-lined combat mittens. At night, I'd take my boots off and slip my feet into those mittens.

The roof leaked and let the snow drift down inside. The Germans hung some blankets over one end of the barracks, and that was the flu ward. If you got the flu, you would die there. They would drag about 10 to 12 corpses out every day.[6] I lost 100 pounds. It took two belt loops tied together to keep my pants up, but I never go the flu.

I'm getting ahead of the story. The first move after interrogation, they put us in railroad cars, 60 to a car. In my car, there were 40 Americans and 20 Frenchmen that got captured the same night we did. We were locked in for four days and nights.

I had dysentery that got so bad I couldn't straighten up. First I had to go every half hour, then every 10 minutes, and then it got to be constantly. There was one five-gallon scheisse can sitting by the door that was for everybody. We took turns sitting next to it. The train would start and stop, and the shit would slop. There was no way to dump it. Guys would come up trying to find the can in the dark, and I'm talking dysentery. I thought if this was what prison camp was going to be, I'd have been better off if they'd killed me.

This French doctor, I give him credit for saving me. He gave me a stick of charcoal to eat; my dysentery disappeared and never came back.

By the third day, those Frenchmen were berserk. Guys were hitting them trying to make them shut up. There was no food. I got on the train with a little bottle of water, that was all. In Karlsruhe, after four days, they opened the doors. We got out and ate snow like crazy. Then we started raising all kinds of hell with the guard. He said the worst was over, and it turned out to be true.

At Limburg[7] they took our dog tags and gave us identification numbers as prisoners. As we walked into that camp, the first thing the leader showed us was a smoldering barrack. "Two hundred and fifty American officers died inside," he tells us. He blamed English night bombers. The English used flares to mark their targets, and a flare fell into the camp by mistake.

We stayed in Limburg possibly 10 days, and it was back to the railcars. One afternoon in the railyard at Frankfurt, they kept us locked in that boxcar while the American Eighth Air Force bombed for two solid hours. I thought no way could we survive. We had a lot of guys go crazy, just blew their stacks. You could hear every damn one of those bombs coming down. Wave after wave, the drone, then the explosion. Our car was sideways on the track when they finally opened the door. The railyard was a mess. I thought, "They'll never run trains through here again." But the Germans had tracks in 20-foot sections with prewelded metal ties stacked up and ready to go. Slave laborers, maybe 50 or 60 men, would load those sections on their shoulders and double-time the track around the craters. Trains were running again inside of two hours.

SEWARD

The boxcar was so crowded somebody would holler, "Shift!" and we all had to turn over at the same time. We were strafed by our own planes, P-38s.[8]

I was in two prison camps, Stalag IX-B at Bad Orb 38 kilometers out of Frankfurt, and Stalag XII-A at Limburg. There were thousands of prisoners in that one. Some were British soldiers that had been captured at Dunkirk four and a half years earlier. I never tried to escape. Some did, but the Germans put the dogs on them.

We were treated all right. There was no brutality. If someone dropped out on a march, though, the guard would drop out with the prisoner. Then the guard would catch up, but you would never see the prisoner again. They evidently shot them. I don't remember which camp it was where they got all the Jewish boys together and marched them out. American Jewish soldiers. They were marched out, and that's the last we saw of them.[9] I was glad I was blond-headed.

I lost 45 pounds in three months. About ten o'clock in the morning, we got a bowl of soup consisting of flour, water, and potato peelings. About five in the afternoon, we got a very thin piece of black bread that looked like it'd been rolled in sawdust. Some people died of malnutrition.

Some of the prisoners, not a lot, but some, would try to steal your bread ration. That didn't set too well with me. It seems like a lot of times, each man was out for his own, to save himself. Somebody stole my field jacket once. I got it back. Yes, I threatened. It was a matter of life or death. But the American soldier is a good soldier, except for a few exceptions.

We slept in barracks on wooden floors, no bed or blanket. You just had a field jacket over you, and it was pretty cold. We spent the days picking lice off ourselves. To keep a positive attitude, we made menus of what kind of meals we were going to have when we got back to New York.

We got some Red Cross packages, but the Americans shot up a lot of the trains. Cigarettes were the biggest thing. People would give up their bread ration for cigarettes. Prison camp was not like "Hogan's Heroes."

SHELLEY

From Frankfurt, we went to Hammelburg,[10] and that was our main camp. All officers. We wanted to work on farms like the enlisted men because you could get food that way, but the old general in charge said no, officers don't work. Once a day, we were fed what we called grass soup and a slice of brown bread. We divided into groups of six and rotated cutting the bread. The guy who did the cutting got the last choice. The soup looked like collard greens. There was no meat in it, but every so often there would be a white worm floating there, a little protein. We didn't get any Red Cross food packages till way toward the end of the war. The Germans shortstopped them. Walking through German towns, we saw American Red Cross boxes sitting in the windows and the people smoking American cigarettes.

The roll was called every day. Right after that, if there were any dead people, we would go to a little ceremony for them. I can't remember a morning when there weren't bodies.

Hammelburg was the camp where General Patton's [George S. Patton, Jr., Third Army commander] son-in-law, Lieutenant Colonel [John K.] Waters, was a prisoner. He'd been captured in Africa two years earlier. Patton knew somehow he was there, so he sent a task force to rescue him. This happened on March 28 [1945]. Reason I know the date is that's my birthday. A task force from the Fourth Armored Division came right up the autobahn 60 miles in front of the lines to liberate American prisoners, primarily Lieutenant Colonel Waters.

The whole story is laid out in a book called *Raid* [Baron et al., 1981]. The tanks knocked down our fences and shot the place up, and we thought, "Well, we're liberated." We went out to greet them, and they were not all that enthused. The task force had information that there were 250 American officers in Hammelburg. Actually, it was more like 2,500. Lieutenant Colonel Waters was so happy to be liberated, he was running up and down the company street with this little American flag, and he got hit. By American shells, I suppose. It didn't kill him, but it ruined his leg, and they had to drag him back to the prison hospital.

We were wearing Serbian army outfits. The Serbian general staff had capitulated at the beginning of the war. Their camp quartermaster had issued us Napoleon hats and big, long coats with red tabs and about five stars. The task force couldn't believe we were GIs. They told us we could do whatever we wanted to—go back to the prison, take off on our own, or stay with them. A lot of the prisoners went back inside, but the Serbians, thinking the war was over, had set fire to all the barracks.

I decided to stay with the tanks. You'd be surprised how many men can get on a tank—30 or 40. We started down the highway, and I'm on about the third tank back. When the tanks would turn, guys would slide off and then they'd run and you'd help them back on. The lead tank got hit by a German bazooka. Bodies went flying, and that stopped the convoy real quick.

The tanks did an about-face, went right back to where we came from, and pulled in under some trees for cover. They told us they didn't have enough gas to get back, so they were going to drain the half-tracks to fuel the tanks.

That meant a lot less transportation, but they still let all of us stay with them that wanted to.

Being in the infantry, I decided to dig a hole. I figured all hell was going to break out come daylight. Those half-tracks had barracks bags full of stuff: tobacco, candy, soap. I was salvaging goodies when all hell *did* break out. The half-track got hit.

I went over the side and rolled underneath, but I knocked over a can of gasoline. A guy from the task force followed me under, but when he saw we were lying in a pool of gas, he got up and tried to run. I was going to run too, but I didn't know where to. He didn't get more than 40 feet when his leg went one way and his body went the other. He got hit by an armor-piercing shell, took his leg right off. He laid there and it was like a pump, blood pumping out of that wound. All these years since, I've thought that fellow was dead, but he wasn't. *Raid* tells how he took off his tie (Patton made combat troops wear ties, you know) and used it as a tourniquet.

Everything was burning. Land mines in the half-track I was under started exploding. Thank goodness, they've got maybe three-quarters of an inch of armor plate. The German artillery kept firing for maybe 10 minutes, and then here came the panzers. They had that hill surrounded and were coming in from all the perimeters. Every American vehicle was hit.

The Germans started the old "Raus mit." They could tell who the old prisoners were by our Napoleon hats and coats, so they didn't search us. I was able to hang on to my goodies, and that stuff came in mighty handy later. That night they marched us down to a warehouse at the railroad station. There was the German general in charge of the camp, real nice English-speaking general, and he's smiling as we get to the warehouse, standing there like he's greeting all of us. "Good seeing you, ha ha, we meet again," things like that.

WOODBECK

General Patton had a son-in-law who was a prisoner in Hammelburg. While we were there, he got guys with tanks to come and liberate the camp. The officer prisoners were in a separate area from us. We could see them leaving their part of the camp, and we waited for them to come over and tell us to take off, but nobody ever came. When they got through liberating the officers, they moved their tanks onto a field, which turned out to be a practice field for German field artillery. The Germans had an easy time of it, throwing in fire. All the U.S. tanks were knocked out. The whole thing ended up flopping. The Germans captured everybody, raiders and escaped prisoners, and put 'em back in the compound. It was a crazy operation.

SHELLEY

The camp was in shatters. The next day, they put us on trains and moved us to Nuremberg; we got in there Easter Sunday morning. I'd picked up a can of K-ration ham and eggs from the half-track. When we got off the train, I heated 'em up with hot water leaking from the engine, so I had my ham and eggs for Easter breakfast, same as the people back home.

WOODBECK

The Germans put us on a train after Patton's raid. A lot of us didn't want to leave Hammelberg. We could see the artillery flashes at night and figured the Americans were getting close. We didn't want to be moved further into Germany, so we kinda held back in the barracks. But the Germans came in the doorway and fired over our heads with machine guns. That convinced us we better get out to the train.

We were locked in a boxcar for three to five days. Before we got on, they gave us a cup of awful smelling German cheese. That was all. At first I didn't eat any. I put it up to my nose, and that was enough. But before I got through, I was eating anything that anybody else didn't want. That was all we had till they opened the cars in Nuremberg. They set a big garbage can by the door of the car, and that was where you'd urinate or anything else you had to do. When it was full, it just ran over.

You had to squeeze into a corner so guys could all sit down. There was no room to lie down. Even during the day, it was dark. There was one little window up in the corner, like the old "forty and eights."[11] We ended up in the freight yards at Nuremberg and were bombed by Americans while we were locked inside. We heard this weird high-pitched sound, then bingo. One bomb hit the far end of the train. It must have killed some prisoners. The guards ran for cover, but they didn't let us out.

SHELLEY

We slept that night in Nuremberg in Hitler's big sports plaza where they had the '36 Olympic Games. But the front lines were getting too close, so we had to move again. Now, we're talking ten thousand prisoners. It took all day to get us out on the highway, and then here came two American fighter planes strafing and dropping their little 500-pound bombs. Of course, they didn't know we were POWs.

Everybody scattered. The Germans didn't have many guards, but they had a lot of police dogs, and they turned them loose on the air corps guys that were with us. The dogs would tree them, and they couldn't come down because the dogs would chill [kill] them. It was quite a fiasco.

That night, we walked all night in a cold rain. It was so dark you couldn't see anybody. The column would stop, and you'd think the guy was right in front of you, but he'd move when you didn't realize it, and pretty soon we were scattered all over the place.

I've often wondered why the Germans worked so hard to hang on to us that late in the war. They must have known it was about over. What I think was, the Wehrmacht, the regular army that was in charge of the prison camps, were pretty regular folks. Supposedly, Hitler gave the order to kill all prisoners at the end. I think they realized they better not, although we did see Russian prisoners that were digging like dogs in their compounds, trying to find something to eat.

I was pretty weak. I didn't think I could walk 15 minutes, let alone all night, but I did. At daylight, they let us build a fire and get halfway dried out. That was the start of a 90-mile walk in the last month of the war. All that time, they never fed us, and we're talking Nuremberg to Moosburg, which is just outside of Munich. At night, we'd get in a little courtyard, maybe 200 of us one place and another 200 somewhere else. We didn't have any blankets, but we still had those Serbian army coats, and that was what really saved us.

We learned to scrounge pretty good. This was potato country where they dug pits to store the potatoes, with two feet of manure on top. The top layer was kind of green and gave you a lot of gas and dysentery, and the guards finally told us, "Nicht eat those." We had sugar beets, too, that they fed to cattle.

My buddy and I would get up early, and the Polish slave laborers milking cows would squeeze us out a drink. They were in sympathy with us, but they had to help us on the sly. Our guards helped us some too. They would warn us when we were coming to a town where SS troops were: "Don't get out of line. Stay in line."

One of the prisoners was a lieutenant colonel named Goode[12] who was almost like a God to us. He appeared in Hammelburg with a group that had been force-marched across Germany when the Russians were getting close. A great physical specimen and a great outlook, and he carried a bagpipe. He became our leader. The first night of the hike out of Nuremberg, he told us, "I'm satisfied you could take off any time you want to, but my advice is, don't do it. You could get into an irate family that has just lost their son, and they might shoot you. This war will be over in another month or two. We should all stay together. There's safety in numbers." And that's what we did.

Every night, Colonel Goode would make sure all the men had a place to sleep, and then about dark, he would sit down and play his bagpipe. You could hear it all over the valley. He was an inspiration.

WOODBECK

In Nuremberg, we were marched to an airport where there were tents set up for the prisoners. We had just enough room to lie down, that was all, feet to feet. The Germans organized us into prisoner companies and battalions, getting ready for a march from Nuremberg to Munich.

The column for that march was at least a mile long, maybe two. We started out at three o'clock in the morning, and it was evening before all those troops finally got out on the road. Thousands of prisoners. Air corps and infantry, mostly infantry. The air corps was glad to have marching soldiers with them. They figured they would do better with us. It didn't exactly work out that way, though. That first day, a P-38 strafed the column. We were told one prisoner was killed.

Our guards were all old-time fellas, 60 to 70 years old. We could have gotten away anytime, and we thought about it. We could see flashes of our artillery at night. But we went on, pulled into farms at night to sleep. We tried to get into a barn at night so we could steal potatoes. We'd save the peels and the next day, we'd add some dandelions and boil them with the skins. We used powdered milk cans from Red Cross packages for cooking pots. The German army supplied very little food on that march. We had to depend on the Red Cross. They met us every three days or so. Not the German Red Cross. It could have been the Swiss.

My health stayed good except I picked up a lot of sinus trouble that I blame on that march. We had to stay in damp, old horse barns. The Germans would have nothing to do with you if you got sick. Back in Hammelburg, there was a hospital, or what they called a hospital, but they had nothing to work with. The Germans didn't shoot you. You just died.

We had American fighter planes all the time. They came out every morning, flew down low, flopped their wings, then did the same thing at night along the length of the column. They never bombed us after that first day. The first plane must have found out we were a column of prisoners.

We weren't in Munich too awfully long before an armored outfit came in to liberate us. Those old guys who had been guarding us threw their guns away and got right in amongst us. They wanted to be taken by the Americans, not the Russians.

SHELLEY

We were in our final camp at Moosburg only about three days when the guards disappeared. Then the 14th Armored Division came in, and we were free. Some of the prisoners started ravaging the countryside. Colonel Goode got everybody together and said, "Now you're pulling just what we fought this war to stop. We don't believe in stealing, and raping women. I don't want to hear of another case of this." Everybody took him serious.

Boy, were we rank when we were liberated. We had to throw away all our clothes and be deloused. Then everything was burned. It was the first time I'd had my uniform off since I was captured.

The air corps flew us out to Reims, France. There must have been a hundred C-47s loading us out. What was so amazing, it took us all that time to get into Germany and only two and a half hours to get out. By the time we got to Reims, the Red Cross was limiting prisoners to one doughnut and one coffee. The first ones out got all they wanted, and one fellow dropped dead from indigestion.

SEWARD

There were some good moments in prison. Sam Neel, a Methodist chaplain in the 106th Division, was in one camp with me. I had known him at Duke. We spent a lot of time walking and talking together, and I assisted at his services on Sunday mornings. I'll always remember the song "Little Brown Church in the Vale." I told my wife I want it sung at my funeral.

We were liberated by the 14th Armored Division. The Germans disappeared one day, and we were freed the next morning. The fastest way to get started home was to go on sick call. The British, who were very disciplined, tried to get their men out first that way, but I said I had bronchitis and I got out too. I was discharged in December 1945. POWs were given discharge priority.

EPILOGUE

For the past four decades, Seward has been a leading businessman and civic figure in Johnson City, Tennessee: vice president of a lumber company, man of the year, Kiwanian of the year, and fund raiser for a cancer treatment center in honor of a son who died of leukemia. He and his wife have three adult children.

SEWARD

The first notification my mother received was that I had been killed in action. She turned gray overnight. My brother, a seagoing marine in the Pacific, had been reported wounded a little earlier. That was another mistake. He was never hurt.

I think everybody owes it to his country to serve his country. What happened to me was just a growing experience. I didn't ever doubt that I was going to make it back.

You can be in the wrong place at the wrong time, but you can also be in the right place at the right time. Hank Iba asked me to play basketball for him at Oklahoma A & M after the war, but I had only one year left at Duke, so I went back there. If I had not, I would not have met my wife, and I would not have had 42 years with the finest person that I know. Til was the most beautiful girl at Duke. I often tell her I ran after her until she caught me.

MATILDA SEWARD

John Seward's Wife

Everyone talked about Bubber Seward. I picked his picture out of the annual and told my sister, "Now, that's who I'd like to meet when I go to Duke." We met at a Sigma Chi dance. Nine months later, we were married in the Duke Chapel. John was president of the student body. I started a scrapbook that spring, and the first article I saved was about his campaign. But the picture I saved wasn't the one in the school paper. I put another picture over it because I thought he looked a little haggard. It was taken when he first came back. I'm sorry I did that. I've thought so many times it was a record we should have kept. But it was just the look in his eyes. It was not a happy picture.

LAURA SHELLEY

Marvin's Shelley's wife

I came back home to my parents in Mooreland (Indiana) when Marvin was sent overseas, and they shared my loneliness. When I heard he was missing in action, I just refused to believe he wouldn't return. My parents tried to keep me interested, and I had our first baby. I never gave up hope. My mom tried to make me realize things could be different, but I just prayed he would return. His nerves were pretty shot, but to find his body still together was just wonderful.

SHELLEY

I still have bad dreams. The worst is the boxcar dream, four days and four nights when I'm helpless. In this dream, it's just black, a black room where a lot of people are crawling around on top of me and I can't get air. I think if I ever have to go to hell, that will be the staging area. Once in a while, my frostbite still bothers me. I wake up of a morning with a place so sore it's like gout, and I can't put on a pair of socks.

LAURA SHELLEY

He doesn't tell me what's bothering him. He keeps things to himself, which I don't think is good. I thought he had to have plenty of rest, and I still think he has to be pampered. Not be storming with people all the time. Marvin needs his own time to think things out.

SHELLEY

The GI Bill sent me to school to get my engineering degree. Until I retired in 1982, I worked in the steel industry. Then I did consulting work till we moved to Scottsdale. Now I'm really retired.

Being a prisoner helped me spiritually. I became more appreciative of the little things of daily life, the fact that you have toothpaste, toilet paper, soap and water. We should not waste anything, especially food. All three of my children quickly learned to clean their plates.

LAURA SHELLEY

We've had our ups and downs. I try to stay out of his way when he's tense. I blame it on his war experiences. He was about as laid back as anybody could be when he went into the service. I don't say we've had a rough life, no, we've learned to cope with one another.

We've made it work.

EDNA WOODBECK

Woody Woodbeck's wife

I was teaching school in Ladysmith [Wisconsin] when Woody asked me to come down to Camp Claiborne for Christmas vacation in 1942. We'd been going together for six years, and our friends said that was too long. We were married the day after Christmas in the post chapel. It was lovely, decorated with poinsettias, and Woody had the whole company come to the wedding.

There was a jeep waiting when we left the church, and a row of crossed guns for us to walk under. We sent a telegram home saying, "We dood it," which was a popular expression then.

I went back to teaching and finished out the year. One night he called and asked me to quit and come down to Camp Howze. Decisions, decisions. Well, you can guess what I decided. When he went overseas, I went home pregnant to stay with my mother in my home town of Mondovi, Wisconsin.

In February, I got the message that he was missing in action. Five of us were at my friend Emmy's house when Witt, the depot agent, rapped at the door. In those days, telegrams were delivered through the train depot.

"This is it. Your husband is missing in action." That's what he said when he handed me the telegram. A month away from having a baby! It was enough to knock anybody off her feet.

My first reaction was, "You've got the wrong person." Emmy's husband and another girl's were missing too. Emmy's husband came home, but the other girl's never did. We all had babies or were about to, so we were sort of a club.

Rowley was born the ninth of March. I was in the delivery room when a box arrived that Woody had sent before he was captured: a great big Nazi flag, a box of silverware with sort of a bone handle on it, a cheese knife, and a pickle fork. Real pretty. Bless their hearts, the nurses brought the box in and let me open it between pains. Usually, they wouldn't have let a dirty box from Germany in the delivery room.

I spoiled Rowley rotten, so he turned out to be a thumb sucker, but I didn't care. He was all I had. Thank the good Lord I had a baby that kept me busy.

You think a lot when your husband is in a POW camp. You lie there at night, and you wonder and wonder, and you think. There were times I doubted if he was alive, but I wouldn't let myself believe it. There was a song I sang to Rowley, "My Bonnie Lies Over the Ocean," but instead of singing "My Bonny," I'd sing "My Husband Lies Over the Ocean," and "Bring back, bring back. . . ."

I never was notified that Woody was a prisoner, just that he was missing. A year after he came home, we got two cards from him from the prison camp.

A friend told me that a boy by the name of John Seward was also missing from E Company. He had been a star player on the E Company basketball team at Camp Howze, and we'd often enjoyed watching him. I sat down and wrote a letter to "A near relative of John Seward" and sent it to Duke University, where he had come from.

Well, that thing was forwarded to his mother in Norfolk, Virginia. We corresponded all through this time. Then she sent a telegram saying that John had been released and to have faith that Woody would be free soon.

I was on the phone to Emmy one night when Central[13] broke in and said, "Edna, your husband's trying to call you from New York. Wouldn't you rather talk to him?" Oh, you know, I just about died. Woody came on, and he didn't know anything about the baby, he didn't know if we'd had one or two or nothing or what.

He came home for a month's furlough, and then he was assigned to Camp Adair, Oregon. I said, "Boy, you're not getting away from us again," and the three of us took off for Camp Adair.

After Woody got out of the service, he went to work at the post office. We didn't have any money, so I went back to teaching.

Now we're retired and enjoying the fruits of our labors.

5

"I NEVER SHOT ANYBODY MYSELF."

With rumors of overseas movement mushrooming, Melvin and Lucille Seiler decided not to wait any longer. On 19 August 1944, six weeks before Mel shipped out, they married and set up housekeeping in Gainsville, Texas, the town closest to Camp Howze. Their honeymoon cottage was a room with kitchen privileges.

The Seilers, teenage sweethearts in St. Louis, met at Mel's church in 1939. In 1942, the year Seiler was drafted, Luci graduated from high school, and he gave her an engagement ring.

LUCI SEILER

My father wanted us to wait to get married, so we did, but when it looked like he was leaving, we didn't want to wait any longer. We had almost two months together. When he shipped out in October, I stayed till I saw the troop train leaving. I had heard stories about women who went home, and the fellas didn't leave after all. Once Mel left, I wrote to him every single day. If I was in bed at night and hadn't written yet, I'd get up and do it.

SEILER

A bunch of us rookies arrived at Camp Claiborne at the same time, where the 103d was forming. They put us in a big field house where platoon sergeants were standing around calling out names. One of them was Woody Woodbeck. Some of those guys looked pretty rugged and tough, but Sergeant Woodbeck was a nice-looking guy who seemed more mellow. I thought I'd like to be in his platoon. Then they called my name and said, "You go with Sergeant Woodbeck." From then on, I was in the First Platoon of E Company.

Woodbeck made you toe the line, but he didn't cuss you out like some of them. We hit it off really good.

When we went overseas in October of '44, I was a staff sergeant leading a rifle squad. Lieutenant (L. B.) Doggett was our platoon leader. Woodbeck had been promoted to first sergeant by that time. The first attack I remember was in the Vosges Mountains in November. We were moving up a road, columns on both sides of the road, when our French guide said, "There's boche up there."

Doggett took our platoon up ahead to see. Somebody spotted a machine gun. We shot the gun crew without any casualties of our own. Down below was a farmhouse. Doggett says, "Let's drop a few mortar rounds on that house and see what happens." They did, and I mean Germans came out in all directions. Our guys had a field day.

SAM NATTA
mortar squad leader

We had a lot of fun. We put one round right down the chimney.

RAY MYSLIWIEC
mortar squad leader

We were on a forced march in the rain about daylight when Doggett shot a German. That's when I saw my first dead German. Colonel Robison [Lt. Col. James C. Robison, battalion commander] says to me, "See if you can get them out of that house." The first shot landed right on the roof. Colonel Robison jumped up and down for joy and told me to fire some more. Boy, Germans just scurried out of that house. We laid a pattern, and with mortar, rifle, and machine gun fire, we counted a dozen and a half dead.

SEILER

I never shot anybody myself. I could have, but I couldn't pull the trigger. I just couldn't kill a man. I fired my rifle, but not at anybody in particular. We fired a lot like that. It was just a lot of noise.

I've always been kind of religious. In fact, my minister wanted me

to go to the seminary to learn to be a preacher. But it wasn't religion that held me back. It was just something inside of me that kept me from shooting at the enemy. If a man was to stand in front of me with a pistol and it was either him or me, it might have been different, but that never happened.

I'm from a German background. My grandparents came from Germany, and all they spoke was German. But that didn't have anything to do with it either. I'm kind of chickenhearted, I guess. I don't want to even shoot a rabbit or a squirrel in the backyard, and we have plenty of them. I don't own a gun.

Schillersdorf[1] is where I did most of my firing. Our company really got it there. It was early one morning when Doggett came around and said, "They broke through the line up front, and they're headed this way." Next thing I knew, SS troops wearing white camouflage parkas and all schnapped up were shooting at anything in their sites.

This was maybe five or six in the morning, before daylight. My squad made for the woods. "Spread out," I told my people, "and hold them off as long as you can. If they keep coming, fall back a little." Pretty soon, we were back in town, and the Germans were too. We held them till almost everybody escaped. Then we piled into trucks and jeeps and got out of there.

After Schillersdorf, we were on a defensive line between Rothbach and Kindwiller. The big problem was artillery. I lived in a bunker that was almost like a room, nearly deep enough to stand up. It got bigger all the time. There was nothing else to do but stay in there and make it better. We had a little gas stove, and it wasn't too bad. It was pretty quiet, till I got shot.

LUCI SEILER

When he was wounded, I never got any word from the government.

SEILER

Maybe because it was an accident. I shot myself in the hand with one of those M-9 burp guns that fired .45-caliber ammunition. The trigger must have snagged on a limb when I picked it up. The bullet went through the fleshy part of my hand between the thumb and index finger and lodged in my upper right arm. For a while, I couldn't straighten my thumb out.

LUCI SEILER

He told me what happened in a letter from the hospital in Nancy, France. Sometimes the censors cut stuff out, but that came through. I was glad it was only that much. It could have been a lot worse. It was his right hand, and he's left-handed.

SEILER

I recovered and went back to E Company, but not in time for the spring offensive. It was the end of April or early May, so I didn't see any more shooting.

LUCI SEILER

We were fortunate he didn't get in any worse battles.

EPILOGUE

SEILER

I was in the 103d Division from the day I left Jefferson Barracks here in St. Louis till I was sent to the 45th Division after the war. I hated to leave my old outfit, but I was glad to be in a division that was coming home, even though we were going to attack Japan.[2]

Did I think of the 45th as a death sentence? Sort of, yeah, but I was still glad to be going home. Mostly, I thought about that 30-day furlough, not about what came next. There was never any thought about going AWOL. Never! I was dedicated, I guess, and patriotic. It seems like I thought, "We have to do it. There's no other way. If we're going to win this war, we have to go do it." Young people today don't know that feeling.

LUCI SEILER

I never really thought about him going to Japan. I guess I didn't think that far ahead. I just wanted him home.

SEILER

That war was different than the two or three we've had since. Not as far as the shooting goes, but the moral aspect. If they hadn't attacked us at Pearl Harbor, I don't think we'd have been nearly as strong about going. Everybody thought that was the worst thing to happen when the Japs attacked us like that.

I liked the army. I almost didn't take my discharge. I was in the army just shy of three years.

After the war, I went back to my old job in the hardware store just down the street from here. On January 1, 1950, I went to work for the post office. For 37 years, I carried the mail, and finally retired in '84. I ended up 10th in seniority in St. Louis. In all that time, I had only three routes, so I got to be quite a fixture. Invited to people's weddings, things like that.

Luci and I started going to reunions seven years ago when I got a call from Tom Fowler down in Memphis. I had both him and Mike Eagan (of West Allis, Wisconsin) in my squad. Boy, you talk about a couple of goof-offs. Mike was only 17 when we went overseas. He lied about his age.

LUCI SEILER

They called Mel the Old Man. He was 20.

6

THE MORTARMEN

Robert Meredith, Ray Mysliwiec, and Sam Natta were three of the "old originals" of the 103d Division, in at the beginning and at the end. Drafted in the winter of 1942, they were assigned to the weapons platoon of E Company as the division was being organized in Louisiana. Mysliwiec and Natta became buck sergeants in charge of the two mortar squads. Meredith, a staff sergeant, was their boss.

Tom Kelly and Ed Fitzgibbons were latecomers. They were spending the war in college as members of the ASTP when they were sent to the infantry in the spring of 1944.

NATTA

The army put me on a train headed south. It wasn't till I got to Camp Claiborne that I found out I was in the infantry. I was so mad I wouldn't answer my name. A sergeant talked to me for two hours, and the next morning I woke up with a little different attitude. There was no use fighting it. That sergeant told me, "You're the kind of guy who's going to like this, but there will be times you wish you were dead." He was right. Before long, I was picked as acting squad leader and then moved up to sergeant. I was competing with a guy for the next jump, but they gave it to him. It wasn't three weeks before he was pulled out as a replacement and sent to Italy and really got busted up. Strange things happen.

When I finally did go overseas, it was with my own outfit. I'll always remember the conglomeration of smells, from gunpowder and a burning town (St. Die), when we went on line November 11. We had our helmet chin straps down, like we were in a parade or the movies. Those Third Division guys [the veteran outfit they were relieving] told us to unbuckle. The concussion from a shell can break your neck if the strap is fastened.

Those old-timers said if you survived the first 10 days, you had a good chance of making it all the way, but I only made it to March 15.

Mortarmen didn't have much combat in the early days. We carried rations up to the riflemen and helped evacuate the wounded. Schillersdorf in January was when things got hot. We were in reserve when word came that the Germans had taken the town. The whole mortar section was thrown in to reinforce the riflemen. We didn't know what to expect.

FRANK KANIA

H Company jeep driver

I was attached to E Company, hauling supplies and anything they needed. We'd been in Schillersdorf about a week, living in one of the houses. There were three jeeps in the courtyard. That morning, the woman of the house came running and yelled, "Boche come, boche come." That was our only warning. We grabbed our belongings, and the sergeant says, "We'll all start the jeeps at once. Then follow me." He smashed through the barnyard door with the rest of us behind him. Here came the krauts up the street from the right. Luckily, he turned left. We got out to the next town. I've always wondered how that woman knew to warn us.

NATTA

A jeep with a .50-caliber machine gun came tearing out of a barn. I jumped on board and tried to fire it, but it froze after one shot, so I joined up with a machine gun sergeant who had a brand-new light machine gun. Whoever was supposed to have cleaned off the Cosmoline (a thick protective grease) hadn't, and that gun jammed too. A concussion grenade knocked us both down. We squeezed in between two buildings, and apparently that's when Dennis Bellmore was out in the street and got hit.[1]

MYSLIWIEC

My squad was asleep in a barn when gunfire woke us up. We ran down out the door, and here were Germans coming around the corner. I was alongside Dennis Bellmore, brave soul that he was. He was the gunner in my mortar squad. He stood there and opened fire with his .45. We didn't know they had a tank with them. That's what blew the building apart and killed Dennis.

Or maybe it was a bazooka. You hear different stories. The wall collapsed, and he was trapped under the bricks.

Two of our guys grabbed a machine gun and took off. I was all by myself. What the hell, we all ran like scared rabbits. The Germans just kept pouring in. I think I was one of the last ones to get out. I ran from one side of the road to the other till I got to the edge of town and saw they'd stopped firing at me. As I lay in the snow catching my breath, I could hear a lot of German singing. They had captured Schillersdorf.

THE REVEREND WILLIAM KLEFFMAN

Catholic chaplain

I was at the aid station. It was still dark. The gunfire got closer and closer, and then their tanks came in. My first thought was to evacuate anybody that was wounded. Our doctor had already fled for his life.

Cecil Shaw [E Company machine gunner] held them off till we got the jeep loaded. I picked him up as we left. We were the last ones out of Schillersdorf. Then the Germans came in and blew up the hospital unit. It was sheer luck I picked the only road out of the town that was still open. [See chapter 3.]

NATTA

Somebody yelled, "Everybody out!" Dennis must have been hit by that time, but we didn't know it till we were 100 yards away. We tried to get back to him, but there was no way. It was a bad thing for us, feeling like there was someone we couldn't help. They recovered his body when the town was retaken. He was badly burned.

MYSLIWIEC

Two days later, some other outfit [the 410th's First Battalion] took the town back in a counterattack, and the news people came in. They called me in to explain exactly how all this happened with Dennis Bellmore, and that's how the story appeared in our division history.

After Schillersdorf, I was more scared. I got to thinking, "This is it. I'm going nuts." We had lost a tremendous amount of men. You may think you're

Schillersdorf, Alsace, 26 January 1945, after it was recaptured by First Battalion.
Courtesy of the National Archives

Two of Schillersdorf's defenders.
Courtesy of the National Archives

going nuts." We had lost a tremendous amount of men. You may think you're brave, but incidents like we'd just been through take something out of you. I think the whole company, what was left of it, had the jitters beyond that point. We were more trigger happy. What we really needed was a good rest, and we never got it.

MEREDITH

We had half of this town [Schillersdorf] and the boche had the other half. I had to get our men in there to give help, but we got too bunched up and too many men were wounded. The Germans were shooting machine guns. I could see dust from their bullets up in front of me, so I run till I about give out. I was just dewinded, deflated, you see. I kinda checked up, and one of our buddies up ahead hollered, "Run, you bastard. They're shootin' at you." That kinda gave me a little more spirit, I guess, and I took off again. So that's how we got into town and helped the other boys. The Germans had them pinned down so they couldn't move.

[Meredith won the army's third highest award for military heroism, the Silver Star, for his action. The official citation says in part: "Staff Sergeant Robert C. Meredith . . . volunteered to lead his mortar section as riflemen in an attempt to dislodge the enemy. In the ensuing firefight, twenty five SS Troops were killed and the lost ground regained."]

It's true I got a medal, but I don't know what I did that was so special. I never wanted to come out and say "I killed so-and-so." Lots of times, you don't know. You're out there in the field and everybody's firing, eyeball to eyeball, and you don't know who got hit by who.

NATTA

There was a long quiet period after Schillersdorf. We just laid around in dugouts and pulled some raids and patrols. The division was getting ready for the big attack on March 15, but we didn't know anything about it till a day or two before. That's when the civilians around our area jumped on their bicycles and took off. They knew before we did.

Our objective was a bridge in a place called Gundershoffen, but I never did make it there. I was carrying the mortar when our section got pinned down on a road. The Second Platoon rushed a hill where the German fire was coming from. They took the hill, but they got cut up pretty bad. I followed and finally caught up with them in the woods. That's where I saw

Jerry Wendt [T. Sgt. Gerald T. Wendt]. He got drilled right through the head.

[Wendt received the Silver Star posthumously. The citation read in part: "On 15 March 1945, near Engwiller, France, Sergeant Wendt's platoon was pinned down by machine gun and sniper fire and part of the platoon was caught in mine fields. . . . Disregarding enemy fire, [he] went forward to aid a wounded man. While rendering first aid, he was mortally wounded by sniper fire." Wendt was from Milwaukee.]

Our guys drove the Germans out of the woods, but then they started throwing artillery in on us. A piece of shrapnel lodged in my arm, tore up my gas mask, and put a dent in my helmet. Bennie Coleman, one of my mortar gunners, was hit by the same burst. There was a large hole in his thigh, and he was all doubled up and just white. What saved me was I was right up under the tree, and he was about five yards behind me.

I think he had lost too much blood to be alive, but we couldn't take the chance. Kelly and Fitzgibbons carried him out with the help of four German prisoners, but one of the prisoners stepped on a Bouncing Betty. It exploded right under Bennie's body, and that finished him for sure. Fitzgibbons's face was black, and his back end looked like it was full of buckshot. Those mines bounced up when you stepped on 'em and shot out BBs.

DR. TOM KELLY

mortarman

Ed Fitzgibbons and I and four German prisoners tried to carry Bennie Coleman out. One of the prisoners stepped on a mine. He was disintegrated, and that was the end of Bennie. The mine went off right under him. I think he was already dead, though. I put my belt around his upper thigh to stop the bleeding, but he had turned white. Then the mine explosion threw him 20 or 30 feet and killed two or three of the prisoners.

Bennie Coleman was a very special man, a perfect Southern gentleman.

Fitzgibbons got banged up too. Bennie was dead, so I picked up Fitzgibbons and dragged him to the road. He'd pass out and come to. I lost my hearing from the blast. I screamed at him: "Can you walk? We have to get help." I finally got him to the aid station in town, and I got back to the outfit the next day. It was a long night.

ED FITZGIBBONS

mortarman

It was late afternoon. We'd been pinned down all day till we finally moved uphill into a woods. Intelligence said there wouldn't be any artillery, but there were tree bursts all around us. That's when Bennie got hit.

Tom and I wrapped a raincoat around some limbs to make a litter and got four prisoners to carry Bennie. I was on the right, and Tom was on the left, holding him to keep him from rolling off. We had to get past some barbed wire, and we should have known why it was there. We hadn't gone too far when the prisoner behind me stepped on a mine and blew us all off our feet.

I had no idea what had hit us. All I knew was the explosion. When I regained my senses, I ran over to where Kelly was. He was trying to find out what condition Bennie was in. I have difficulty talking about Bennie. He was a mess. I couldn't look at him. I was nauseated and sick. The mine probably went off under his head. Kelly was reluctant to leave him, but there was nothing we could do.

When we left, three of the prisoners were nowhere to be seen. The one who stepped on the mine was on the ground. I assume he was dead. We didn't know which way to go, and it was getting dark by that time, but we could see the burning town behind us, so that's the direction we headed. On the way, we ran into the prisoners. One was wounded, and the other two were trying to help him.

Tom wanted to shoot the three of them. I had to fight him to put his pistol away. He was pretty upset. We left them there and wandered on down the road, and somehow we ran into those prisoners again. The injured fella was on the side of the road. This time, Kelly put a tourniquet on the leg of the guy he wanted to kill an hour before.

Kelly was a real gentleman. He had lots of personal discipline too. It's a mystery why people behave as they do sometimes.

When we got to the town, there were fires all over the place. We just kept going till we saw the red crosses at the aid station. There were a lot of wounded there so we had to wait a while. I didn't think there was anything wrong with me except a fragment in my right forearm, but there were fragments in my leg too. I didn't have any permanent injuries. I even rejoined the company, but not till the war was over.

NATTA

Kelly wasn't hurt bad. I gave him my carbine. A week later, he showed up at the hospital with two bottles of beer stashed in his jacket and a French combat medal he'd rigged up. I still have it. He was that kind of a guy.

MEREDITH

There was hot fire going both ways. We lost several men. One in particular was a best friend of mine, Bennie Coleman. He got it when a shell hit into the timber. When I went back to him, I could see he was really hurt bad. They were still throwing in shells. Something hit me on the shoulders and back that I thought was shrapnel. It was only dirt, but I took a headache from the concussion that lasted all night long.

MYSLIWIEC

Artillery was coming in like crazy. "How you holdin' up?" I says to Sam Natta, and the last thing I remember after that was flying through the air and slamming into a tree. I woke up in a hospital in Dijon, France. I have a hazy recollection of being put in the first aid wagon, but nothing cleared up till three or four days later. Sam took my sheeplined jacket when they picked me up. He knew I wasn't going to need it anymore. But he got hit himself not long after that.

My back, my leg, my spine, and my neck were messed up, and my right hip was dislocated. The whole conglomeration took away my thinking power for a while. It was two weeks before I could walk, and then I got a tremor in my hand and arm, shook so bad I couldn't write. That ended after four weeks or so. I never got a Purple Heart. They said the skin wasn't broken.

NATTA

Believe it or not, I was sent back to the company toward the end of April. I was not ready to go back, not mentally, not physically. I still had bandages and my arm felt like it was going to split. I was back only a couple of days when G Company got cut off in some little town in Germany. [See chapter 24.]

EPILOGUE

For Bob Meredith, combat infantry service was just a blip in a long, stable life spent in the rural industrial town of Elizabethton, Tennessee. He was drafted exactly one year after Pearl Harbor when he was 30, old for an infantryman. He spent his entire working life in the huge rayon factory that dominates the skyline of Elizabethton.

He and his wife, Veda, were married in 1934. Just down the street from the house they built in 1935 is the East Side Free Will Baptist Church, their church for many years. Meredith was a self-described "Christian boy" even when he was in the army, though he did manage one visit to La Rue Pigalle ["Pig Alley"] while on leave in Paris.

Veda Meredith died in October 1988 after 54 years of marriage. She and her husband were interviewed for this book four months earlier.

Bennie Coleman, killed in action, 15 March 1945, and Claudia Coleman Howard.
Courtesy of Claudia Howard

VEDA MEREDITH

Robert wrote to me, "I can't write you anything about the war. The censors would clip it out. I couldn't even write you if my best friend got killed." I knew it was Bennie because he and Robert were real close. We got to be friends with him and his wife while we were stationed in Texas. After the war, she came here to talk with Robert about what happened. We were with her when she had Bennie's body brought back. It was a sad occasion. She's like a sister to me.

CLAUDIA HOWARD

Bennie Coleman's widow

Bennie is buried at the Primitive Baptist Church in Healthy Plains [North Carolina]. That's about 12 miles out in the country from Wilson.

His daddy was afraid when he went off 'cause he didn't know if he'd come back. But I think he accepted what happened as God's will.

Bennie and I were married August 23, 1941. He was a farmer, but he was drafted the next year anyway. I stayed with my people for the first two years. He didn't think it was safe for me to go with him, the way the army boys were. But in 1944, I told him I was going back to camp with him. I knew others had done it, and I was going to too.

He wrote the night before he was killed. That was why it was so hard to understand.

MEREDITH

I never talked to anybody about the war. I guess I've talked more to you than anybody. Veda used to rag me about what happened, but I wanted to forget it, see? I'll just turn it off again after we finish this conversation.

VEDA MEREDITH

I never heard these stories before. It was, well, so horrible, I thought what I didn't know of what he went through, the better. I was a country girl, born and raised right here in a family of ten children. I had six brothers in the service. I learned to live one day at a time.

While Robert was gone, I wrote him every day. I wanted him to know I loved him and I was all right and I was really backing him and I knew he was going to make it through. Sometimes, I got awful down. I went to Mama's so she could give me comfort. But there wasn't much comfort for me because she was worrying over all her boys, including Robert.

When he told me he was coming home, well, I felt like shouting. I never shouted in my life, but I felt like shouting then. I sat up all night waiting. That was the longest night I ever spent in my life. Then I heard the step on the porch. I'd heard that step so many times.

The next day, I had near all my people and all of his over. I didn't know what I was goin' to feed 'em, but I called and told 'em all to come. My sister and his sister cooked the dinner. We had his mother and daddy, my mother and daddy, his sisters, my sisters, everyone was there. We had a happy, good time.

As many years as it has been, I have never got to the place that I don't thank God because I know it was through God that he made it back to me.

*

Mysliwiec, who grew up back of the yards in Chicago, was an advertising man when he was drafted. When he was discharged in February 1946, he returned to his old job and stayed until he retired in 1984 as art director.

MYSLIWIEC

I was lucky I wasn't hurt worse. I've never looked on it as a million-dollar wound. It was worth something, but I've had to live with the consequences ever since. My hip still gives me trouble.

My time in the army was the most valuable experience I've ever had. I went in a boy and came out a man. Before the war, I was a little shy and backward. When I came out, wasn't anybody going to push me around.

Why did I survive? Dumb and stupid. Those were the ones who survived.

*

After he left the army in November 1945, Natta spent 31 years as a career federal employee.

Tom Kelly, of Coquille, Oregon, became a chiropractor and is still in active practice there.

Fitzgibbons became an accountant and now lives in retirement in Boxford, Massachusetts. Although they have not seen each other since the war, he and Kelly still stay in touch.

7

TRENCH FOOT AND THE GI SHITS

"N/B" stands for "nonbattle" casualties in the Second Battalion records. During the combat winter of 1944–45, N/B casualties made up 57 percent of the total casualties.

While soldiers suffered from a number of diseases, including jaundice, trench foot and diarrhea took the heaviest tolls. Trench foot was a terrible condition. The soldier's feet sometimes turned black and gangrenous, and literally rotted. Diarrhea, popularly known as "the GI shits," probably accounted for more N/Bs than trench foot, but it was also more treatable. Aid stations passed out paregoric by the quart, and it had a magical if temporary effect.[1]

Joe Meadows, executive officer of G Company, reports that he "had the GIs for 70 days. You'd go along and all of a sudden the urge would hit. No matter what I was doing, I'd drop my drawers, and then get going again. My weight dropped from 190 to 163 pounds in two months."

One of the common stories in the battalion was of two cannoneers who were shot by a sniper when they were forced to stop to relieve themselves.

Trench foot, which caused permanent disability for many of its victims, was preventable. Soldiers who were able to take care of their feet didn't get it. Combat conditions at times, however, made proper foot care impossible.

Dan Higley, an H Company machine gunner who kept a wartime diary, said his squad took special precautions during the coldest part of the winter, when they were holed up in static positions: "Nearly every day, we took the trouble to change two pairs of wool socks as well as the felt pads that lined our shoepacs. No one in our squad ever had much trouble with his feet."

In his book, *Death of a Division* (1980), Charles Whiting blames the large number of nonbattle casualties in the 106th Division on poor discipline and morale. A. J. Torrance, G Company commander, reports, "We were supposed to use the buddy system in foxholes, whereby one man massaged the other's feet. But I think it was rarely practiced." Meadows notes, "We had a procedure to prevent trench foot. Every night, you'd take off your shoes and rub your feet, dry 'em as much as possible, and put on dry socks. Then we'd put the wet socks up under our jackets, and they'd be dry the next night. But it wasn't easy to make sure every man did what he was supposed to. People that didn't ended up with trench foot."

Two of the trench foot victims were in E Company, Mike Egan of West Allis, Wisconsin, and Syd Fierman of Malvern, Pennsylvania. Egan, at 18, was one of the youngest men in the company. Fierman was one of the thousands transferred from the Army Specialized Training Program.

EGAN

The Germans sent an awful lot of mortar fire in on us that first day of combat. There was several wounded by a tree burst, and one man was killed. I was totally green and totally scared. I says, "If I ever get out of here alive, I'll work the rest of my life for nothing." One of the other guys says, "What do you think you're doin' now?" And I says, "Prayin'."

I was loaded down with bazooka shells. I was so tired I wasn't going to dig in till a shell landed nearby and knocked my helmet off. It felt like a technical knockout. When I came to, I could hear myself shivering. I was in shock. I dug a hole so fast you wouldn't believe it.

Right next to me, a guy was wounded pretty bad. I remember he had two children. Nobody could get him out of there, the shelling was so bad. I'm trying to find out if he survived.

When we got up there, what do we see but 13 dead Germans scattered all over the place. They must have been hit by one of our big shells. That was another shock. From time to time as we moved through the mountains, we would see German graves with a bayonet stuck in the ground as markers.

I got calmer as time went on, but I kind of prayed for a small wound to get out of there. Million-dollar wound, they called it. There were guys, I guess, that took off, that couldn't take the shelling, but no one I knew. It was just talk.

I got a little wound from a tree burst. It didn't amount to anything, but I thought Lieutenant Doggett [1st Lt. L. B. Doggett, at that time a platoon leader] was going to get us all killed. He was crazy, just one patrol after another. He'd go right through the lines, the Germans would be talking, it didn't mean anything to him. He was a great guy. He kind of protected me and helped me at different times.

Father Kleffman [Capt. William C. Kleffman, battalion chaplain] was another good man. He was watching over us all the time. I told him the other night [at a battalion reunion], "Father, you gave me all the blessings up there, and that's why I'm here today."

Around the middle of December, my feet go so bad I had to go to the aid station. They turned black, like with gangrene, to the top of my stockings, and swelled to double their normal size. Boy, was it painful. You lose all your tissue veins. One kid, they cut off both his legs, it was so bad.

I was in a couple of field hospitals and then the 100th General Hospital in Paris, and finally the 120th Station Hospital in England for two and a half months. When I went for a physical, there was a guy there I knew from basic training. He kind of felt sorry for me and he said, "We'll put you in the air force." He did it on his own. I was assigned to a bomb group in March 1945.

FIERMAN

To be very frank and very honest, I'm not going to sit here and tell you war stories because I wasn't in too many of them.

There was quite a number of us that went from North Texas State College to the 103d—Red Dolbie, Ivan Fagre, Bernie Flanagan, Miller, Mel Jacobs, Dennis Bellmore. Jeez, it all comes back to me. I was assigned to the captain as his radio man, but once we got to the combat area, they handed me a rifle, and that's the last I ever saw of the radio.

I was standing in my foxhole one day reading a letter when I was hit by sniper fire. Boy, if that isn't something. Uaaaannnnggg! I hit the bottom of that hole and screamed "Sniper." The helmet did its job. The bullet hit right above my ear and bounced off. I got down so low in that foxhole my buttons were in the way. They sent two fellows out and got the sniper. They found him in a tree.

I wasn't hurt at all, just had a headache for a while from the helmet banging around. There was no blood, so I didn't get the Purple Heart.

It wasn't long after that that I left the outfit with foot problems [on 1 December 1944]. I tried to keep the helmet as a souvenir, but the stretcher bearers didn't want the added burden.

My feet were in good shape when we went on line. I was wearing shoepacs like everybody else, but those things were "one size fits all," and they were way too big for me. Over the course of 20 days when we couldn't take our shoes off for any length of time, I developed blisters. My feet swelled up to where it was difficult to walk.

We took a small village one morning after walking five miles. I asked to go to the aid station, and when I did, my feet were so swollen the sergeant had to cut off my boots. A medical officer told the sergeant to fix me up the best he could and send me back to my outfit. When the doctor left, the sergeant hung an evacuation tag on me and told me to get into an ambulance

World War I dugout taken over by Second Battalion during static winter defense, which produced many trench foot casualties.
Courtesy of the National Archives

and stay out of sight. So I wound up in a field hospital where I can remember very pleasantly an army nurse massaging my feet with something that felt like a million dollars.

I had trench foot and frozen feet and blisters. My feet were a total mess. At the hospital in England, they operated on the small toe on both feet. The toes had become very hammered. That was in March of '45. It was six months before I could put shoes on again.

THE REVEREND RICHARD STEFFEN

private, F Company

To my father, being drafted was about as low as you could be. He thought you should volunteer, so I volunteered to be drafted in March 1943 when I was in my second year of ministerial training at the University of Illinois. The understanding between the government and the church was that if you had completed two years, you could be given a 4-D [deferred] classification. I missed by one semester.

When we got overseas, I was platoon messenger in the First Platoon, but after a month or so, I was made company messenger. It was a cushy job, carrying messages from company headquarters to the platoons. I didn't see any combat, and on March 14, I got sick with yellow jaundice and didn't get back to the company till they were in Austria and the war was over.

Well, I did get a minor scratch. I was kind of embarrassed to get a Purple Heart when other people were hurt seriously. It happened at the end of November at Nothalten. I had taken a message to one of the platoons when the shelling started. I crouched down in a muddy ditch till the shells got closer. I didn't want to get real messy. Then the shells got closer, and I laid right down. Shrapnel wrecked my rifle, and a chunk went through my jacket sleeve and frayed my undershirt. Another sliced open a can of beans I was carrying on my hip. I had an air pillow that my father had carried in World War I. When I went to blow it up a couple of days later, it leaked. Inside was a piece of shrapnel. I still have it. Somewhere in all that, I got a shrapnel scratch on my hand.

A guy in the ditch with me was deafened. The shelling left him kind of bewildered, and he had to go to the rear.

A close call, you say? Yes, but it was coincidence I wasn't hit. I don't have the kind of religious faith that would say God was protecting me.

What I remember most about that winter was the sheer misery, the cold and the wet. I'm from a cold climate, yes, but I didn't spend much time sleeping outside in Wisconsin. Down sleeping bags were issued, but there weren't enough to go around, so we didn't get them in company headquarters at first. As casualties occurred, we got their bags. Of course, coming off the front lines, they were a muddy, dirty mess. The guys had been sleeping in them with their boots on.

In March, I got sick with a headache, and I couldn't eat. They hung a tag on me, "NYD," not yet diagnosed. I was four or five days in the field hospital before a nurse finally showed me to a doctor. He could see clear across the room that I had yellow jaundice.

On VE-day, I got out of the hospital. I was only back with the company a few days in Innsbruck when I was transferred to the 45th Division. [See his further comments in the conclusion.]

[N/B (non-battle) victims got no Purple Hearts even though their injuries were sometimes more disabling than combat wounds.]

EPILOGUE

EGAN

My feet have bothered me ever since. They're bothering me right now. I can't sit very long. Cold and then hot weather is when it gets bad. When I sit very long, everything goes dead. I'm afraid to drive a car with air-conditioning. The chill bothers me. That's why all these years I've had a job as a fireman and engineer. I got by that way.

FIERMAN

I flew home in May [1945] to a rehabilitation unit in North Carolina. They discharged me in September. For the first few years, I had severe discomfort walking. Even today, there's some difficulty.

My time in the army was important in my life. I wouldn't want to repeat it, but having survived it, I can say I'm glad it occurred. The army taught me discipline and respect for authority. It taught me a great deal about living, and a few things about dying.

8

"DON'T SCREW HIM. SHOOT HIM."

In 1944, E. Robert Brennan got a form letter from the chief of staff of the army air corps, Gen. H. H. (Hap) Arnold.

Dated "1 April 1944," the letter announced that Brennan was no longer an air cadet. He and all other cadets who were not yet in preflight training were ordered to return to the "Ground and Service Forces" from whence they came. "It is essential that every one of these soldiers be made available for pending operations." Within weeks, Brennan was a member of E Company, 410th Infantry.

He was not a typical infantryman. A graduate metallurgist, he was building 1,000-pound bombs for the air corps when he was drafted from the steelmaking city of Lorain, Ohio.

"They called us quiz kids and college boys," Brennan recalls. "For my part, I looked at some of the officers and said, 'I'm better than they are, and here I am a private.' But it's true that misery loves company. There were so many of us in the same boat I couldn't take offense."

In six months of combat, he rose from buck private to staff sergeant, and still relishes memories of his feats of arms. Most of the men in this book fired their weapons blindly, but Brennan remembers at least three enemy soldiers "who specifically belonged to me."

BRENNAN

I think I captured the first German in the outfit by being ridiculous. I was on a roadblock when here comes a German soldier. I stepped out in the dark and challenged him, and being the trained, expert combat infantryman that I was, I dropped my rifle and grabbed his, and we struggled for possession. My buddy says, "Don't screw him. Shoot him." When the German knew there was more than one of us, he dropped his rifle and surrendered. I don't tell that story to many people.

Those krauts could be brave. I remember one prisoner who wouldn't answer questions, so one of our sterling characters put a cocked .45 against his head. The guy still wouldn't talk. I thought that was a hell of a man.

When we relieved the Third Division, those people said half of us would be dead in a week. We respected what they'd been through, but we figured, "What the hell, we're probably better than they are." We did pretty well.

For the first month, we did a lot of marching in the Vosges Mountains without always being aware of our objective. We'd go two, three weeks, maybe a month without seeing the other platoons, we were so scattered. When winter settled in, there wasn't much activity. That was when we started to move out of the mountains into the villages.

I was a BAR man when we went overseas. A lot of men couldn't carry it. I guess there was a little bit of bravado there. I made damn sure I wasn't a target, though. It took a real touch to get off single shots, but I learned. Automatic weapons drew fire.

Our platoon was out in an open snowfield one freezing night [22 January 1945] when all hell broke loose behind us. Company headquarters had been captured. Seven or eight of us were missing in action for a couple of days. We used abandoned American antitank guns and other equipment to guide us back to our lines. For two nights, we slept in ditches. In one village, we were standing next to a house when someone inside said, "Don't go that way. German soldiers." I thought, "Jesus, am I in a trap or do I listen to this?" But it was good advice.

My feet were frostbitten. They never turned black, but there was intense needle like pain that was so bad I couldn't stand the weight of a sleeping bag. It would take me two or three miles in the morning before I could walk comfortably. I was never evacuated, though. It was a matter of pride.

I had a very low opinion of guys who were looking for the million-dollar wound. I noticed that the quiet, friendly person was a better infantryman than the braggart, the loudmouth. The guy who said he was going to do this and do that to the Germans, watch out for him. He wasn't going to hold up.

But I can't think of anybody I was personally involved with that ever failed to do what was required of him. I saw all of us hesitate at times, but there was always somebody who would start the movement in the right direction. There might have been some wavering, but I never saw anybody turn tail and run except one sergeant.

I always felt nothing was going to happen to me, until maybe two or three weeks before the war ended. I got to thinking, "This is ridiculous. I've taken enough chances." Only five of the original guys in the platoon hadn't been killed, wounded, or sent back with illness. I didn't want to be the last man killed in the war.

My luck held. I have scars from a tree burst where the explosion lifted me clear off my feet. Another time, the stock was shot off of my rifle, but I never got a Purple Heart.

At the end of the war, we were in Innsbruck. Everybody was building up a liquor supply when I got another letter from a general. This was in July of '45. Here's the letter, from the commanding general of the 45th Division: "You have just been transferred from your old outfit. . . . We begin today the friendships which will carry us with swiftness and certainty to complete victory over our remaining enemy, Japan."

I didn't think much of that. I wanted no part of the attack on Japan. I'd done my bit. The greatest thing that ever happened was when Truman decided to drop the atomic bomb. I'm sure he saved a lot of lives on both sides.

But if he hadn't, I'd have been ready to go. There was never any thought of going over the hill. If you're an American citizen, you owe a debt to your country. And the better trained a man is, the more experience he's had, why, that's the man to give the job to.

EPILOGUE

LORRAINE BRENNAN
Brennan's wife

I was depressed when I found out he was going to the infantry. I was visiting him at the college down in Memphis on April Fool's Day in 1944 when he told me. I thought, "Golly, the years that will be wasted." He deserved better than that. He could have been a leader, and then to be stuck in the infantry. That's when I remembered how one of the doctors at the hospital where I worked said, "Sign up early or they'll put you anyplace." He waited too long to go in.

We were married June 15, 1943, in Cleveland. My parents wanted me to wait till Bob returned from service. Maybe they meant "if he returned," but they never said that.

BRENNAN

Your mother did.

LORRAINE BRENNAN

Well, she probably thought it. While Bob was overseas, I enrolled at Western Reserve University for nursing and psychology courses, thinking that if he didn't come back, I would improve my nursing career. I quit when he came home. We were interested in having a family, and Bob wanted me to stay home with the children.

He was drafted one day, and we were married the next. I immediately went to work nursing at St. Luke's Hospital. Many of the nurses were going into the service and into industry, where the pay was better, so hospital nursing was extremely hard. I had 46 patients and no help. But hard work was one of the facts in maintaining my mentality, I think. I worked till I was exhausted. Having Bob in the infantry was a constant worry. Every morning, the first thing I did was check the *Plain Dealer* to see where the Seventh Army was. I was doing an awful lot of praying. I think it helped.

BRENNAN

Here I am.

LORRAINE BRENNAN

Every night when I got home, I wrote my letter. There wasn't always enough to tell, but I wrote anyway. Bob was an only child, and his mother would call; she'd be so worried. I tried to reassure her he'd be all right even though I didn't believe it myself.

When he got home in March of 1946, he didn't talk much about the war, but he seemed normal. No bad dreams or things like that. He wanted to go on job interviews right away. I wanted him to relax a little bit like our friends were doing, but he said, "Nope." I was washing and ironing white shirts every day.

BRENNAN

I have trouble believing those guys who talk about their bad dreams. I might as well tell you. I used to feel good when I saw dead Germans. When you've lost some friends, you feel pretty good about it.

LORRAINE BRENNAN

When Bob was in Innsbruck, he sent me some big wooden crates full of souvenirs: Nazi flags and badges, a sword, a helmet, bayonets, rifles, and a dagger. My friends—this is a terrible thing to think of now—were getting fine silver and linens and china.

BRENNAN

Their husbands were in rear-echelon outfits, Dear. They had time to pack it and get it to the post office.

LORRAINE BRENNAN

It wasn't right. It was stealing from those poor people. Things that women treasure in their homes.

BRENNAN

I've always been patriotic. During Vietnam, our second-oldest boy said if they drafted him he was going to Canada. I just could not believe anybody would do that. I feel if you're born and raised here, you have an obligation to your country.

My combat service will always have a special place inside me. I met a heck of a lot of fine people. It was traumatic and interesting, and I'm glad I lived through it.

LORRAINE BRENNAN

Bob used to display his souvenirs in the church parlor and at school. He talked to our three boys about the war, and they all listened, and they all played with guns when they were little. Now they don't want a gun in the house. The boys are so fearful of war. They think it's horrible, a thing they never want to experience.

9

"FUCK YOU, SERGEANT."

Joseph Skocz grew up in Chicago and as a youth was "just shooting around in part-time jobs" when the army gave him a focus in life by drafting him into the infantry.

Skocz, who died 7 November 1989, was a staff sergeant and rifle squad leader in E Company's Second Platoon. He was interviewed on 18 June 1988, at his home in Crystal Lake, Illinois. Like many other members of E Company, his memories centered around events in late January of 1945, when German troops twice overran the company's positions.

SKOCZ

We got kicked off the outpost line [on 22 January] and had to make our way back to the MLR as best we could. The next day, they needed people to close a gap in the line where the 36th Combat Engineers were supposed to be. These two people from G Company [James Teague and John H. LaVelle] guided me and six others from E Company into the gap when a machine gun opened up. We made for a shack out in the middle of an open field. There wasn't a shred of cover except that beat-up building.

JOHN H. (JACK) LAVELLE

G Company

The shed was full of land mines the Germans had stored there. We were halfway there when a tank started firing up the hill from Rothbach. A lot of stuff was coming through the walls, but they couldn't shoot low enough to hit us. We kicked the boards out on the side away from the tank and went out, one at a time.

SKOCZ

The amazing thing is that all nine of us got out. I was the only one wounded, but there were people with slugs through the front of their jackets, slugs through their packs, one man with bazooka shells on his back who had slugs glancing off the shells. A man had the back of his boot split open. Another got his rifle shot out of his hands. But I'm telling you, no broken skin on any of those guys. We finally made it out with the help of a BAR man that was on our flank. We would give him signals to fire, and every time he opened up, someone took off.

Me and another guy from Clinton, Iowa, was all that was left. The gun opened up again, and I'm hit. This guy says, "We gotta get our butts moving outa here." I says, "I'm hit." He says, "I don't think so." Instead of getting out of there, we were talking back and forth. I reached back and wiped my hand across my butt and showed him the blood on my glove. "What is this?" I says. And he says, "I don't know. I don't think you're hit."

Finally, I told him, "Get your ass moving because it may take me forever. I don't know yet how bad it is." He wouldn't do it. "Sergeant," he says, "I know you're giving me an order, but I want a request. I want to come out last to see how you move. If you don't move, I don't move. You've got to go out with me."

I gave up and said I'd go first. The guy with the BAR opened up, and I took off. When I got to my feet, I found I could move. No bone had been hit. One of the slugs that hit me flattened out and tore up inside. I got it in the left thigh, right thigh, and the butt. One slug. Another inch lower, it would have shattered my knee cap. To this day, I don't know who to thank, the Lord or the Germans.

That BAR man is who really saved all of us. I never found out who he was. He must have been from the closest rifle company. G Company? Without him, we would never have got out of there.

LAVELLE

Whoever he was, he was in G Company's Third Platoon. Murphy? It could have been Murphy. He was a BAR man at the time.[1]

SKOCZ

I got halfway back to cover when I stumbled in the snow. My steel pot [helmet] came whipping down and hit the bridge of my nose. At the same moment, there was the crack of a single shot. You know how those suckers sound when they're close, like a tiny sonic boom. I thought the guy had shot my nose off. There were tears coming out of my eyes, that's how bad it hurt, and it made me drop my rifle.

After that, I didn't run anymore. I crawled. The other guy passed me on the way. When I got close enough, the others yanked my arms and dragged me into cover. The first thing they said was, "Why did you go back for your rifle and helmet?" I didn't know I had. I wanted to go after that machine gun, but everybody was hollering, "You're getting out of here." I refused to go out on a litter. It was too hard for the guys to carry me up that steep hill. So they walked me out, but one of them lifted up on my rifle belt to help me out.

I don't blame Teague and LaVelle for what happened. They'd gone across that open area before, and nothing happened.

JAMES TEAGUE

private first class, G Company[2]

There was this boy from E Company got seriously hit across the legs. It was years and years at our reunions I would ask about him, and I finally found him. He thought I was the one that gave the orders that got him shot, but it really wasn't that way. Finally, I told him I'd introduce him to the man who was responsible, just teasing, you know, and went and got LaVelle. It was friendly. LaVelle gave me my orders, but he got his from someone else.

SKOCZ

Before I was wounded, I had another guy give me a hard time in a hairy situation. We were on a patrol out in front of Welferding. This guy was my scout, moving through a woods, when all of a sudden everything stopped. I went up to see what was what. He points and says, "There's people out there. They're waiting to nail us." I says, "They're not moving." He says, "Neither are we."

I'm the squad leader. What do I do? I tell him to go up there and see what he can find out. He leans up real close to my head and he says, "Fuck you,

Sergeant. You wanta find out, go up yourself." That brought on a lull of quiet.

But I didn't have any choice but to check the situation out, so I walked ahead a ways, then crawled as fast as I could, watching for movement. Nothing. When I got up to where he had been pointing, I could see the problem: Bushes! It was bushes that got clobbered with sticky snow that hung on the branches.

When we got back, I told him I never wanted to see him on the front lines again. "I won't report you; just go in and ask for a transfer, and remember that I won't forget what happened." I never saw him again.

Some of my strongest memories are dealing with other soldiers. I was in a hospital in December, before I got hit, to get my stomach straightened out. I was gone maybe a week and a half. A lot of replacements come in from the air force while I was gone, and every one of those guys was a noncom. So when I got back, there was somebody in my spot. In I walked, saw the guys, says "Hi ho" to them, this and that, and I tells this new sergeant I'm taking over. He resented it, but I said, "These are my people. I'm taking over the squad." I don't know what ever happened to him. Seems like he just disappeared.

Being wounded kept me away from the company for four months. At one time, the doctors hung a ZI tag on me. Then for some unknown reason they sent me to England instead. After I was well enough, they wanted to put me in some other outfit, but I insisted on going back to E Company. When you're an original and you've lived with your people for so long and you depend on them, you become family. Besides, I didn't know anybody else in Europe. So they finally put RTO on my papers, and I took off looking for the outfit.

By that time, the 103d was on a fast chase through Germany, and I never did catch up till they were in Innsbruck and it was all over. The division was starting to break up, and I got stuck in the 36th Combat Engineers. Yep, the same outfit we were looking for when I got hit.

EPILOGUE

SKOCZ

I still feel my wound at times. The bullet must have touched a nerve. Sometimes I get a funny feeling in my right leg. But I don't complain. I never asked for any disability. I don't feel I'm crippled in any way.

As soon as I got home, they discharged me. I might have re-enlisted if they hadn't broken up the old outfit. But once you've been whipped into shape by a guy like John Rhye,[3] nothing else can be as good. He was eight or nine years older than I was. Maybe he was like a father figure. He was a big, rugged individual, very rough and very firm, but he could be gentle too. He watched you to make sure you didn't make a misstep. He would go out and have a hell of a time with the guys, and if you got into an argument with him, you could patch it up, and he'd forget it ever happened. He meant a lot to us young ones that came in.

INTERLUDE: CASUALTIES

Casualties fascinate veterans. At Second Battalion reunions when the hour is late and the stories and the whisky are flowing, one of the favorite phrases is "over 100 percent."

The reference is to casualty rates, and a look at the statistics show the yarn spinners are right, probably more right than they realize. Casualty statistics for G Company, which was the hardest hit, show a total casualty rate of 128 percent. Actually, it was higher. The statistics assume that the company was always at full strength when in fact it almost never was. Combat strength varied from day to day. A. J. Torrance, G Company commander, remembers that his company was 25 percent below full strength when the final assault on Germany began on 15 March 1945.

But there are casualties and there are casualties. In the Second Battalion, more than half were "N/B," or nonbattle. [See chapter 7.] Missing from the table that follows is "SIW," or self-inflicted wounds. SIWs were part of the daily folklore of combat, like the threats by soldiers to kill hated officers. Murder of officers never happened, at least in this battalion, but there was deliberate self-wounding once in a while. No record of the number was kept.

Stripped of the nonbattle figures, casualty rates still demonstrate that "infantryman" was a hazardous position. E Company, which had the fewest, suffered 50 percent combat casualties: killed, wounded, and missing in action. The combat casualty rate for F Company was 56 percent, and for G Company, 69 percent.

Why was G Company's rate so much higher? Every outfit thought it was called on for more dangerous jobs than any other, but that may have been true for G Company. Robert Loyd, a G Company rifleman, thinks it was because "they asked us to do a lot of things they wanted done right, and they figured Al Torrance was the guy to do it. A price had to be paid."

Still, casualties were not out of line. B Company of the First Battalion had more men killed. The highest number of wounded in the regiment was in A Company.

These figures are similar to those of other units that entered the war in its closing months, but they pale beside outfits like the Third Division, which fought for three years in Africa, Italy, France, and Germany. The Third Division had 4,280 killed and 15,208 wounded, the highest total of any American combat unit in World War II. The 103d Division had 821 killed and 3,329 wounded.

Tactics made a huge difference. The marines in the Pacific fought short but extremely violent engagements. At Tarawa in November 1943 in a battle that lasted just three days, the Second Marine Division lost 990 men killed and 2,391 wounded.

In the table that follows, KIA stands for "killed in action," WIA for "wounded in action," MIA for "missing in action," and N/B for "nonbattle."

CASUALTIES
410th infantry, 103d Division

	KIA	WIA	MIA	Total Battle Casualties	N/B	Total Casualties
First Battalion						
Hq. Co.	0	10	20	30	57	87
A Co.	19	105	12	136	113	249
B Co.	32	77	18	127	144	271
C Co.	15	72	19	106	134	240
D Co.	8	31	9	48	62	110
Totals	74	295	78	447	510	957
Second Battalion						
Hq. Co.	7	7	4	18	48	66
E Co.	13	53	29	95	162	257
F Co.	14	93	0	107	149	256
G Co.	28	70	34	132	113	245
H Co.	4	21	10	35	48	83
Totals	66	244	77	387	520	907
Third Battalion						
Hq. Co.	4	6	0	10	49	59
I Co.	12	46	3	61	132	193
K Co.	2	39	1	42	132	174
L Co.	15	52	2	69	90	159
M Co.	2	13	2	17	56	73
Totals	35	156	8	199	459	658
Regimental						
Hq. Co.	0	2	0	2	32	34
Cannon Co.	1	2	0	3	23	26
Service Co.	0	0	2	2	28	30
Anti-Tank Co.	3	3	0	6	35	41
Medical Det.	4	17	8	29	49	78
Totals	8	24	10	42	167	209
Grand Totals	183	719	173	1075	1656	2731

Source: Adjutant General's records, National Archives and Records Administration, Suitland, Maryland.

TWO

F Company

10

FIGHTING IN EVERY DIRECTION

The late John S. Clark was the most admired soldier in the Second Battalion. Tough and brave and solicitous of his men, he was a Regular Army professional in the best sense of the word.

Comments Paul Fussell, writer and F Company platoon leader, "Clark was tough. I thought he was a real pig before the war when we were training, a real brutal bastard, hopelessly uncultivated. But he was very, very good, just a brave old army man who turned out to be an excellent combat leader. I developed great respect for him. We needed more like him."

Dr. Robert E. Lawler, F Company platoon leader, says "The one man who had the most effect on me, drawing my respect, teaching me, was John Clark. He was just one of those people you had to look up to. I admired him tremendously. If anybody made a man or a soldier out of me, it was John Clark."

When Clark went overseas, it was as first sergeant of F Company, but he soon earned a battlefield commission to second lieutenant.

CLARK

I joined the army in '32, but things were pretty slow till the war broke out in 1941. The Japs, they opened up promotions pretty good.

I was down to the border with one of those chemical warfare companies when the first [sergeant] asked me if I wanted to be cadre [permanently assigned trainer of troops] some place. I could see my old outfit was breaking up, and I didn't like it a little bit, but so what? It was breaking up. So I told the first I wouldn't mind, but not as a mess sergeant, which was my job for a long time. He says, "Well, we'll think about it," and pretty soon there was orders cut that had me on the cadre as first sergeant.

Me and a lot of those ol' boys from Fort Sam Houston went to Camp Shelby, Mississippi, to organize the 85th Division, but we only stayed two or three months and went on to Camp Claiborne to activate the 103d. I went to F Company, and that's where I stayed.

Throughout my army career, I always tried to stay associated with the best people I possibly could, and it was tough with all the turnover. We got all those boys trained up, and then the word came we had to fill up the 88th Division to go overseas. So we started the training all over again, and we sure picked up some good men. Those college boys from the ASTP filled in real good. And the draftees were good too. A soldier was a soldier. He had a job to do, I had a job to do. If he was under me, he was going to do that work of his, and whoever I was under, I would try to carry out whatever he wanted.

When we got overseas, we went on line the 10th of November to relieve the Third Division. Two of our platoons replaced one of their companies. I think they had about 30 men in the company, that's how bad they was beaten down.

Those Germans had the place well zeroed in. I got hit that first night. We got up to where the Third had a CP. I was trying to patch a broken telephone wire when a mortar shell blew me and the wire and two messengers right out. I never did see the messengers again. I was wearing a big, old heavy trench coat some truck driver threw away. If it hadn't been for that, it would of been a lot worse. Fragments hit me in the back and along the side, but I had the first aid man put sulfa powder on the cuts so I could stay up on the line. That sulfa was good. Kept me from getting infected.

They give me the Silver Star a few days later for helping get our men in position. Mostly, I think they give it to me for publicity. I don't know. It was the first one in the division.

[The citation in part: "On the night of 10–11 November, 1944 in the vicinity of [censored] France . . . 1st Sergeant Clark's company was proceeding through a dense wood [when] intense artillery fire began to fall among the men, causing disorder and a threat of serious casualties . . . 1st Sergeant Clark, with utter disregard for his own safety, and hampered by sleet and snow, on his own initiative moved among his men dispersing them, leading them to places of greater security and restoring order."]

When we pulled back a few days later to get a little rest, I found out someone had left a man up on the line in a foxhole. I decided I'd go git that boy, and I finally found him. Must have been three miles up toward the German lines where I finally found him. He wasn't out of position. Whoever was in charge of his platoon had pulled out without checking and left him there.

Before we went overseas, the company commander [Capt. Cornelius Scott] bet me a fifth of liquor the war would be over by November 11. He got shot through the legs not too long after that [on 30 November 1944 at Nothalten] in our first real scrap. We lost 27 men and three officers. It was a horrible fight. Seemed like there was fighting in every direction. One ol' boy named Fontenot even got hit with a bayonet. Far as I know, that was the only bayonet wound in the war.[1]

I did something I probably shouldn't of done. We were so short of men I used some Germans we'd captured to carry our wounded back to the aid station, and then had them bring back ammunition so we could continue fighting. I might have been a little in arrears in that, but I didn't have any men to get it up otherwise.

Another time, I can't remember where it was, that cost us a man. This boy was walking wounded, so he was sent to the rear with some prisoners. It wasn't but just a few yards from where he started that they killed him and got away.

That battle at Nothalten left us pretty short. When we got replacements, we put some of the old men with some of the new men. Even when a squad was beat down to two men, they didn't want to be moved. It was home, that squad. It sure was.

Gibbs [Spilman Gibbs, who had taken over as company commander] says, "How about making you a lieutenant? You made one out of me," meaning the training I'd given. At first I said no, but I thought about it a while. I'm probably going to get bumped off anyway, is the way I figured, so I might as well be an officer, and my wife would get a little bit more compensation. That's the only reason I took it, and only if Gibbs saw to it I came back to the same company.

When I came back with the commission, the men all wanted to be in my platoon, the Third Platoon. It made me feel pretty good. I won't say the men liked me, but they respected me, they knew I wasn't going to do anything wrong for them.

I used to tell them, "I'll carry 5,000 rounds more rather than get one of your hands hurt." I tried to lay down a blanket of fire. You never knew who did the killing. I never knew, and I don't think anybody else does.

Before we jumped off for the Rhine [on 15 March 1945], the colonel called me up from Battalion and said, "John, I won't think a bit less of you if you don't want to do this, but I need you and three men to reconnoiter behind the German lines to see what it's like where we got to go."

Well, three men volunteered to go with me. One was a big ol' sergeant [Mike Engle; see the epilogue] out of the Second Platoon, and the platoon sergeant out of the First Platoon, and the jeep driver for the Old Man 'cause he could speak German. We jumped off about nine or ten o'clock at night (on 12 March) and made it about three miles out between our lines and the German lines. I wanted to lay up in a line of trees, but maybe we made a little too much noise. Somebody set off a flare, and we had to freeze right quick. I could see we ain't going to get back by daylight, so we were going to hide in manure piles till I realized the Germans would see us if there was fresh manure turned up.

The best thing was to get out in a field. The four of us laid there flat all day long. Couldn't turn over, couldn't eat, couldn't smoke, and I lived on cigarettes in those days. We found little trenches where the farmers had plowed, getting ready for spring, you know, and made 'em a little deeper with our trench knives. We spent the day marking down German mortar positions.

On the way back that night, one of those ol' boys, he wanted to get a prisoner. I said "Uh, uh. We got back this close. I ain't going to take a chance." We were out there about 36 hours, and when we got back to Regiment, the division commander was giving attack commands for the next day. He says to me, "Could I infiltrate a battalion through where you were?" I says, "Sir, you couldn't get a platoon through there." He turned to the colonel and said, "We'll knock that plan in the head."

I thought I'd have a couple of days rest, but the attack started the next bloomin' day. We had a rough time of it. There was Germans above us to the left and right, and they got to firing those mortars down on us. Fortunately, we were caught in a little marsh. Mortars won't do much in swampy ground. They get buried before they explode.

When we got through the swamp, we had to cross about 800 yards in the open to get to the Germans in the woods. I had to get out in front of my men that time. The Germans were firing at them, and my men were shooting right into the ground. I told 'em, "Git those damn rifles up. You're not hitting anything."

We had a problem with people gittin' diarrhea when they was scared. I didn't blame 'em. It was hard work.

JOHN J. KAISER
squad leader

We never had a BAR when we went into battle 'cause he [the gunner] always had diarrhea.

CLARK

Nobody's perfect. A German truck started to pull out in front of me. I pulled up my carbine to take a shot at him and pressed the safety. Except I pressed my bloomin' clip release instead, and there were my shells all over the place. I got a little excited, I guess. I could surely have got that truck, but I was sitting there empty.

A lieutenant from H Company [2d Lt. Raymond F. Biedrzycki] got killed in those woods and Fussell [2d Lt. Paul Fussell] got wounded when a tank started firing in front of them. [See chapter 11.] When I saw that, I pulled back into the trees. Let 'em hit the trees and go off 'fore they git to me. That was the only time in my life I ever saw American soldiers run. I got 'em stopped after maybe a couple of hundred yards. We dug in there that night.

The next morning, it was a sight to see all those boys laying there dead. They'd got some of the wounded out, but not the dead. I went to the company CP to get orders. Sittin' at a table waitin' for the company commander, I was so knocked out I just slid down and slept till he came in. I appreciated that sleep.

[The next day, F and G companies attacked the village of Gundershoffen across an open field. See chapter 22. Clark completes his story in chapter 24.]

EPILOGUE

After the war, John Clark served two more tours in Germany and rose to captain before he retired in 1955. He was living in Lugoff, South Carolina, struggling against debilitating illness, when he was interviewed on 12 April 1988. He died on 26 September 1988, at the age of 78.

Mike Engle, the "big 'ol sergeant from the Second Platoon" on the 12–13 March patrol behind enemy lines, was shot in the jaw by a German machine pistol two days later. Extensive reconstructive surgery was required. He spent eight months in military hospitals before his discharge in October 1945, when he returned to college. In 1952, he was ordained an Episcopal priest and served several Mississippi parishes until his death on 14 January 1988.

MIKE ENGLE, JR.

Engle's son

As a child, I remember feeling the bullet in the back of Dad's neck. It had to be removed around 1960, but many fragments of teeth and bullets were left in. He and I went back to Alsace a few years before he died. He led me right to the place in the woods where he was wounded. He told me the sensation was like someone grabbed his collar and punched him in the face as fast as he could. It spun him around, but he didn't lose consciousness. He never saw the man who shot him.

JIM McCARTHY

F Company machine gunner

Mike stood up to shoot at a German machine gun, and the guy hit him three times in the face. When we got up to him, he was still standing up, spitting blood and teeth and everything else. One of our guys said, "Get back with the medics." Mike says, "I can walk." I realize now he was in shock. That was the last I seen him till the reunion in 1985.

MIKE ENGLE, JR.

A medical aid man came by with a morphine shot, but he took a look at Dad and told him to wait for a stretcher bearer. He wasn't going to waste a shot on someone who was going to die. Dad knew he'd bleed to death if he waited, so he walked back on his own. He could still remember how men coming forward averted their eyes.

But he had very little disfigurement. He thought it was worse than it was. He had to learn to talk again. One of the bullets shot half an inch off of his tongue.

I was never in the military myself. I secretly wanted to go to Vietnam, but I would have had to drop out of college. Dad thought it was horrible, a bad war, and he didn't want to lose his only son. But he was not an antiwar activist or a pacifist. I'm sorry he missed the Persian Gulf. He'd have been glued to the set for that one.

It hurt that I could never really understand what he went through. Here I was, 20 years old like he was, and all I was worried about was the dance that night. Dad tried to make me feel better. "Then is then, and now is now," he would say.

11

2D LT. PAUL FUSSELL

Abrasive, iconoclastic, controversial, sentimental: Paul Fussell is these and more. Today, he is a distinguished man of letters at the University of Pennsylvania and a widely known commentator on war, but this chapter is about the 20-year-old second lieutenant who was a rifle platoon leader in F Company.

He began the interview by announcing that "luckily enough, I came from an upper-middle-class family in Pasadena." He once described his fellow soldiers as "hillbillies and Okies, dropouts and used car salesmen and petty criminals."

Fussell got into the army in 1943 through the Enlisted Reserve Corps. He joined while in college with the promise of an extra semester of school and an eventual commission. After basic training, he was commissioned and assigned to F Company in the spring of 1944 as leader of the Second Platoon. It was just what he wanted.

FUSSELL

Edward Hudson [to whom he dedicated *The Great War and Modern Memory*, 1975] was my platoon sergeant. Very experienced, very cynical, very calm and cool. I respected him deeply, and I hope he did me. I was 20, and he was like 37, but, quite amazingly, he accepted my leadership. It was a great dramatic act, actually, because half the time I didn't know what to do and he always covered for me. When I dedicated my book to him, I sort of hoped his family would get in touch with me, but I never heard a word.

We went on line for the first time at La Bolle, outside St. Die. A night relief, and it was grotesque. Absolutely pitch dark. We had no idea we would be close to the Germans. There was so much racket they heard us and began shelling.

The next morning I got orders to take three men and set up an observation post in a farmhouse in front of our lines. "Do what you like if they attack," were my orders. "If you think you can make it back, do it. Or hold to the last man. But give us warning." Well, all day long I watched out of an upstairs window and didn't see a thing. But that night, the Germans started digging new defenses and were perfectly silhouetted against the flames from St. Die, which they had set on fire. I called for mortar fire and our gunners put 20 incredibly effective 81 [millimeter mortar] shells onto those people and blew them up in the air. Immensely satisfying.

It was a dumb second john's trick to be up there, though. The Germans figured out where they'd been observed from. Ten minutes later, they practically blew the house apart. No one was hit except the daughter of the French family living there. She got a shell fragment in her calf. The family was very disturbed. We spent the rest of the time in the basement.

It went on like that for a while, attacking small Alsatian towns, half of which proved to be full of Germans who would leave after a show of resistance. Once, we gave a town a barrage with our 60 [millimeter] mortars and then attacked. We were met by an absolutely distraught woman. We had killed her husband, a harmless civilian. There were no Germans in the town at all.

DANIEL HIGLEY
H Company machine gunner

[From his diary] "Nov. 29—We moved forward at 0600 and set up our guns on a hill. . . . Our riflemen advanced into town and found that the krauts had withdrawn during the night. Capt. [Cornelius] Scott of F Company had already called for mortar fire on the town, however, and two or three French civilians were needlessly killed as a result. They were blown to bits, and as we passed through the town we could see the victims' family grieving and crying in a manner none of us will ever forget. That incident gave us one of our most vivid pictures of the horror of war."

FUSSELL

That was sort of typical of our procedures, our willingness to substitute firepower for intelligence and subtlety. If we had sent in even one man to talk to the natives, they could have told us the Germans had left.

Captain Scott was shot through the knees along about this time [at the village of Nothalten on 30 November 1944]. My platoon was out ahead of the company. I'd sort of gotten out of control at that point, very gung ho. Finally, a messenger told me to hold it where we were and come back after dark. I found Scott delirious in a dugout. He was in great pain and in his lunacy very unanxious to relinquish his command. Gibbs[1] [1st Lt. Spilman Gibbs] told me to pay no attention to what Scott said. "I'm in command. We're going to remove the captain." And we did. It was the right thing to do. Captain Scott was incapable of command anymore.

From that point on, Gibbs was the company commander. His style was very different from Scott's, cool and ironic where Scott was solid and stolid and phlegmatic.

Like the other officers, I carried a carbine, a contemptible little weapon. But not after the time I was out with my men on one of those mad patrols. We got lost and stumbled into three Germans. I'd sent my men off to see what they could see, and several of them left their M-1s leaning against a tree. When three soldiers came from the direction they had gone, I stood up and waved. Then I saw that their helmets were cut square. Germans! I leaped for those M-1s. Thank God, the one I grabbed had something in the chamber. I pushed off the safety and fired all eight rounds.

One of the Germans had a side of bacon on his belt. His blood was leaking all over. It looked like a slaughterhouse. One got away limping. We never found him. The third man ran into my own men as they were returning and surrendered. From that moment on, I carried an M-1. I had great faith in that weapon. And it helped me look like an enlisted man.[2]

The first town names I remember were Neiderbronn and Bischholtz. We retreated through the snow one night from Neiderbronn [on 21 January 1945] and took up positions overlooking Bischholtz. The engineers had to blast out holes. The ground was frozen solid.

The Germans broke through and got into Schillersdorf, but my platoon wasn't involved. The thing I remember most about that time was going back to company headquarters and finding everybody distraught. A couple of U.S. soldiers, coming up to replace us, had been killed because they didn't know the password.

I caught pneumonia and had to be evacuated. When I got to the aid station, there was this second lieutenant who'd been commanding a machine gun post about 100 yards to my right. When the German attack began, he fled out the back of his dugout without saying anything to anyone, he and five or six of his men.

There he was, sitting in a corner of the aid station full of shame, a psychoneurotic battle casualty. In those days, we were pretty tough on people like that. I ignored him; he had cut out. He was a new fellow in our company, very smart, a replacement. I don't think he'd been in combat at all.[3]

[Two months later, Fussell found his own nerves had cracked. In an article he wrote for *Harper's* magazine in January 1982 titled "My War," Fussell said that "when I returned to the line early in March (after recovering from pneumonia), I found for the first time that I was terrified, unwilling to take the chances that before had seemed rather sporting. . . ." When I asked him during our interview what had happened to change him, he said:]

I don't know what happened. I think it was that I'd had time to think about it in the hospital. I developed a sense that I had become vulnerable, which was quite irrational. You can be hit the first day as well as the 101st. Just before that, I'd been on several night raids that I disapproved of very highly. Those raids struck me as absolute folly, stupidity, and I almost refused to go on them, but not quite. On one, I led a squad, and on another, I led the whole platoon, trying to surprise a German machine gun nest. Those scared me very badly. By March 15, I was pretty tense and nervous.

We were one of the lead platoons that day. The objective was one of those towns that begins with G [Gundershoffen]. It was a very long day. We took off at port arms, sort of, walking through a smoke screen. Gradually, groups of terrified German prisoners would come back toward us, and we would gesture them to the rear. We ended up on the forward slope of a hill and stayed there most of the morning in this most dangerous, exposed position while Gibbs consulted with us and tried to get Battalion on the radio. We didn't dig in at all, and we should have, immediately. We just lay there. Thank God the Germans at that point didn't have any artillery observation, or they would have wiped us out.

The Germans were in a woods. Finally, Gibbs got orders to cross a road that was under machine gun fire and take cover in a ditch. Every time one of my men ran across, there would be a short burst down the road, and somehow that terrified me.

I kept urging the men across. I probably should have crossed right behind the scout, but I stayed where I was till the whole platoon was across.

That was when a lieutenant colonel who was trying to find out what was holding us up told me, "Fussell, I've got my eye on you. Look out. Any more of that and you're going to get in really deep trouble." I said, "Okay, I've got it." He was right. It was a deserved rebuke.

SPILMAN GIBBS

F Company commander

I don't think so. He tried his best. I'll be perfectly frank about it. He should have had a little more drive. I thought he was a pretty good officer, but there were times when he was lacking, let's put it that way.

JOHN S. CLARK

second lieutenant, F Company, leader of the Third Platoon

Fussell's a professor at one of those colleges. He wrote an article just the way he saw it, and it was a good job. I guess there was a lot of men felt that way about the war. His combat performance? Well, there was very little of it. I don't know where he was all the time after we jumped off. He was like a lot of the rest of the officers. They was scared. I was too, but I knew somebody had to do it so I done what I could. Fussell wanted to be a good soldier, but I think he was a little bit afraid.

FUSSELL

Battalion ordered a Civil War–style attack on a copse about 500 yards away where the Germans were dug in. It took an hour to get organized, but we did it, so-called marching fire across an open field, shouting and trying to scare the Germans, fixed bayonets, the whole act. [Second Lt. Raymond] Biedrzycki's heavy machine guns fired along the edge of the woods to keep the Germans down as we crossed. I was certain it would be a disaster, but, remarkably, nobody was hit.

Twenty yards into the woods, they pinned us down, as we used to say, with machine gun fire. Sergeant Hudson and I were together, which was a mistake. We should have separated to be more effective. We stayed there a minute or so, trying to figure out where the machine gun was and what to do about it, when one of my sergeants without any orders sneaked around to the left and killed the gunner with a grenade. The gunner was the German that I mentioned in the [*Harper's*] essay.

[In *Harper's*, Fussell mused: "Why did the red-haired young German machine-gunner . . . not go on living—marrying, going to university, going to the beach, laughing, smiling—but keep firing long after he had made his point, and so require us to kill him with a grenade?"]

Once the machine gun was out, my platoon moved gradually through the woods, capturing various people. I was out of contact with Gibbs and the other platoons, advancing on a skirmish line till we reached the end of the woods, where we captured more prisoners. There was nothing in front of us but a field. I didn't see any enemy, so I thought this was the place to consolidate, see who's missing, get organized, and decide what to do next. It was about four or five o'clock, too late to do any further attacking.

We were out of breath, sort of recovering our senses, when we became aware that a German self-propelled 88 was firing very systematically across the front of the woods. About 200 yards to my left, a shell struck right at the edge of the woods. Another one hit 50 yards closer, then another 50 yards closer. We didn't quite know what to do. My men, though, rushed into a deep German dugout.

DAN HIGLEY

There must have been 30 or 40 of us in that dugout.

FUSSELL

I was still aware of the colonel's rebuke earlier in the day and very conscious that I shouldn't be seen taking cover. So I didn't run into the dugout. If we had, we would have been untouched. None of those in the dugout was hurt at all.

Hudson and [2d Lt. Raymond F.] Biedrzycki and I were flat on our stomachs under a tree, so close our shoulders were touching, planning what to do next with Biedrzycki's machine gun. I was in between them. A shell hit the tree 30 feet above us, an immense crack and bang that left me deaf for five minutes. Hudson and Biedrzycki were killed. I was hit through the back and the leg.

DR. CARL G. NICHOLS, JR.

second lieutenant, leader of F Company's Fourth Platoon

It was flat trajectory 88 fire. You couldn't hear 'em coming. I was running for a dugout we'd just cleaned out when one of the shells went off. I fell between some other people that turned out to be Fussell, his platoon sergeant, and a machine gun platoon leader. A shell exploded right over us and knocked my breath out. Fussell rolled over on his back and said, "Nick, I'm hit, I'm hit." Biedrzycki and Hudson were both dead. Their faces were black. I dived for the dugout. It was every man for himself.

FUSSELL

[In *Harper's*] "[The shell fragments] felt like red hot knives going in, but I was as interested in the few quiet moans, like those of a hurt child drifting off to sleep, of my thirty-seven-year-old platoon sergeant."

[Sitting in his peaceful, cloistered university office 43 years later, Fussell's memories of those brief minutes of smoke and blood have not faded.]

The first thing I did was take a deep breath to see if my lung had been penetrated. It hadn't been, so I knew I would be all right if I could get out of the shell fire. My medic wrapped me up and pulled me part way. Then I leaned on another man, serving as a crutch, and staggered to the bunker where the wounded were being assembled. We stayed there till dark, when gradually the medics began to take out the people who could walk. I could still walk at that stage, but in the morning after lying in the cold all night, I was so stiff I couldn't move anything. From then on, I was a litter person.

NICHOLS

I found Fussell in a dugout kind of pale. He asked me to look at his back. He had a little ol' hole near his kidney and another one in his leg, but he seemed to be doing all right, so I laid down and fell off to sleep.

FUSSELL

I don't remember Nichols at all. Lawler [2d Lt. Robert Lawler] was the only one in the company who came to see if I was okay. Lawler was a good friend of mine, very cool, a very good officer. He asked me if it hurt. I said, "Not at all," 'cause I was under morphine. "Liar," he said, and walked away. I haven't seen him since.

My medic had been hit in the calf, but he wanted to go back and help other people. He was a great guy. John something . . . [After consulting the casualty list, Fussell concludes the man's name was Juan Medellin of California.]

When we were being removed to the rear, I was very noble. I was conscious that I had a small disgrace to overcome. I insisted that I be the last one out. By that time, I was really feeling quite fine. Juan had given me morphine and tied me up, and the bleeding had stopped. I knew I would survive.

German prisoners carried me out on a litter. One of them was a kid about 17 whose ass I had kicked the day before. He was wearing American ODs when we captured him. We had this thing about not wearing the enemy's stuff. [GIs believed they would be subject to summary execution if captured with German souvenir pistols or other gear, and reacted violently when they caught Germans with American equipment.] The next morning, there he was at the end of my litter, about to carry me out. I felt guilty about what I'd done the day before, so to expiate, I gave him some K rations.

From then on, I was treated very well. They gave me more morphine at the aid station. At some point, there was a hospital train and an evacuation hospital that looked like the film of the battle of Atlanta [in *Gone With the Wind*]. A paved area maybe 200 yards square in front of the hospital was covered with litters.

That's where I had my first operation. My right leg had been torn open by shrapnel and fragments had entered my back. That night, I had this emotional breakdown that I've written about. It just seized me, and I couldn't stop crying. The other people in the ward paid no attention. They'd seen enough disaster to realize there must be some reason and to interfere would do no good.

Several days later, I was moved to another hospital and operated on again. I guess that's when they sewed me up. They used to leave wounds open for a while to air out. Then I was in another hospital in Épinal and stayed there a long time. The wound in my leg didn't heal. I was on penicillin shots every four hours for two weeks. Finally, the doctor said he'd have to open up the leg again.

That operation left an immense gash in my leg. In another war, I would have lost it. Penicillin is what saved me. My leg doesn't bother me at all now, but it's got me $300 a month for life for pipe tobacco, booze, and so on. You feel you can spend a little money irresponsibly.

I was in the hospital quite a long time. Roosevelt died, and the war in Europe ended. Then I started to learn to walk again after two months in bed. In June or July, I went back to my own company, but very shortly, they broke up the division, and I went to the 45th Division.

EPILOGUE

Fussell came home with the 45th Division and spent the next eleven months in various minor assignments before he was discharged in August 1946.

FUSSELL

The minute the war was over, I decided that I had been spared by some sort of curious accident, and I had better do something worthwhile. That's why I became a college professor and tried to direct young people for very little pay instead of becoming a highly paid journalist for *Life* or *Time* or *Newsweek*, which is the career I was aiming for before the war.

You felt you were paying a debt because you had been spared?

FUSSELL

I wasn't quite that superstitious. I had a sense that I had wasted my life to that point in frivolity, and I didn't want to waste it from there on.

Why do you think you survived?

FUSSELL

Just good luck. I was not at all religious. I may have prayed once or twice in the war, largely with my medic, who always carried a Bible. But except for moments like that, I had no truck with religion whatever.

I finished college at Pomona, then was at Harvard for my Ph.D. from 1947–51. I got married there in 1949. I propose to stay here [at the University of Pennsylvania] until I'm 70, which is the retirement age.

Other Second Battalion veterans are unhappy about the way you described them as a bunch of dropouts and hoods.

FUSSELL

Petty criminals and used car salesmen, actually. Well, everybody should realize that a writer is not a nice guy. I was actually very kind. I didn't say how utterly incompetent we were, how badly trained. Like lying out on that hillside exposed to German observation for two hours.

Nevertheless, my time in combat was the crucial moment in my life. I found out about myself, my strengths and weaknesses. I learned that my career was somehow in teaching and explaining things. Having barely escaped with my life taught me a lot about the conditions of life and death, irony and tragedy, crucial subjects which I had not thought about at all before.

The war: I'm still in it. I think about it every single day.

12

"I DIDN'T CARE WHAT HE DID. I JUST WANTED HIM TO COME HOME."

Harold Motenko met Adele on a blind date when they were teenagers in Chicago. He was going to De Paul University, and she was a secretary. When the war started, he joined the Enlisted Reserve Corps, which permitted draft age men to stay in college until they were called up.

MOTENKO

I was in the army, but I lived at home and went to school at home. By the time I was called to active duty, the only OCS that was open was the infantry, and I didn't want that. Instead, I went to ASTP for a few months, till the program closed down. I wasn't too happy. Here we were, supposedly the cream of the crop, the highest IQs in the army, stuck in the infantry without any rank at all.

But ASTP at Texas A & M was a pleasant time in my life. We lived a life of luxury, really as uniformed civilians. We stayed in the dorms, had our meals served in the dining room, and never pulled KP. Back home, I'd been putting myself through school, and here I was with my tuition paid, living in a beautiful place. It was the lap of luxury.

ADELE MOTENKO

We were married in Chicago February 2, 1944. He got home the night before the wedding. He wasn't even there for the rehearsal.

I was 20, and I had never been away from home. I had never been on a train till we rode down to Texas A & M together. We had to sit on the floor all night. When I asked him where we were going to stay, he said to take a look at the shacks we were passing to get an idea. Just teasing, of course, but our first place was a tarpaper barrack called a guest house. There was one washroom for the whole building. I wasn't too used to that.

There were only a few married men in ASTP. Everybody knew they went home on Saturday night, so we used to get a lot of razzing on Sunday morning.

MOTENKO

Sunday mornings, we were allowed to bring our wives in to have breakfast with us in the mess hall, so there would be 5,000 guys saying, w-e-l-l-l, I won't say.

ADELE MOTENKO

I was only in College Station a couple of months before they canceled his college program and sent him to the infantry at Camp Howze. I was very upset. I just could not visualize anybody coming from a sheltered home, and not just him but other men too, and going out and killing. But that's where he was, so I moved to Gainsville [the town nearest Camp Howze]. I made friends there with other servicemen's wives.

You talk about anti-Semitism! I used to get a lot of comments. Gainsville had three Jewish families, and I guess they knew I was Jewish, but people would forget every once in a while, and I'd hear some smart-ass remark. But what could I say? I had to live there. I couldn't defend myself.

MOTENKO

I went AWOL the night before we left camp so I could say good-bye.

ADELE MOTENKO

I never knew that. Can you imagine? I've been married to a criminal all these years!

MOTENKO

We had dinner that night and spent the evening together. About three o'clock in the morning, I called a cab to take me back to camp. As we kissed to say good-bye, that was the most horrible time of my life. She collapsed in the middle of the street. There was nothing I could do. I had to get back before reveille.

ADELE MOTENKO

It was just the trauma of him leaving. The people I was living with came out and picked me up. I knew he was going overseas, and we were newlyweds. I went back to my parents in Chicago and worked as a secretary. Every single day, I wrote him four letters, 15 and 16 pages. What I had for lunch, what I had for dinner, every detail I could think of.

MOTENKO

Listen, I was as bad as she was. In the States when I'd get a pass, I'd go to the USO club and write a letter, go to lunch and a movie, write another letter and go to another movie, write another letter, have dinner, and write another letter. When I was wounded, I wrote every day. My hands still worked.

ADELE MOTENKO

When he was in the front lines, I wrote him once that if he got a pass, I didn't care what he did; he didn't have to make excuses for anything. I just wanted him to come home.

MOTENKO

There are a lot of kids over there with my looks.

ADELE MOTENKO

His father had a grocery store. I used to come by and visit with his parents. One night, the phone rang, and my mother-in-law answered. She talked for a minute and then turned the phone over to him. It was Harold's little brother calling.

My father-in-law turned white. Then he turned to us and said, "Harold is missing in action." My mother-in-law was a very emotional person. I used to think we'd have a basket case on our hands if anything ever happened to Harold. But strangely enough, she kept her cool, and I was the one that fell apart. I screamed and screamed. I screamed so much that for three days, I couldn't talk.

MOTENKO

Calm down, Adele. It's been 42 years.

ADELE MOTENKO

I'm all right. They took me into the back of the store. My mother-in-law kept saying, "Shh, the customers, the customers." I couldn't walk. They had to drag me. When we got home, I pulled the telegram out of the boy's hand. He hadn't even opened it. It said, "Slightly wounded in action." He thought Harold was missing because the telegram had some kind of star code on the envelope that he thought meant "missing in action."

Well, then my mother-in-law started falling apart. "Maybe he lost an arm or a leg," she said.

MOTENKO

And all I had was trench foot. That's what the telegram was about. Later, when I *was* badly wounded, I got a chaplain to send a wire saying, "Slightly wounded. I'm all right." I didn't want them to learn about it from the government.

ADELE MOTENKO

The one I'll never forget was the first one.

MOTENKO

[Motenko tells the story of his wounding in chapter 22. He credits the late John Clark, his platoon leader, with saving his life.]

Clark was first sergeant when I got to Camp Howze. The division was getting ready to go overseas. An order came down for carpenters to build shipping boxes. I was in Headquarters Platoon then with no particular duties, so Clark picked me. This colonel came by and wanted to know what I did in civilian life. When I said I'd been studying to be an accountant, he dragged me down to Clark's office and says, "Sergeant, I sent a request for carpenters, and you sent me a man studying to be an accountant."

Clark says, and I'll never forget this, "Colonel, when you show me a carpenter on the MOS of an infantry company, I'll give you a carpenter. Until then, you'll take Motenko, or you'll get no one." Just like that. The colonel sort of stuttered and walked out.

Clark was commissioned not long after we got overseas. When he was assigned to the Third Platoon, he asked that I be transferred there. He made me first rifleman, I believe was the terminology. [Actually, the term was *first scout*, the rifleman who led the squad on the attack.] The sergeant in charge of the platoon said, "Why are you giving me that Jew?" Clark said, "Don't worry about the Jew. He'll take care of himself. You just take care of *your*self." We never had any problems. After the war, that same individual came to me and said, "I want to apologize. You're the first Jew I'd ever had a chance to meet." Unfortunately, he thought we all had horns, I guess.

There weren't any anti-Semitic incidents in combat that I know of, but one man had a great job, the burial detail. I'm not going to say it was anti-Semitism, but I always felt it was.

The platoon was cut off that winter on a defensive line for three days [January 1945 near Bischholtz, Alsace]. It was about 14 below zero. We couldn't dig in, so we blasted holes with dynamite and covered 'em with railroad ties. Our mortars knocked the hell out of the Germans. There was plenty of ammunition because Clark saw to it that everybody in the Third Platoon carried mortar shells.

I never shot anybody that I know of. I was probably one of the softies. We took a lot of prisoners. I probably had more reason than most to dislike their philosophy, but I could never take their watches and other booty like the other GIs did. The watch my dad gave me meant so much to me, I just couldn't.

When we were in Innsbruck at the end of the war, I was walking down the street one day, and here came a couple of men in striped uniforms. They looked like bean poles, Jews who were coming from concentration camps. One of my buddies and I confiscated a hotel, threw everybody out, turned it over to the Jews, and got 'em food. They gathered others from the area.

EPILOGUE

MOTENKO

While we were in occupation duty in Austria, I was made vocational and occupational counselor for the 410th Regiment. Captain Gibbs put me in for that. He remembered I'd said I had the highest IQ in the division. I think it was 152. But then the order came through that we were going to the 45th Division to fight in the Pacific. I volunteered. Everyone was going home for a 30-day leave first. I made up my mind if I ever got back to the States, I would never go overseas again.

[After his discharge, Motenko enrolled at Roosevelt University in Chicago to study accounting.]

In 1948, I went into the women's apparel business. I still am. We moved out here [to Mission Viejo, California] in 1984 to be close to our two children and our grandchildren.

My marriage was a very fortunate occurrence in my life.

ADELE MOTENKO

I'm just glad he came home.

13

"THEY THOUGHT IT WAS HOPELESS."

Ray Offerman suffered terrible injuries when a sniper bullet struck him in the left chest. The bullet shattered as it entered and drove pieces of his clothing and glasses into his body. Fragments of metal, bone, glass, and lead kept coming out of his side for the next four years. Some pieces are still there.

The man who saved his life with prompt battlefield first aid was Lester "Doc" Duckett, medic for the First Platoon of F Company.

OFFERMAN

I was the supply sergeant in an anti-aircraft unit that was sent to the South Pacific. They never saw combat down there. I couldn't go with them because I was legally blind in my right eye: 20/200. I almost didn't get into the service. I was turned down by the draft the first time they called me. I was classified limited service, and before I went to the 103d, there was a court of inquiry to determine whether I should be discharged. Two other men with eye problems were discharged, but they told me I had too good a record to let me go. Next thing I knew, I was in the infantry.

DUCKETT

We was gathered in the field house at Camp Claiborne [where the 103d Division was being formed]. Some guy asked who'd ever shot a rifle before. I told him I'd been shooting one since I was five years old. "We'll put you in the medics," he tells me. They didn't want nobody that knew how to shoot.[1]

Even though I was a medic, I was really part of F Company. Medics slept in the same barracks and did everything with the riflemen.[2] There was one of us assigned to each platoon. I didn't have no prior experience in this line of work, but we had good schooling, first aid, giving shots, bandaging.

Overseas, I never worked in the aid station or a hospital. I was always with the company.

The first time I heard that cry of "Medic!" was the night we relieved the Third Division. I was 50 yards back in the column in the blackest night I ever seen. We didn't know the Germans was so close. Everybody was shining a light 'cause you couldn't see the man in front of you. The Germans called us the Flashlight Division.

MARTIN DUUS
G Company

A friend of mine in the Third Division said he remembered how we came up on the line with the truck lights on and canteens banging around. They were very much concerned we'd bring artillery down on them.

DUCKETT

They started shelling us. The word passed down the column, "Medic!" Well, you just do everything by instinct. I went up to see what was the problem. Shells were falling. I had to feel around. You couldn't see nothin'. The man was still conscious. He'd got a piece of shrapnel up side the head. While I'm bandaging him up, the outfit moves off and leaves us. It was raining, freezing cold. I gave him my raincoat and shelter half to be kind of comfortable. We spent the night together. I didn't sleep. Too many noises. He had a hell of a headache and a skinned place on his head, but the next morning, he could walk. I sent him to the rear and caught up with the company.[3]

OFFERMAN

I never had any infantry training. When I got to F Company, I told 'em I was a supply sergeant. They had supply sergeants up to their eyebrows, so I was made a rifle squad leader. My men were old timers who knew more than I did, but they accepted me. I was 29 when we went overseas. I think I was the oldest one that went over.

We still had Springfield '03s. We didn't get M-1s till just before we went overseas. I wasn't allowed to qualify at first because I had to aim with my left eye, and the rule was you aimed with your right eye. But then some general said they were getting so many limited service people that they could quality left-eyed. In combat, it didn't make any difference. You never aimed from the shoulder. You fired from the hip.

[Offerman came through F Company's first major encounter on 30 November uninjured.]

After that one, the whole company had 30 or 40 men left and only two noncoms that could still sit up and take nourishment.

Nine days later, I led a patrol across a river. We had a rubber boat with a rope on both ends to pull it back and forth. We got into a large German patrol, and a firefight started. As we pulled back, I was the last man to reach the river. The boat was on the other shore. I threw my rifle across the river and swam across. Burp guns cut the water all around me, but they missed.

DUCKETT

We had two squads on the raid, and me as the medic. I stayed with one squad on the American side of the river. Offerman took his squad across in boats. We heard the shooting start, and then we were pulling them back over the water when the Germans started spraying the water with bullets. Ol' Murph [1st Lt. Warren Murphy, Vanderpool, Texas] says to me, "I don't mind them drivin' us back across the river. It was the staying across I didn't like."

Two of us grabbed the pontoon boat and carried it to cover. It must of weighed 400 pounds. Later we couldn't even lift it.

OFFERMAN

I got kinda wet. Bullets hit my shovel and went through my pants, but I wasn't hit. The next morning, though, I had a bad feeling. I told Doc [Duckett], "Today's the day. Stay on my tail."

A machine gun started lining in on us, so I went up to see what the situation was instead of sending a scout. I never expected a man that served under me to do anything I wouldn't do. I had my glasses in my pocket. There was all that mist in the morning, and you couldn't keep 'em clean anyhow.

A sniper shot me. He was hidden in a pit with camouflage over him. I caught a glimpse of him out of my left eye and tried to get a shot off, but he got me first. The bullet hit me in the left chest. As I lay on the ground, a machine gun started digging up the dirt in front of me. I didn't think I could move, but I ran maybe 15 feet and dove behind a log.

Duckett was right there, him and the lieutenant [Robert E. Lawler]. They looked at me and shook their heads. They didn't think I was gonna make it. I fooled 'em.

DUCKETT

Well, he was badly hit. His glasses case deflected the bullet. Instead of going straight in, it went down through his stomach and further down thataway, which I understand caused him a lot of problems. But in my estimation, the glasses case saved his life. Otherwise, the bullet would of hit his heart.

He kept asking me if he was gonna die. I told him, truthful as I could tell him, that he was gonna be in a lot of pain and suffer a lot, but he had a chance 'cause he was still alive. I bandaged him up, and our outfit moved on. I left him for the stretcher bearers to pick up. You had to do that. My job was to treat them immediately and stay with the outfit.

OFFERMAN

The bullet went through the pocket of my coat, through my eyeglasses and everything else in the pocket, and shattered my ribs. All I had showing on the outside was one little hole, but there was massive bleeding inside.

I had at least 35 pints of blood in the first 10 months. In the X ray, the bullet was just like a spider. Went every which way. The doctor said it must have been notched, a dumdum. I lost my left kidney and spleen. It tore my stomach apart and nicked my lung. For 10 months, I had a colostomy, but I got rid of that.

DUCKETT

Medics weren't supposed to fight, but there was one time that winter [near Bischholtz in January 1945] we were on the edge of a ravine, snow on the ground. The enemy was attacking our lines in white parka camouflage outfits at three in the morning. By seven o'clock, we'd drove 'em off with grenades. Someone wanted to put me in for a medal, but when they found out I was a medic, they said, "No way."

Later on, they told us we was gonna take this town [Gundershoffen, 15–16 March] at all costs. Fifteen hundred yards of open terrain. We had a lot of wounded. I must of helped a dozen men, zigzagging across that field. You had to use your best judgment. If I could get to 'em, I'd take care of 'em. I had a Red Cross on my helmet, but it was no protection at all. I think they were shootin' at me. You'd be surprised how much of yourself you could get into a little furrow. I found two holes in my mess kit when I was eatin' supper that night.

[Duckett won the Bronze Star for his work those two days.]

The worst time I had was after a mortar attack. I can't remember where it was. People laying all around with arms and legs off. Stuff like that. But I never thought of quitting. If I could help, that was my job, what I was there for.

When the war ended, I went to an outfit that was gonna attack Japan. Then they dropped the atomic bomb, and that ended everything. I don't know why we didn't do it sooner. I wouldn't want to go through it again, but it was quite an experience. On a scale of 1 to 10, it was 10 in my life.

I was never wounded. Don't know how they missed me. Guess I missed them. Two days after I got home and went back to work, I smashed my finger.

EPILOGUE

OFFERMAN

I had three operations. The first one was right there, four miles behind the front. That's where they took out my spleen and kidney, gave me the colostomy, and took out my ribs. I don't have any ribs on the left side. It's just a big hernia there. I didn't lose my lung, but I had to have it drained about four times when it filled up with fluid.

See, I had all this foreign matter inside. The doctor would go in with a scalpel and puff up the incision to run the pus out. Pieces of my glasses, pictures I'd had in my pocket, clothing, all of it was driven inside. In 1949, stuff was still coming out. A little boil would start on my side. When it festered and came to a head, a piece of bone or metal would come out.

For the first five days, I wasn't given any water, just a wet cotton bat I pressed against my lips. I dreamt I was dying of thirst in the desert. For five months, I was on a liquid diet. Except at Christmas, when the ward boy set a turkey dinner with all the trimmings in front of me. I asked him if he was sure this was for me, and when he said it was, I dove in. Halfway through the meal, I thought I was gonna die with stomach cramps. They had to go in with a stomach pump and pump me out.

The doctor was going to fly me to the States right away, but I got a fever. For 100 days, my temperature was 100 or 101. They put me on penicillin till I couldn't stand the shots in the butt anymore. In February '45, I was sent to a hospital in Charleston, South Carolina, and put in a paralytic ward. They gave good service, one nurse to each patient, but I kept looking at these other guys and thinking, "Jiminy Crickets, I'm not that bad, am I?" It wasn't until I was moved again, to Benjamin Harrison Hospital outside Indianapolis, that I got out of bed for the first time. That was around the first of April '45. When I did, I slid to the floor, my legs were so weak. I'd been on a liquid diet all those months. My weight dropped from 195 to 90 pounds.

That summer, I went home on furlough and ate with my family and gained 100 pounds. The wound finally healed too. The doctors couldn't understand it, but I explained my mother fed me the foods I liked. If I couldn't handle something, I wouldn't try it again, but I ate about everything.

When I came back to the hospital, I was supposed to have one more operation, to put a screen in my side to support the muscles where the ribs were gone. But they told me there was a fifty-fifty chance I wouldn't make it. I didn't like the odds. The last operation I had was in July '45, when they hooked up my plumbing and took me off the colostomy.

I've been limited in what I can do, but I coached baseball for the church and worked steady. I was a timekeeper for Borg-Warner when I was drafted. After the war, I went to the personnel department till I retired in 1977. I do lots of church work. Sunday is a church day for me, and I brought my children up the same way.

I don't go to battalion reunions. I like the fellas all right, but I'll be quite frank with you, I'm not a drinker, and most reunions, all you do is sit around and booze it up. I did go one time. I was talking to this one fella who kept bragging what he did in the war. I finally said, "Boy, oh, boy, I can't understand why it took us so long to lick 'em." He got mad.

*

Offerman and Duckett live within 35 miles of each other, Offerman in Detroit and Duckett in Wayne. They never see each other. Unlike many veterans, the war ended for them in 1945. Duckett married after the war and had three children.

DUCKETT

My medic training didn't carry over when I was discharged. My job prior to the war was production worker making auto windshields. I went right back afterwards and stayed for 29 years, till they suddenly said, "Today is your last day." All I got was two weeks vacation pay, and the union wasn't no help. I went looking for another job. A retail tire dealer took me on as a salesman, and I stayed there for 17 years. I retired in 1988.

14

"EVERYTHING WAS MASS CONFUSION."

Spilman (Spil) Gibbs was a star in semiprofessional baseball in West New York, New Jersey, when the Japanese bombed Pearl Harbor. The next day, he enlisted as a private and was soon selected for Officer Candidate School. In the infantry, his job was sports. His Second Battalion basketball team won the division championship. When the division moved from Louisiana to Texas, Gibbs went to F Company as leader of the weapons platoon.

Dr. Robert Lawler, a South Dakotan, was in college learning to be a pharmacist when he was drafted in 1943. After earning his lieutenant's bars at OCS, he became leader of F Company's First Platoon. In the most hazardous job in the infantry, Lawler escaped unscathed. Why? "Luck and faith," he believes.

Except for the war, Dick and Selma Pearson have never strayed far from their hometown of Piqua, Ohio. They started dating in their senior year at Piqua High School, married there, and raised their family while Pearson taught in the Piqua schools.

Pearson spent a year in the Signal Corps after he was drafted in 1942, but he wanted to be a bombardier or navigator. The army air corps (there was no independent air force) agreed and sent him to pre-cadet school at the University of Missouri. All went well until the spring of 1944, when the program was canceled and he was sent to F Company.

GIBBS

When we went on line near La Bolle, I was in the advance party [on 9 November 1944] sent up to scout the Third Division positions we were going to take over. To be very frank with you, I was damn frightened. I never saw a German, but they started a counterattack till the Third finally threw in enough artillery to stop them.

Their company commander was showing me how to call in artillery when an 88 round came right through the roof of our house. The blast killed one man and blew my shoe off. I was afraid to look down. I thought I had a foot missing, but it wasn't bad, just a shrapnel cut on my toe.

I believe I received the first Purple Heart in the 103d Division, but all I was thinking about right then was running back to Marseilles, jumping in the goddamn Mediterranean, and swimming back to New York.

One thing I learned real quick. I watched the 411th Infantry on an attack in those early days. They followed the book, hit the ground like they were taught to. The next thing you know, mortars came in, and they got butchered. We'd been taught in infantry school that you ran 25 or 30 yards, hit the ground, fired, got up, and ran again. I decided that was wrong. The first thing you do is head for a building or some other cover.

It was while I was sitting in a foxhole at La Bolle that I got a letter telling me I had a son. Written on the back was "It's a boy, it's a boy, it's a boy." Th Red Cross got the letter to me. "Well," I said, "I sure hope I get to see him." My sergeant and I had a drink of schnapps to celebrate.

[On 30 November, F Company fought its first real battle outside the village of Nothalten.]

We lost 3 officers and 22 men. The company commander [Capt. Cornelius Scott] was hit in the knee. It was almost completely decapitated. [See chapter 11 and "Interlude: He Never Cried Till Vietnam."]

LESTER (DOC) DUCKETT
company medic

Ol' Bushelfoot. He was quite a fella. Had about a size 14 shoe.

GIBBS

The Germans were all over—in the woods, on the high ground. We were in a narrow confine. They had us really pinned down.

I was told to take charge of the company. I was the only officer left. Things seemed to quiet down that night, and we got reorganized. First Sgt. John Clark was promoted on the spot to second lieutenant, and we got another officer from E Company.

One incident stands out in my mind. At dawn the next day, two big German Red Cross people carrying white flags brought one of our wounded machine gunners back to our lines. They said they had no transport and no medicine, so they brought him to us. We said, "Thank you," and they took off back to their lines.

In December, while we were on a static line above the town of Saarguemines, I had the machine gunners and BAR men fire every morning to make sure their guns hadn't frozen. Not much happened there, but we got in some excellent replacements from the air force or somewhere in a higher part of the service than the infantry. They were intelligent, fit in right away.

In January [1945], we dropped back into the Saverne Gap. Later, we learned this was where Hitler was supposed to make his big drive to Paris. The orders were to dig in above a town called Bischholtz. We no sooner did than, thank the Lord, a beautiful snow came down and covered our diggings. Natural camouflage.

That night [22 January 1945] we could hear gunfire out in front of us where E Company had two platoons on an outpost. A lot of them were captured.

Now we come down to the real meat of it. On my right, my machine guns were tied in with the machine guns from another battalion. The Germans came through a gap over there when this other company pulled out of position.[1]

Everything was mass confusion. All I knew at the time was something was wrong. I could see these figures coming toward me in white capes. Battalion radio told me they were Americans from B Company coming to help me. I told 'em I didn't want 'em. They were Germans. Sure enough, they hit us on the flank and from the rear.

PEARSON
staff sergeant

Lieutenant Clark says, "If those are B Company, they're B Company from the Germans," and kept on knocking them off. They were coming from our rear and the right flank, all in white. They plastered us. Shells hit the trees above us and burst downward. One piece of shrapnel slammed all the way through the timber on top of our dugout. You could see it sticking out on our side.

GIBBS

This was the Sixth SS Mountain Division, probably the finest troops we fought against. Brought down from Finland or Norway.

CLARK

I'll say this for the men. We held our own. I was outside the goddamn bunker firing to the rear.

GIBBS

I told Clark to get out of the bunker before he got racked up. [The bunkers, open only on the front, were useless when the enemy got behind F Company.]

PEARSON

The tip-off to the attack came when a guy by the name of Bury [Albert J. Bury, Little Falls, Minnesota], who was out about 200 yards, was attacked and fended 'em off single-handedly. He got the Silver Star.

CLARK

The Germans captured one of my gun positions. From there they'd try to get a machine gun set up. They'd throw the tripod over, then the gun over, try not to expose too much. Well, I had my aid man [see chapter 13] and my little messenger, Allen, in the hole with me. I took all the ammunition I could carry and laid up there on top and told the aid man, "You fill these guns up fast as I hand 'em to you."[2] I told Allen, "You get out of here and get us some help."

Those were SS troopers we were fighting. I know. I got me a good Luger off of one of the officers I killed. He come back there and jumped on my rear, but we had our rifles and machine guns turned around by then, much as we could.

I kept askin' Battalion about artillery. I guess it was that afternoon before we finally got it.

G. GARDNER WILLIAMS
rifleman

We were in the snow there for many days. Dombrowski[3] got a little stir crazy, I guess. He got out of his hole, and they hit him with an 88 shell. After some days, our people found us. Like to scared me to death when this guy came crawling up in a white snow suit to see if we were still alive.

My feet were frozen. The doctor knocked me out to kill the pain while my feet thawed. [He was evacuated 3 February 1945.] I woke up about 10 days later having my feet bathed with some sort of purple stuff. It was the most wonderful feeling. I was okay. I walked back to the company. [See chapter 22.]

GIBBS

We pulled back to Bouxwiller in February to get supplies and rest. McAuliffe [Maj. Gen. Anthony McAuliffe, division commander] ordered F Company to raid Bischholtz [on 3 February] and get six prisoners. Bischholtz is where they'd attacked us from, so we were mad. We cleaned the place out, shot up 36 and captured six.

DAN HIGLEY

private, H Company machine gunner

[From his wartime diary.] "F Company was supported by our platoon. . . . The town wasn't of any great importance, and most of the krauts had already cleared out. . . . The net results of the raid as far as we could see were six prisoners and a cleaning job on the machine guns, but the 'brass' hailed it as a great success."

GIBBS

After the raid, McAuliffe says to me, "How long you been a lieutenant?" I told him I was the oldest ranking lieutenant in the goddamn regiment, and he says, "Congratulations, Captain."

PEARSON

The raiding party left early in the morning. We were about to enter the town when our white phosphorus and HE hit. A round came in, zinggg. I'm not sure whether it was a short round of ours or a German shell. It exploded right behind me and this kid [Pfc. Edward A. Luebke] got a piece of the shrapnel. It killed him instantly.

I was a bit overcome. I'd known Luebke since the previous June. The next night, me and two or three other people went out to bring his body back to Graves Registration. Things like that you think about all the time. It's still very vivid, the white phosphorus and the artillery flying all over the place. It's something you just can't erase from your memory.

LAWLER

We were going through the town cleaning out houses when someone threw a grenade through a window. It must have landed in a cook stove. Pieces of iron came hurtling back through the window and took off part of my sergeant's head. [S. Sgt. Sanford Sloan and Luebke were killed and four were wounded on the Bischholtz raid.]

PAUL FUSSELL

F Company platoon leader

Lawler was a phlegmatic guy, but there was one thing that shook him very badly. He threw a grenade through a window where he knew there were Germans. The explosion blew the eye out of one of his squad leaders. Bob never recovered from that, kept saying, "It was my fault," that sort of thing. I used to tell him, "It's not your fault at all. It's the fucking war's fault. Anybody might have done it." He was deeply damaged.

LAWLER

There was another time too, during the spring push (15–16 March). I lost one of my men, a guy that shouldn't have been with us, really. He was much too old to be in the infantry. [Pfc. Arthur Schnabel, killed in action 16 March; see chapter 22.] Those losses had an effect on me.

GIBBS

We spent the rest of the time in Bouxwiller getting ready for the spring push. We took off on that attack on March 15 under a chemical fog so thick you couldn't see a damn thing. We were down under an embankment when the battalion commander says, "Gibbs, you gotta take F Company across that field to the woods." So I told the platoon leaders, "I'm gonna blow a whistle and over we go," just like World War I. We made it across, firing from the hip, and never lost a man.

We cleaned out the woods and captured a lot of Germans, but when we started off again, they kicked the shit out of us. Hudson [T. Sgt. Edward K. Hudson, F Company] and Lt. [Raymond] Biedrzycki out of H Company were killed. [Second Lt. Paul] Fussell was wounded [see chapter 11]. It was a real nasty little battle. Shrapnel was coming down like rain.

Doggett [L. B. Doggett, E Company commander] and me, we kept the men circling there in the woods. When the 88s would hit one place, we'd move, and just seemed to keep a step ahead of 'em. Right around in a circle we went. Men dropped into ditches or anything they could find for cover, but we had quite a few casualties.

The next day, let me tell you, that was rough. We had to cross an open field to get to this town. [See chapter 22.] American fighter planes bombed us by mistake. No casualties, but it scared the shit out of us.

[With the capture of Gundershoffen, the next obstacle was the Siegfried Line.] They didn't defend it much. When they resisted, the engineers would throw 50-pound sacks of dynamite against the doors of the pillboxes. The sound drove 'em right out.

Now we were seeing German civilians for the first time. They were scared, very. We didn't bother them. We'd chase 'em out of their houses when we needed a place to sleep and, let's put it this way, took what we wanted. Our theory was you went to the best houses, so you chased out the biggest Nazis. Oh, you lifted everything, but that was the spoils of war. I never figured that as theft. I think the Germans expected it. You should have seen the French. The Austrians thought we were saints compared to the French.

We did have one bad incident. Near Stuttgart. The mayor of the town said a girl had been pulled off her bike by this soldier, taken into a house, and raped. He was guilty. She came right up and pointed him out. I had to appeal to Division to get his sentence knocked down to 20 years.

Along about this time, I conked out. Got a terrific pneumonia just before Munich on the way south toward Austria. I was sent to a hospital in Dachau, not the concentration camp, the town. I got back to the company just before we got to Innsbruck.

EPILOGUE

Only a few incidents stand out in Lawler's memory. Two of those, in which enlisted men he knew well were killed, turned his attention to medicine. After the war, he gave up his pharmaceutical studies to become a doctor. Since 1957, he has been in practice in Oxnard, California. His unusually strong rapport with his men carries over to this day. The late Reverend Mike Engle of St. Grenada, Mississippi, a sergeant in F Company, wrote him a letter in 1986: "Dear Bob, It still seems strange calling you by your first name. You were always 'Lieutenant Lawler' to me and probably always will be. . . . Mrs. Lawler, . . . I want you to know how much Bob's men thought of him. He was by far the best liked and respected of any of the platoon leaders."

Gibbs was in the photoengraving business in New York and New Jersey for almost 50 years, but the six months as an infantry commander produced his premier memories.

Not so his no-nonsense wife, Helen. She went to several battalion reunions until she was "sick of you fighting the war over and over. You go and have a good time. I'll stay home." They understand each other. In 1989, they celebrated their 50th wedding anniversary.

HELEN GIBBS

While he was gone, I wrote him every day. Maybe just a short note, but I wrote him. I told him, "I don't care if it's nothing but a piece of paper. Put your name on it and send it just so I know you're there." We had a real nice mailman who'd known us since we were children. If a letter came in after the last delivery (we had two deliveries a day then, you know), he would drop it off before he went home.

It had been quite a while since I'd heard from Spil when I got a telegram one day. This messenger kid just handed it to me and ran out the door. I thought, "Oops." I didn't know whether to open it or not. It said, "Thanks for my son, and Happy Mother's Day."

Some of the time he was gone, I worked as a legal secretary and court stenographer. Two nights a week, I did volunteer work in a hospital in North Jersey where very seriously injured men were recuperating. We'd play cards and read to them. I got to know one young man who didn't have a mark on him, but he wouldn't talk or do anything. When I read him his mail, he'd just nod.

We were only allowed to stay in one ward for a certain time, so I thought I'd better tell him I was leaving. I went over and shook his hand and said goodbye.

"Thank you," he said. I almost fainted. Those were the first words he'd ever said. I heard he gradually got better.

Spil got home from the war a day late for Phillip's first birthday, on October 31, 1945. For a while, he used to get up in the middle of the night and go outside to walk. Just walk. He never said too much. I didn't ask. That went on for a couple of months. Then he sort of simmered down.

GIBBS

I couldn't sleep. The biggest thing on my mind was wondering if I did right—replaying what happened, some of the senseless things, the deaths. What better way could I have done it? But I got through that period by myself. No psychiatrist or anything like that.

HELEN GIBBS

I knew if he wanted to say something to me, he'd say it. I felt like if I asked one question, it could be the wrong one. It was best to let him work it out. I figured, "One day at a time."

We had another little crisis when he first got back. "In Innsbruck," he tells me, "we had this place where a nice, big German girl served us breakfast in bed of eggs and fresh-caught trout."

I looked at him. "You were Captain Gibbs there. You're Mr. Gibbs here."

*

Dick and Selma Pearson had always planned to be married.

SELMA PEARSON

We got married in spite of the war, not because of it. We just had seven days together before he had to go back to camp. All the time he was gone, I kept the letters flying. I didn't miss a day. It was just part of the daily routine.

I stayed with my parents while he was gone. Sunday afternoons, several of us would go to the theater. That was the highlight of our week. I tried to keep track of where he was, but by the time we would hear about it, it had already happened. I did lots of praying, and I definitely feel it helped.

When he got home, we went down to Cincinnati to see the Reds play. That's the thing that stands out.

15

"THE GROUND WAS COVERED WITH BODIES"

The ranks of the veterans of the Second Battalion reunions grow thinner as the years pile up. Paradoxically, the number attending reunions increases. As men get older, interest in their wartime experiences increases.

Dr. Carl Nichols, M.D. of Leland, Mississippi, is typical. With his wife Mary Jane, he attended his first reunion in 1986.

NICHOLS

When I went in the army, I was just a college kid. Like everybody else, I wanted to get into the air corps, but I had some problems with the visual part of it, so I joined the ROTC at Ol' Miss and left in 1943 to go on active duty.

MARY JANE NICHOLS

We got married when he graduated from OCS, a big church wedding in my home town of Cleveland, Mississippi. They were shipping OCS graduates directly overseas, so he didn't know if he'd be there or not. But we sent out 500 invitations, and it worked out beautifully. We left for Camp Howze right afterward.

When we drove into Gainsville, there was a line 200 yards long trying to get rooms in a hotel. I said, "Carl, there's no way. We are going to be spending the night in this automobile."

He said, "I don't know what to do." I said, "Well, I do. I'm going to call the Baptist minister." He had a list of emergency rooms. That night, we had a clean bed and pillows. That's all I can say. There was a sheet dividing the room, with a bed on both sides.

The next morning, I put on my going-away dress and said, "Let's drive over into the prettiest section of town." Off we went till he slammed on the brakes. I thought, "My God, what is happening?" A lady was taking in her laundry, and he ran up to her and offered to help. She smiled and said, "Soldier, you're looking for a place to live, aren't you?" From then on, we had no problem. Texans, I'll never forget 'em. They were great.

NICHOLS

When I went to the 103d in April 1944, my first assignment was as a platoon leader in I Company, and that's how I went overseas. Not long after we went on line, I got pneumonia. While I was recuperating, I got to know a captain from that nisei outfit, the 100th Battalion.[1] The captain was an occidental, and he took a liking to me, wanted me to go back with him. "It's the greatest outfit in the army," he told me. "All the officers are white, and they really treat you good."

Those Japanese had horrendous casualties. I could see the handwriting on the wall. When you came out of the hospital, they sent you to a repple depple, and from there you went to wherever they needed you, and that meant to the place that had suffered the most casualties. I didn't go over there just to be wasted. On top of that, one of his men—he was white too—came in to see the captain and was telling him about shooting some prisoners. That chilled my bones.

So I went slightly AWOL and found my way back to my unit. I was so weak I couldn't even carry my own duds. When the regimental commander saw me, he said, "Boy, you can't go back on the line right now. We'll hold you a few days, and let you get your strength back." Around Christmas, he called me in and said, "Carl, we need you. You ready to go?" I didn't want to go, of course. I liked it back there at Regiment. But he told me, "[Capt. Spilman] Gibbs needs a platoon leader up there. You can't go back to I Company. We've already replaced you there." So I said, "Yes, Sir," and that's how I got into Fox Company.

I never feared the responsibility much. But I wasn't a big leader. It was the company commanders that carried that load.

My first taste of battle was just before we pulled out in that retreat in January. I was up in the third floor of a building to see what I could see and, frankly, to catch a little nap if I could. German artillery started up, and I thought, "I'm gettin' the hell out of here." I started down the steps. There was a huge window right in front of the steps, and that window hit me right in the face. It knocked me down and blew my helmet off, but I only got one little cut.

I didn't ask for the Purple Heart. There were a couple of other times that bullets went through my clothes, and I got a shrapnel burn on my leg. I still have a scar there. I don't like to talk about it. I was superstitious about talking about injuries. Still am.

The companies rotated onto the line through February and March. We had a foxhole about as big as this hotel room, under a tree. If they ever hit the roof, you'd wonder where the troops went. I never did like that hole. But I didn't like it outside either.

One of the guys was going out to his relief on the machine gun one time and accidentally fired a shot from his rifle right between my legs. It got kind of quiet for just a minute.

[There was another, more serious, accidental shooting not long after.]

We were cleaning our weapons when a shot nearly burst my eardrums. I spun around and realized that the boy behind me was hit. He sank slowly and silently to the floor. I cut away his trousers, exposing a clean, black hole just above his left knee. The white-lipped youth looked up and said, "Do you think this'll get me home, Lieutenant?"[2] I never saw him again. This sergeant was cleaning his M-1, and the darn thing went off.

I always tried to be careful. I never tried to hide my rank, but I will admit I carried an M-1 one time. The Germans knew very well that junior officers carried either a carbine [a conspicuously smaller rifle than the M-1] or a pistol.

The main thing I want to talk about is that March 15 and 16 thing. The artillery began firing at 0630 March 15, and for 15 minutes, they fired as fast as they could pull the lanyards. At 0645, our attack began. We were going to try to capture a bridge in a little town [Gundershoffen] and then breach the Siegfried Line before the Germans could back up and man those fortifications.

The smoke cover the artillery fired would choke you to death. "When I stepped into the smoke, it was like opening my eyes in a bottle of condensed milk." You're running, and it feels like your lungs are being burned out of your chest. You couldn't lose sight of the guy in front of you in the smoke 'cause he was leading you, and if you lost sight of him, you'd be leading the whole battalion. It behooved everybody to stay in touch.

We found ourselves in a little town where we weren't supposed to be. [Ingwiller, according to his memoir, but more likely Engwiller.] Shells were falling and slate shingles were raining down like confetti, and it was just absolutely miserable. The snow had begun to melt, and the barnyard was muddy and filthy. The krauts would fire down a street, and the only thing that saved us was we were as quick as they were. We killed off all the livestock, and the chickens were running around with all their feathers blown off. We were milling around like a bunch of lost ducks when old Robbie [Lt. Col.

James Robison, battalion commander] says, "We're not supposed to be here. They [U.S. artillery] are gonna shell this town to the ground. Let's get outa here." So we pulled out.

We were going pretty good. I didn't see any but dead Germans for the next 30 minutes or an hour when, all of a sudden, the smoke blew away, and it was broad, open, and beautiful, and we were standing right out in front of the Germans on this bald little rise.

Mortars started hitting. Two of my men were wounded. I remember their names: [Vincent L.] Jackson and [George P.] Dallara. Dallara was flung around, saying, "My eyes. My eyes." Jackson was hit in the jaw. I jumped in a foxhole the Germans had dug. It was full of ice water, and I do mean ice water, right up to the top. I sat on the edge at first. I really didn't have any desire to get in. But watchin' those shells get closer, it looked like the next one would be right on us. T. Sgt. [Edward] Hudson had eased up to that same hole. So here comes the next round. Shhhhhhhh. In I went right up to my neck. Hudson too. It was big enough for two, a nice, big tub of freezing water.

Maybe 15 minutes later, Hudson got out and sat on the edge, ready to get back in if the situation demanded it. I told him, "Damned if I'm gittin' out. I'd rather freeze to death than git blown to pieces."

Along comes Colonel Robison in a protected spot across the road and says, "Platoon leaders, move your platoons across the road to better cover." So I came out of my hole and fell flat on my face. My legs were useless. I started pulling myself with my hands. I wondered, "Am I so scared I can't move my legs?" Two men grabbed my arms and drug me 30 or 40 feet to cover. When I got my boots off and rubbed my legs, pretty soon I got the use of 'em back. I know now it was hypothermia.

"Our own artillery was doing more damage to us than Jerry's. One man had his head cleaved completely off his shoulders by a cannister from a white phosphorous shell that fell short."

We had to attack across an open area up to a woods. The riflemen were told to fire one clip and then go over the top while the machine guns fired over their heads. We fixed bayonets and took casualties before we got started. The machine gunner up above me got shot through the chest.

"One of the water cooled [heavy, .30-caliber] machine guns was set up directly above my head. . . . Jerry must have been waiting for him because the impact of a bullet knocked the gunner back and spun him around. . . . The gunner crawled, cursing vehemently, back to his gun and put on one of the most magnificent displays that I have ever witnessed. Reaching forward with his right hand, he knocked the swivel latch loose and began firing a swinging traverse . . . raking German positions with a continuous stream. . . . The water in the jacket [which cooled the barrel] was boiling. . . . The assistant gunner jerked off his helmet and . . . scooped up muddy water [to] pour into the jacket and go back for more. . . . The wounded man was heedless . . . as he ran another belt through the smoldering weapon. When the gun was so hot that expansion was causing frequent stoppages, the gunner ceased firing, voiced his opinion of the krauts to all of us, and walked nonchalantly to the rear."

We ran and ran and ran until we got to the woods. I didn't care whether they killed me or not. A two-year-old baby could have whipped me. In the woods, the Germans started surrendering, but that was nothing but their outpost. Their main defenses were several hundred yards back. We had small arms fire at a 20- or 30-feet distance, and it was hot and heavy. That's where Mike Engle got hit in the face. [See the epilogue in chapter 10.]

I was on the ground, and this sergeant, you talk about me leading my men, this damn guy gets up and says, "Let's go," and they went, so I got up and went too. We were gonna throw grenades in their dugouts and blow 'em out, which we did, but in this one, they came streaming out.

Okay, we milled around there. The casualties were being picked up by our medics and the German medics (I haven't talked this much about the war, ever), and they were draggin' them maybe 100 yards back. The ground was pretty well covered with wounded. The dead were allowed to lie there for GRO.

We were doing pretty good, you know, considering. We'd taken a bunch of casualties, but we were regrouping. I'm saying, "Who's around? Who's in charge?" Just about that time, there came an explosion and then another and another, in rapid succession. We didn't know what it was. We couldn't hear 'em coming. It turned out it was flat-trajectory 88 fire. I was right next to two people who were killed. [See chapter 11.]

I dived into the dugout. It was every man for himself. It was filled with wounded. When they saw I was a lieutenant, they said, "Lieutenant, what are we gonna do?" You asked a while ago did I ever feel inadequate as a junior officer. I did then. I didn't know what to do. But I told 'em, "Look, I know one thing about the kraut. He'll counterattack whenever he gets an advantage. If he ain't got but one man, he's gonna come atcha. We're gonna meet them outside, not in this hole. So when this fire lets up, I want everybody out of here. If you're wounded and can't go, your buddy can drag you out."

We withdrew to a road behind us. The ground was literally covered with bodies, the wounded screaming and crying and moaning. I remember one guy pulling his buddy along on a shelter half [tent], just pieces was all there was. Couldn't possibly have been alive.

JIM McCARTHY

F Company machine gunner

We were in bad trouble. There was this young soldier layin' there. His stomach was all torn up. American. He musta been standing when the burst hit him. I said to him, "You're gonna be all right." I got him on my raincoat and pulled him back. Some other guys came over and gave me a hand.

NICHOLS

As we fell back, I caught up with one of my machine guns and set him up at one end of the road, with one of the heavies at the other end. If it was a rifleman, I'd stop him: "Here, this is as far as you're goin'. We're waitin' for the krauts." But the krauts never did counterattack that night.

[There was more bitter fighting the next day. See chapter 22.]

The fighting ended for me the 17th of March. That's when the pursuit through Germany began.

Sometime in April, I got pulled out to pick up DPs coming out of Dachau, Buchenwald, and Belsen [German concentration camps] and help repatriate 'em. UNRAA was supposed to do it, but they were overwhelmed, Red Cross types, and they didn't have but a few trucks. So we were sent in, about a dozen armed combat soldiers in my little group. We requisitioned food wherever we could find it to feed those people. And to keep 'em from killing the Germans. They were out for revenge, you know. That lasted till a more orderly and reliable source of supply was established.

EPILOGUE

Nichols shared his wartime memoir with his fellow veterans when he came to his first reunion in 1986. The reception was cool, to say the least.

After it had been passed around and chewed over, reviews ranged from a gentle "That's not exactly how I remember it" to "It's a bunch of crap." Thus it is strange that it is in essential agreement with the recollections of other veterans. It is, in fact, a valuable piece of history, one of only two unofficial eyewitness accounts. (The other is by H Company machine gunner Daniel Higley of Wilmington, Delaware.)

Nichols was aware of some of the reaction.

NICHOLS

In the Civil War, they used to ask, "Have you seen the elephant yet?" It's the story of the three blind men trying to describe an elephant. One feels the tail, one feels the trunk. Each one has a different picture of the same thing. Same with combat.

MARY JANE NICHOLS

Carl was gone two Christmases, but he got home, which was just a miracle. When he got home, we had a little fourteen-month-old girl that he had never seen.

NICHOLS

I was talking to Big Jim [McCarthy] here at the reunion, and he said, "Hey, Nick, what did you have, a boy or a girl?" I looked at him. "What? You remember that?" He said, "I remember it like it was yesterday." While we were waiting for the barrage to start for that March 15 thing, I got a cable telling me I was a father.

16

"I STILL THINK ABOUT WHAT HAPPENED."

James W. McCarthy is a product of the strange rural-urban environment that seems unique to New Jersey. An old pol in the local Democratic Party and a past commander of Veterans of Foreign Wars Post 625 in Cedar Grove, his roots run deep in northern New Jersey. He was born on his grandfather's truck farm in Cedar Grove in 1923, and now lives in Verona, the next town over. Of Irish and German descent, he calls himself "a good mixture of a tough bunch of people."

Growing up in suburban Newark, McCarthy developed a tough-guy aura that he carries to this day. He and his closest friend, Bill Mahoney of nearby Brick Township, were fast with their fists, as McCarthy likes to say. They are still friends.

At 17, McCarthy was nearly blinded in his left eye when he was hit by a horseshoe. He tried to enlist when he was 18, but was rejected.[1] The army drafted him in 1944. Five months later, he was a machine gunner in Alsace with F Company.

McCARTHY

Those are my vividest memories. I lay in bed at night thinking about what happened, especially since I been goin' to reunions the last few years. I don't talk to my family. How can I get started tellin' 'em about the horrible things that I seen? People I'm the closest to know the least about it.

You're gonna think I'm crazy, but I enjoyed the thrill of combat. I did, really. But I also did what I could to help the odds. I was very religious during that period. I used to go back and see the good Father [William] Kleffman [the battalion's Catholic chaplain] and get a recharge. I'll tell you, for what it's worth, I used to say to myself, "If I live, I live. If I die, I die."

As long as I was in what we Catholics call a state of grace, I accepted my fate through the faith I had. It didn't hurt, either, that I react quick. I used to fight fast, and I think I acted without thinking about the consequences.

Coming through was part luck, though. How long can you go in combat? The average was 45 days. At the end, I might have been a little more cautious too. Most of the guys who trained with me at Camp Blanding in Florida were killed or wounded. Our training was cut short in the 10th week [normal training period for replacements was 17 weeks]. I think they needed replacements after the Battle of the Bulge.

Mahoney and I went over with fifteen thousand men on the Aquitania as replacements. I told the first sergeant in the repple depple that Mahoney and I had always been together and could he fix it for us. Next thing I knew, we were on a 103d truck to F Company. Mahoney said to me, "Boy, I like that patch." The cactus, I guess.[2] This was around January 8 [1945] in the Vosges Mountains. Snow on the ground and real cold.

The captain [Spilman Gibbs] went over our papers and said, "Trained on machine guns, huh? Good, you're machine gunners." We were introduced around and were very well accepted. I had a lot of respect for them. They'd been in combat, see?

Not too much happened till the big attack on March 15. Nichols [Dr. Carl G. Nichols] was our platoon leader. He joined us shortly after I came to the company.

I was an ammo bearer when that attack started. The whistle blew, and we took off, running like hell. I had three cans of [machine gun] ammo on my back, and one in each hand, 20 pounds a can. All of a sudden, we were lost. The first dead Germans I seen were a bazooka team layin' there. I looked at Mahoney, and he looked at me, but it didn't bother us. We both figured, "Better them bastards than us," and from that moment, we started to become soldiers.

We had to cross a road under fire, then laid out on a slope there for an hour and a half till we attacked a woods. Once we got in the woods, Mahoney and I got out too far. We're blazin' away, shootin' anything we thought moved or didn't move. Mike Engle was about 40 feet away from me when he got hit. [See the epilogue in chapter 10.]

There was a couple more skirmishes before we drove 'em out of the woods. All of a sudden, a tank comes up to the edge of the clearing and opened up on us and give us a pretty good shellacking—tree bursts. Gilbert [Pfc. Leon H. Gilbert] was hit in the heel, and O'Brien's [James A. O'Brien, Jr.'s] legs were shot up. These were men in my squad. A redheaded sergeant 10 feet away from me was hit in the head. He hadda die, it was so bad. I never heard anything more about him. I got a very fine piece of shrapnel in my upper right hip. It was like somebody took a razor and sliced me, but I wasn't thinking about that. We were in bad trouble.

Two days later, the medic came up to bandage me. He was gonna put me in for the Purple Heart, but I told him no, I didn't feel I had a wound that warranted it after the way I'd seen those other guys butchered. Time passes, though. After the war, when I found out a Purple Heart was worth five points [toward discharge], I took a couple of witnesses down to the medics to claim it. This guy looked at me like I had clap or somethin' and says, "I'm gettin' so damn sick and tired of you guys comin' in here for Purple Hearts. One of yous is lyin', and the others swear to it." I called him a lousy noncombatant son of a b. and told him to take his Purple Heart and shove it up his backside. I never did get it.

We fell back to a road that night and slept in German holes. It must of been a German officers' headquarters 'cause they had rabbits. Those damn rabbits were all around the place, spookin' us, but it stayed quiet as far as Germans were concerned.

[McCarthy tells of the next day's heavy fighting in chapter 22. At the end of those two days, he had moved up from ammunition bearer to acting machine gun squad leader. On 23 April, the company helped to relieve G Company, surrounded in a subalpine German village. See chapter 24.]

That was the end of our combat. We had one incident there that didn't look good [See "Interlude: A Painful Part], but that was the exception. The men in our division were brave and honorable, I believe, as much as you can be in combat.

Toward the end, our people were a little more cautious. Nobody wanted to be the last one killed. With me, it was like boxing. There's a nervousness till you get hit once. Then you're right in there. Same thing happens with a soldier. I only knew two out-and-out cowards, and one guy for whom "scared" would be a better word. A coward can't face life, period, but any man that has this swelling fear of losing his life, psychologically, can you call him a coward? That man shouldn't be there.

EPILOGUE

After the war ended and the 103d was disbanded, McCarthy and his hometown buddy, Bill Mahoney, stayed in Europe with the Ninth Division. McCarthy's postwar army career was nearly as violent as the combat period.

McCARTHY

Me and Mahoney, he's back from the hospital now, [he had been wounded; see chapter 22] were stationed where the Germans had been making buzz bomb juice. Guys were drinking the stuff and going blind. At first, they told us we were gonna be the first wave in Japan, but after the Pacific war ended, it was pure idleness. Mahoney and me joined the boxing team. He won the light heavy title, and I became the heavyweight champion of the division.

I was talking to a guy from G Company at the reunion the other night, and he says, "You know, those Ninth Division guys were crazy. They tried to kill me. I saw two of them kill an American GI, and they came after me. I saw two guys with the 103d patch on and ran to them for help."

That was Mahoney and me. He was from our old division, and we backed him up.

We signed a three-month enlistment with the Army of Occupation. You could do that then. We were in London for New Year's [1946]. Got drunk as skunks. Everybody was shootin' off flares and pistols. The next day, we went AWOL to Ireland and stayed three months. When I got back to London, MPs were draggin' soldiers right and left outta the Red Cross club. I played it cool, got my uniform cleaned and pressed so I'd look like I'd just got there, and sat around reading comic books.

When I made my way back to the company in Germany, they put me in an MP outfit. We had a problem with returning German servicemen. They were castrating American soldiers in the parks, robbing the Red Cross girls' quarters. One time, I heard someone at my door. There was about six Germans my age. They took off when they saw me. I grabbed a .45, and my partner and I chased 'em in a jeep. They wouldn't halt, so we fired and hit one. I don't know if it was me or my partner. He was a hard man. He had no love for the German soldier.

"He don't look so good," I says.

"I'll fix the son of a bitch kraut bastard," says my partner, and gives him a kick in the back. Well, that was not to my liking, but whadaya gonna do? People in the street could see him do that. When we got the German to the hospital, he was dead on arrival. We blamed it on the jeep driver to avoid the paper work and went about our business.

The German's friends were gonna do a job on us, but we beat a couple of 'em up, and they swore they wouldn't bother us again.

I left Germany in August 1946 and came home for discharge. I had a carpet business for about 20 years, got into politics, and then came down here to this [mental] hospital to run security. We have to go to war around here once in a while too.

I was 31 when I got married, and I was too young then. We have four children.

INTERLUDE: HE NEVER CRIED TILL VIETNAM

Two generations of the Scotts of Duluth served their country in the infantry in this century. Cornelius (Neil) Scott enlisted when World War II began and was the commander of F Company until he was seriously wounded 30 November 1944, at Nothalten, Alsace.

He recovered from his wounds and was for many years an administrator in the St. Louis County (Duluth) Welfare Department. He died in 1981 of cancer at the age of 68.

His son, Terry, was a rifleman and radioman in Vietnam with the Fifth Battalion of the 60th Infantry in 1969 and 1970. Drafted when he finished college, Terry spent 11 months "in country" and emerged uninjured. He is now a certified public accountant in Duluth.

The senior Scott never said much to his children about what had happened to him: that a machine gun nearly took off his kneecap, that he refused to leave the battlefield until his wounded men had been evacuated, that he won a Silver Star for bravery. The citation says in part, "Captain Scott . . . [was] confronted by a well dug in enemy less than 100 yards away. . . . Captain Scott pushed on magnificently and fearlessly until he reached the limits of his day's objective. . . . He was seriously wounded, but . . . refused evacuation . . . until he was assured the last man was safely removed." (See chapters 11 and 14.)

VIVIAN SCOTT

Cornelius Scott's widow

It was his right knee. He was not crippled, but he had a lot of problems with it aching and hurting. He didn't say much about it. He was able to lead a full life. For 15 years, he coached Pony League Football.

TERRY

Sometimes I'd see a medal of his and ask him about it. "Oh, it's something I got," he'd say. I could see his knee was pretty banged up. But we never heard any stories.

PAUL FUSSELL
platoon leader under Cornelius Scott

Scott was solid and stolid and phlegmatic.

TERRY SCOTT

When I left for Vietnam, he just told me to keep my head down. When I got back, we never talked much about Nam.

VIVIAN SCOTT

The only time I ever saw my husband cry was when Terry left for Vietnam.

TERRY SCOTT

Like Dad, I don't feel like I've had any serious repercussions from the war. I'd have to say our feelings are similar. It's something he passed on to me, I guess.

But come to think of it, I got into a fight not long after I got home. Some antiwar protesters at the U [University of Minnesota–Duluth] ripped the flag down. I didn't feel too good about that. It happened at the time of the Cambodian invasion, and I knew quite a few of the guys who made that trip.

No, I haven't visited The Wall [the Vietnam Memorial in Washington, D.C.]. Maybe I'm afraid to. If I went, I would look up the names of guys I knew. I'm not sure what my reaction would be.

Some day, I'd like to go back to Vietnam and see the Mekong Delta again.

THREE

G Company

17

"MY GOD, I SHOT ONE OF MY OWN MEN."

Alfred J. Torrance was the highly respected commander of G Company through most of its combat history. Robert Schroeder was his faithful messenger and scout.

"I still feel like I'm talking to my superior officer," says Schroeder, "but it's getting better." Torrance, for his part, has the greatest respect for his former subordinate: "Bob was a boy just born to the woods. I'd have been lost without him." Torrance created the position of reconnaisance sergeant for Schroeder.

A draftee in 1942, Torrance quickly won an appointment to OCS and rose to captain. His first two and a half years of service were in the United States. His wife, Ann, whom he married shortly before he was drafted, and their new baby followed him from their home in Pennsylvania to such exotic locales as Bunkie, Louisiana, and Phoenix, Alabama. Four months before he went overseas, Ann's brother was killed in Italy with the 36th Division.

Schroeder nearly missed serving in the army. He was 22 years old when he reported for the draft on 7 December 1942, from Alexandria, Minnesota.

SCHROEDER

No one called my name, and the bus was ready to leave. One of the people in charge told me I'd been redlined 'cause I was a farmer, and did I want to be deferred? I told him, "No, I'm here. I'd just as soon go." Later on, there were times I regretted my words, I'll tell you, but that's how it worked. I got right on the same bus. I was one of the first assigned to G Company at Camp Claiborne.

[With Torrance, he trained with the division at both Camp Claiborne and Camp Howze, Texas. Through two and a half years of stateside training and six months of combat, Schroeder was Torrance's messenger.]

All that training over and over got boring. I volunteered out a couple of times, but I never got picked, and I wondered why. Torrance said, "I had something to say about that."

I had a lot of respect for the man. He could have asked me to tell him something I'd heard amongst the ranks, but he never did. We had a good relation.

CLYDE RUCKER

a Regular Army man who had far more experience than Torrance

He was a hell of a good man, a man everybody felt they could trust. He was concerned about the guys' welfare. I don't know if all the officers were.

JOHN WOODSIDE

machine gunner

A good leader, not a glory hound. He always told us he didn't want a bunch of heroes; he wanted a bunch of live soldiers. In training, we thought he was too hard on us, but we found out he was right when we got overseas.

[The battalion went on line 11 November 1944, but G Company saw little action for the first few weeks.]

TORRANCE

When we started out, I was scared, like everybody else, but I was more apprehensive about how well we would perform. I needn't have worried.

We made our first major attack near a little town called Nothalten about ten o'clock on the morning of the 30th of November. We fought there most of the afternoon. Both G Company and F Company took heavy casualties.[1] I knew all of them. It hurt. They had all been with us before we left the States. Several machine gunners were knocked right off their guns.[2] F Company lost its commander, Cornelius Scott, who was shot through the knees. [See chapters 11 and 14 and "Interlude: He Never Cried Till Vietnam."]

The Germans had the commanding high ground as we were trying to come up a hill. They pinned us down till I got some artillery onto their positions. That seemed to clean them out. After dark we had to reorganize. E Company came up to reinforce the line, which was more or less broken between F and

G. We evacuated our wounded under cover of darkness. Several wounded krauts were brought in too. The surgeon wouldn't treat them till he took care of our men, which was right.[3] The next day, we attacked right after dawn and discovered the krauts had pulled out of Nothalten.

[There followed a series of marches and skirmishes through the Vosges Mountains before G Company went into defensive positions overlooking enemy-held Saarguemines on the Saar River in late December. The weather was bitterly cold.]

Around Christmas or New Year's, I got orders to get across the Saar River and take some prisoners. I sent a man named Valentine across with a rope. He fought that stream up to his neck and finally got the rope tied to a tree on the German side. Each man held on to the rope for guidance. The minute we got out of the water, our clothes froze, but all 15 of us got across.

There was a sheepherder in Saarguemines who claimed the Germans had pulled out except for an outpost down the road. I thought he was telling the truth because I threatened to kill him if he wasn't. I don't think I would have, but I never had to find out. Just like he said, we found two German guards a half mile down the road and captured both of them.

SCHROEDER

The clothes they gave us had been sprayed with some kind of water repellant, so when we tied our pants legs around our boots, the water kind of leaked in slowly. Coming back, this little wire man lost his footing, the air ballooned up his pants, and he turned upside down. [Stanley] Niciporek had to reach way down in the water to get ahold of his collar to set him on his feet again. The guy came up cold and wet and madder than hell. He was gonna shoot our prisoners, he was so mad. Somebody knocked his gun down and explained to him, "If you shoot those two, we're only gonna have to go lookin' for more."

TORRANCE

I wanted to keep one of the prisoners. Battalion was always after us for prisoners, and it wasn't easy to get them, so one in cold storage wouldn't have hurt. But a major who'd been sent along to check up on us said nothing doing, so they both went back to the interrogators.

[G Company remained in its defensive positions until 20 January 1945, when it joined a general retreat, termed a "line straightening" by the public relations officers, of the U.S. Seventh Army. Disruption of Allied offensive operations by the massive German attack to the north, the Battle of the Bulge, forced the retreat.]

We were told to set up new defenses along a line between Rothbach and Schillersdorf in Alsace. We hardly had time to get set when SS troops came in screaming like banshees and hit E Company.

They captured the E Company CP, the company commander, and a lot of other people. [See Chapter 4.] I considered sending some of our men out to counterattack, but I wasn't allowed to. Our job was to hold. We followed the prearranged plan. My rifle platoons pulled out of Rothbach and went into holes above the town. But one of the machine gun squads was somehow left behind.

SCHROEDER

G Company was in houses in Rothbach when the Germans hit us. E Company was on an outpost somewhere out in front. We didn't expect anybody 'cause we hadn't heard any firing from Easy. First thing I knew was when a guard outside our CP shouted a challenge. The guy answered in American, so I didn't get suspicious, but our guard said, "You kraut son of a bitch," and opened fire. All hell broke loose.

Torrance sent me down the street and told me, "Watch while we get our equipment up the hill. When we can't move any more stuff, come and tell us." I waited till the Germans were raiding the house across the street. Then I pulled out. Why our machine gun crew didn't get the message, I don't know. Maybe because I didn't run over and tell them. But I did what I was told to do.

TORRANCE

The next morning, I was walking the line on the mountain up above Rothbach with Schroeder to see how many men we could pull together. Down below, I saw a head move behind the curtain in the house where my gunners had been. The Germans must have taken over the house. I waited till the head showed again, took a good aim with my carbine, and squeezed off a shot. BOOM! The head went down. Then it was real quiet.

I was mystified why we didn't get any return fire. Suddenly somebody started hollering from the house: "Be careful. A sniper just shot Elmer Brawe." Oh, my goodness, that was no sniper. That was me. There were four of our men in that house.

SCROEDER

I was ahead of Torrance a ways. There was a shot, and I hit the ground. Torrance said, "Well, I got the son of a bitch." Next thing we knew, somebody was swearing in American from the house, and Torrance says, "Oh, my God, I shot one of my own men."

TORRANCE

The bullet hit Elmer along the side of his right eye and went all the way around the right side of his head and out the back. It knocked him down and stunned him, but it didn't kill him.

JOHN WOODSIDE

machine gunner

He hit him with his carbine. If it'd been an M-1, it would of blowed his head off.[4]

TORRANCE

What fooled me was he wasn't wearing his helmet. All he had on his head was one of those wool stocking caps that made him look German. I was almost in shock, but we had to go down the mountain to help him. When we got there, Johnny Woodside, one of the machine gunners, was in the worst shape. His leg was almost blown off. [See Chapter 18.] Elmer had a bad headache, but he was able to walk. How do you apologize for something like that? I don't know what I'd have done if I'd killed him.[5]

SCHROEDER

It was a few days after this that Torrance told me to take the forward [artillery] observer up to a foxhole before daylight. Our company headquarters was about a quarter mile back. I wanted to leave earlier, but the FO was a first lieutenant and I was a private, first class, so we didn't go when I wanted to.

Anyhow, I got him into a foxhole, but it was getting daylight by the time I started stringing his phone line.

I was wearing a white camouflage suit I'd picked up on the battlefield. They weren't issued to us guys in headquarters, but the medics must of thrown this one off a guy that was wounded. The trouble was, he had been a lot shorter man than I was, so my legs were showing out the bottom with OD.

When the Germans opened up on me, I was maybe 50 or 60 yards below the crest of the hill, out in the open. I made it, but for a while I thought I wasn't going to.

Usually, I tried to spot out a hole I could use if I needed one. I moved around too much to dig my own. This other guy and I were fixing a broken wire one night when artillery started coming in. I dropped my rifle, something an infantryman is never supposed to do, and dove into a hole. This other kid came right on top of me. "Well, they got Schroeder," he says. "I saw his rifle out there."

There was a brewery in Rothbach. Some people didn't get the word that Rothbach was in Germany now. One day, here comes a jeepful of rear-echelon people, out to get a beer supply. We had no way of stopping them. They barreled into town and then, BRRRRP!, that was the last we saw of them.

There was a power plant in the next town that was still working. I'd done some work with electricity and wiring, so I thought we might be able to get some power into the foxholes. It cost me a liter of schnapps, but I got a half mile of somebody else's wire off of a wireman's jeep, and we had electricity in the headquarters bunker. When there was music on the radio, the other holes could listen in with their phones.

Did anybody tell you about the Polish kids we captured on a patrol? They were German soldiers. Lots of the soldiers we faced were Polish and Russian that the Germans forced into their army. These two guys were sneaking up on the Second Platoon. One of our guys who was Polish heard 'em talking and got 'em to come in. They wanted to be American soldiers, so we used them as interpreters.

Later on, one of 'em took a bullet through his jaw. It cut his tongue so he couldn't talk. One of our Polish guys gave his dog tags to this kid, and he got all the way to London to a hospital before they found out he wasn't American.

[After five days of confused fighting, the German counterattack at Rothbach-Schillersdorf was halted, and G Company went into defensive positions until 15 March 1945, when the final assault on Germany began.]

TORRANCE

It wasn't till two or three days before the attack started that we found out anything. Rifle companies never were told the big picture. Colonel Robbie [Lt. Col. James C. Robison, battalion commander] told the officers that "something's cooking. I don't know what exactly, but I believe we're going to make a push right through to the Rhine." That's when John Clark went behind the German lines for two days to assess their strength and came back with the report that they were dug in with machine guns andd mortars. [See chapter 10.] Our division intelligence people claimed there wasn't an organized squad between us and the Rhine. We soon found out John was right.

The official word came down the day before the attack. It was going to be a platoon fight, not thousands and thousands of massed men, just one platoon at a time hitting and controlling its front. I told my platoon leaders and noncoms, "I think we're going to have a tough fight on our hands. I hate to tell you this, but I'm afraid we won't all be here tomorrow night."

I can remember how [platoon sergeant] Joe Bonacci laughed a little bit at that. He was there the next night, but the second night he wasn't.

The responsibility of life and death decisions weighed on me constantly, but I didn't agonize. We had some officers who did, and I don't think it was a good thing. If a decision was made, you couldn't take it back. I did the best I could, and most of the time I think I was right.

We jumped off just about daylight on March 15 at 6:45 A.M. E Company was leading the attack followed by F Company. G was in reserve. The battalion objective was two little towns along the Moder River, Gumbrechtshoffen and Gundershoffen. We were supposed to seize their bridges to permit other troops and materiel to get across to attack the Siegfried Line. Gundershoffen was nearly five miles away, and we were supposed to get there by 9 A.M. It was a very optimistic goal.

The artillery laid down smoke shells to cover our advance, which turned out to be a great hindrance. The leading companies got lost in the smoke, and the whole battalion was scattered. We had to navigate by compass.

When we came out of the smoke, we surprised 30 Germans, who surrendered. One or two who tried to run were shot. As we moved forward, E Company ran into heavy opposition. That stopped the whole column, and that's when we got hit by a heavy mortar barrage. The Germans were very accurate. All three companies took a fair number of casualties from that fire.

The concussions lifted me right off the ground. I wasn't hit, but I was dizzy and had headaches for quite a while. By noon, the battalion had suffered 40 or 50 casualties. The 103d Division Band, which normally stayed far to the rear, was brought up as stretcher bearers that morning.

SCHROEDER

We got in this terrific bombardment that took out quite a few of our people. It was really bad. In his panic, one guy dug in beside a stack of artillery shells, which was not the thing to do. That's where [Stanley F.] Niciporek, our bugler, got killed, a Polish kid from Hamtramck, Michigan. I was about 10 feet away when he got a direct hit right between the shoulder blades by one of those large mortars. It completely destroyed the upper part of his body. The only way I recognized him was by the peculiar way he had of lacing his boots. Later on, four of us signed a certificate identifying the body, so they didn't have to send a "missing in action" report to his family. The dog tags were gone, everything.

Another round hit a tree 10 feet from where Niciporek got it. A piece of the primer made a hole in the sod about two inches from my helmet. Dirt blew up inside my helmet, through my hair, and out the other side, it was that close. They were using giant mortars, comparable to our 4.2s [inches of diameter].

I lost track of Torrance for a while. He sent me into this town, I don't remember why, and I got challenged in German. I slithered out of there so fast on my belly I lost most of my hand grenades. I caught up with him in the woods.

TORRANCE

Around two o'clock, G Company came out of reserve with orders to cross 200 yards of open ground to the woods where German fire was coming from. We made it across with less casualties than I expected, firing from the hip as quick as we could reload. The noise and the hooting and howling that went with it upset and demoralized the enemy so much they kept their heads down.

All hell broke loose once we got in the woods, though. The Germans readjusted their mortars and artillery and laid it on us pretty heavy. Shells detonated in the trees, and those tree bursts brought fire down on the men as they were lying on the ground. G Company was engaged in heavy small arms fire. It was trench to trench for a little while, getting rid of one and then organizing a couple of squads to go forward and hit another one.

SCHROEDER

There wasn't a whole lot of resistance, but it was hard resistance. I remember laying behind a tree. I was covered with the stuff that flies out of the back side of a tree when bullets go through it. Somebody right close to me got killed. He was standing behind a tree. Those armor-piercing bullets went right through.

TORRANCE

The whole battalion pushed through the woods, but Gundershoffen was still three and a half miles away at nightfall. I put the prisoners to work digging a CP with logs on the roof for protection from artillery. We expected to be shelled during the night because we hadn't captured any artillery pieces. It turned out to be quiet, though.

All the wounded were on the ground around the CP. Lieutenant [Theodore] Rustejkas, the First Platoon leader, was bleeding heavily from a wound in the back, but he could still walk. I put him in charge of the walking wounded. He assembled about 30 American wounded from several companies and some wounded Germans, and got everybody to the rear. G Company had 25 wounded and 4 or 5 killed that day.

[There was more heavy fighting the next day in the capture of Gundershoffen, described in chapter 22.]

TORRANCE

There wasn't much action after Gundershoffen, but the Siegfried Line[6] gave us some trouble.

SCHROEDER

One of our platoons [probably the Third] got up against a Siegfried Line bunker. We called up the antitank company, but all three antitank guns ran into a tank ditch. We made the assumption they didn't want to face that pillbox. There they were, their guns poking into the ground on the other side of the ditch. We finally got past the bunker, firing into the aperture. There were a couple of dead Germans inside. I looked at the soldier's book that they all carried. The guy was 63 years old. But he'd been to good target practice. The Germans we faced were good soldiers. It only took one or two of 'em to stop us.

Our guys threw hand grenades into another bunker. Two Germans came out. They were bleeding from the ears a little, but they were alive. Our hand grenades weren't as good as I thought they were.

TORRANCE

Once through the Siegfried Line, the breakout was on. We rode trucks, sometimes for two days at a time, passing dead horses, broken tanks, farm wagons, oxen. The Germans used every kind of conveyance you could think of in their retreat.

We crossed the Rhine at Worms, and then crossed the Danube at Ulm. It was about that time I left the company to become executive officer of the battalion [and was promoted to major]. Joe Meadows took over the company.

I've never had any negative feelings about my combat experience. It was my assignment. I didn't like it, but on the other hand, I would have hated to miss it. Of course, that's easy to say if you're not all torn up. I was lucky. It's either your time or it's not, and I don't know who determines that.

SCHROEDER

I was careful. And I was lucky. That's why I was never badly hurt. Brave and reckless, one carries into the other. I wouldn't qualify myself as very brave.

EPILOGUE

Torrance stayed with the 103d Division until after the war, when he became a battalion commander in the 80th Division. In 1946, he quit the army and went into the precious metals refining business. Now retired, he and Ann live in Virginia and Florida.

Schroeder stayed with G Company and served the next company commander, Joseph Meadows (see chapter 25). Discharged in November 1945, he returned to farming near Hunter, North Dakota. He and his wife, Marian, have raised six children. They now live in retirement in Hunter near their old farm.

Torrance and Schroeder stay in contact through the battalion's annual reunions, which Torrance helped start in 1948. He has attended nearly 40. It is the highlight of each year for him.

"If you've ever quarterbacked a Superbowl team, everything else looks a little different," he explained.

Schroeder has attended 30 reunions. He missed for a number of years because the timing conflicted with his harvest season, so the reunions were moved up to June.

18

"HE WANTED TO BE DRAFTED."

John Woodside was married, 28 years old, a highly skilled screw machine operator in essential war work in Detroit when his number came up for the draft in 1942.

His was a draftproof combination, and he had every reason to stay at home. He and his wife, Frances, married in 1933, in the depths of the Depression. Jobs were scarce back then, but their world was looking up now, what with burgeoning war work and the demand for his craft.

WOODSIDE

Deferment? My boss in the war plant wanted me to get one. He said, "Why not? I'll get you one." I said, "You want one?" He said no. I said, "I don't either." He was drafted too, even though he owned part of the plant.

FRANCES WOODSIDE

John could have had a deferment, but I don't think he could have lived with it. We had no children. We were no better than anybody else. He didn't want a deferment, so I didn't want him to ask. I don't think I could have lived with myself if I'd tried to talk him out of going when he felt like it was his duty to go.

[Woodside was inducted in December 1942 at Ft. Custer, Michigan.]

WOODSIDE

There was 500 of us there for induction. How many you think were culled out? Three. One was so blind he couldn't see, another one was on crutches, and another one had a newborn baby. The rest of us got in line. 'Course, they were democratic and diplomatic, and they said, "Tell 'em what your occupation was and what you've done and what group you wanta be in." So I went through all the routines and got up to where they asked where I wanted to go, air force or navy or what have you. I said, "Infantry." This other guy in line says, "Are you stupid?" And I said, "I'm not stupid. That's what we're gonna get."

The next week, I was in the 103d down in Louisiana, one of the original members. The Fourth Platoon of G Company was the only outfit I was ever in.

It was the luck of the draw that made me a machine gunner.[1] You didn't volunteer for nothin'. A machine gunner was a prime target. You know what the average life of a machine gunner is? One hour. They told us that in training. I beat the odds. [But not by much. He first fired his machine gun at the enemy on 22 January 1945, in Rothbach, Alsace and was wounded the same night.]

The Germans kicked us out of Niederbron. Our officers said it wasn't a retreat, but when the heavy artillery is going back side by side with the infantry, getting out at the same time, you know that's what it is.

We were told to set up a final protective line in Rothbach. Both of our machine guns were down in the town, with this mountain right behind us. E Company was on an outpost somewhere out in front of us, but a lot of 'em got captured. We heard their commanding officer sung like a pigeon. [See chapter 4.]

Torrance [A. J. Torrance, G Company commander] called his platoon sergeants and platoon leaders back to a meeting to give 'em a little information about what was going on. While he was talking about what was going to happen, it started happening. Loren Becker [Woodside's sergeant] never could get back to us. Those storm troopers come off that mountain and hit us like a bat out of hallelujah.

I was firing out the window when a bazooka round hit just below me. The next one come over the window sill and exploded. It knocked out three of my men, blew my leg almost off, and set me afire. I got the brunt of it. The other three men was all right when they woke up. One of 'em was Bert Irwin of Winter Park, Florida. I don't remember the others.

I never lost consciousness, but I got very cold. It must of been shock. They drug me out of the room and packed blankets around me, but they didn't know and I didn't know I was on fire. I thought my guts was blown out. I finally asked someone to see what kind of shape my guts was in. He took the blanket off; I was burning down there. All the clothes in my middle was burned off. I had nasty burns on my stomach and groin. It was painful, but it didn't amount to a great deal.

BOB SCHROEDER
G Company messenger

There wasn't much bleeding, but he was in terrible pain. To get him out of there, we had to carry him up an icy 45-degree slope that was covered with snow. Once or twice we lost him off the litter.

WOODSIDE

From then on, I never saw anybody from my outfit till after the war, except one guy who had frozen feet. I didn't even know Elmer [Brawe] got hurt. [See chapter 17.] I was what you call semiconscious. I don't remember who carried me out of there, but when I was back in the States, there was this guy at Percy Jones General [Hospital] come up to me and says, "I've been trying to figure out how I know you. It just now dawned on me. I helped carry you out." I don't know who he was. From the 103d Division, tank duty of some kind. Torrance was one of the ones helped get me out too. [His voice breaks.]

After Torrance and them got me up the mountain to the aid station, I was evacuated to the 21st General Hospital. The doctor cleaned up the wound and told me my leg was going to be all right. I knew it wasn't. There was no possible way 'cause there was nothin' there.

SCHROEDER

A piece of his shinbone, maybe three or four inches long, was gouged right out of his leg.

WOODSIDE

They didn't do anything much at the hospital in France, just evacuated me to the States. I wound up in Fletcher General in Cambridge, Ohio. I'm not faulting anyone. The doctors grafted bone and skin; they done everything they could to save my leg, but it would of been short even if they had. This doctor kept saying it would be all right. I knew it wasn't.

Finally one morning, I said, "Doc, don't you think it's about time we stopped kidding each other? I've done everything you've asked me to do 'cause I want to get out of here. I'm no spring chicken, and I'm not getting no younger layin' up here in this bed. [Woodside was older than most infantrymen—30 when he was hit.] You can't save my leg, and you know it. Why don't you send me to an amputation center and get it over with, so I can go ahead with my life?"

He agreed. I went to Percy Jones General in Battle Creek, Michigan, where the same thing started all over again. Doctors are a funny breed of people. They tried for a long time to save it till finally I went to see the general in charge and told him I wanted it straight. Could they save the leg or not? Yes, he says, they could save it, but it wouldn't be any good. I told him I was a screw machine operator. "Well," he says, "I think you can do that again with a good artificial limb. We have the best. When do you want it off?"

"What about next Tuesday?" I says. So they cut it off, four and a half inches below the right knee.

FRANCES WOODSIDE

I told him I'd come. I knew he was having his leg taken off. But he didn't want me there. He said it wouldn't of helped any.

That was a very bad day for me, but the worst was when I got the telegram saying he'd been injured. The War Department only said he'd been wounded and "details will follow," but I never heard any more for a week. A chaplain was supposed to get in touch with me, but I never heard from him.

WOODSIDE

I don't like to say this. I'm not a Catholic, been a Protestant all my life, but our Protestant chaplains, they didn't stack up to our Catholic chaplains. The Catholics just seemed to know more how to talk to people.

FRANCES WOODSIDE

When he got back to this country, he phoned me, but I still didn't know how seriously hurt he was. He said he had some burns. I didn't find out till I went down to the hospital how bad it was. I was shocked, but I could look around and see many of them so much worse off. And I knew he wasn't depressed about it.

WOODSIDE

That's one thing about an army hospital. You go into a civilian hospital with a broken arm and you're in a room by yourself. In an army hospital, you look in the next bed and see somebody with both legs and an arm off. You get the feeling, "I'm in bad shape, but look at him."

When I first got back to the States, my burns were still hurting like crazy, and I had a moment of weakness. Then they wheeled a guy in, in a tub of oil. He was burned all over his whole body. Just layin' there in a tub of oil. I looked at him, and I looked at me. It made me feel a little bit different.

After they did the amputation early in 1946, I had to go through quite a bit of rigamarole learning how to use an artificial leg. It was two years before I got out. One of the last things was what they called vocational counseling. These super brilliant officers with all their charts and stuff said I could be a concrete mixer. They urged me to give it consideration.

I told them the consideration I'd give it was to get back on my old job and do the best I could. I knew I'd be all right. I didn't need any crazy advice like that. I went right back to the screw machine shop in Detroit. We stayed a number of years till we came down here to Parsons [Tennessee].

EPILOGUE

Though he says, "I just don't care about war stuff," John Woodside was one of the founders of the Second Battalion reunions, and as a preliminary each year, he and three other Fourth Platoon machine gunners have their own minireunion. Frances Woodside was a housewife from the time of their marriage until the war, when she joined the ranks of women war workers in Detroit.

WOODSIDE

Nobody even knew I had an artificial leg till I came to work on crutches one day. This here leg is the one I left the hospital with. It's had to be reworked now and then, but it's over 40 years old.

I got a new foot on it last Christmas a year ago. We were going over to my wife's brother's for Christmas dinner. Had the car all packed full of gifts, hot turkey baked and ready to go. I got out to the car, slipped on the ice and fell. When Frances got me back in the house, I got down on the floor and beat the leg back into shape where I could wear it, but I had to have a new foot built.

I can't walk too far. I can't go nightclubbing and dancing and things like that. You got to be awfully careful not to make the stump sore, or you're in trouble. That's happened a few times. I have to do the things I can do and be satisfied with that.

I retired in 1979. I've been taking it easy ever since. If I took it any easier, I'd have to get somebody to chew my food for me. We did a lot of traveling, but we both have heart problems, so we pretty much stay home now, watch television, and take it easy. But I don't watch war pictures. I wouldn't say they're painful to watch. I just don't care about war stuff. Shiloh [National Military Park] is near Parsons. I've never gone out there.

FRANCES WOODSIDE

I'd never been out of the house till I became an inspector in the factory where he'd worked before he went in. When he got home in 1947, I quit.

From time to time, I got to see John while he was in this country. Once, I sat on my suitcase most of the way from Michigan to Texas. There weren't any seats on the train. I stayed a month in Gainesville, the town near Camp Howze, before he went overseas.

Housing was a very big problem. One place we had, the couple lived in a screened porch and rented us their bedroom. When their garage came vacant, they rented us that. It was a single-car garage with a dresser, a two-burner stove in the corner, one corner fenced off for a bathroom, and a bed you let down out of the wall. You had to raise the bed to have a space to eat in.

But you should have seen some of the places we didn't rent. One was a converted chicken house that still smelled like a chicken house. The taxi driver thought I was stupid for not taking it.

When John went overseas, I went back to Detroit. I wrote him every day. Yes, every single day. As a matter of fact, I wrote three letters every single day. I had two brothers in the service too. John wrote often too. I'd get 12 or 15 letters all at once, in packages.

You know, this country has changed since the war. It used to be more patriotic than it is now. We felt military service was a duty everybody owed their country. I don't think I could have lived with myself if I'd tried to talk him out of going.

I haven't been sorry. It's been a struggle, but we've managed. I think he feels like he served his country well, and I feel like he did, too.

Frank Cook, G Company mortar gunner; J. J. Morris, mortar squad leader; Bill Perty. Cook and Morris were wounded 15 March 1945.
Courtesy of Russell Rath

19

THE MINEFIELD

The lives of J. J. Morris and Oscar Hundley have touched only once.

On the night of 15 March 1945, Hundley and two other men risked their lives to pull Morris out of a minefield. Hundley has wondered ever since who it was he rescued.[1]

It was pitch-dark that night. Morris knew two of his rescuers, Russell (Rusty) Rath and Roy England, both fellow mortarmen, but Hundley was a stranger, a machine gunner from H Company who happened to be handy when help was needed.

MORRIS

I was running a G Company mortar squad. Earlier that day, my gunner, Frank Cook, took a bullet across the side of his head.[2] He was bleeding pretty badly and pumping a lot of blood, but he had to lie there till almost dark, when two of us carried him to the aid station. I think it was Roy England[3] that was with me. By the time we started back to the company, it was so black you couldn't see a thing. We ran into Colonel Robison [Lt. Col. James C. Robison, battalion commander]. I didn't know the password. Probably nobody did. I heard all these clicks go off, the safeties on M-1s. He asked me who I was, and I gave him enough names that he knew I wasn't a spy, and he let me come up.

The colonel said to contact F Company off in the woods to our right flank. I went back and told Rucker [2d Lt. Clyde Rucker, leader of G Company's Third Platoon], and offered to go find them. Rucker told me I didn't have to, but I said, "I'll go anyway." He told me to take one man with me.

I picked Sam Johnson.[4] We went back maybe two and a half miles to where the battalion had gone up into a woods [the Engwiller Woods]. There were a few Germans, some of them wounded, but we didn't find F Company. When we started back, I got about opposite where I thought Rucker ought to be and figured, "I'll just cut across this field, and I'll be in business." I walked down a little ravine and up and over the edge about five steps when BLOOIE! I stepped on a mine.

Johnson tried to drag me out, and *he* stepped on a mine. I should not have laid there like I did. I should have gotten myself out. I knew exactly how I'd come in. But you don't always do the right thing. Johnson was smarter. He hopped right on out.

JAMES TEAGUE

Third Platoon squad leader

Morris started calling for Rucker, just screaming for him, every few minutes. It was after twelve o'clock before they took him out and he quit screaming.

CLYDE RUCKER

J. J. don't remember I told 'em to go around the minefield. They went around it on the way out, but they either got lost coming back or just decided to take a shortcut. You could see those mines. They were laid in a hurry, and a whole lot of 'em weren't even covered. They were laid in little rows, right on top of the ground.

We talked Johnson into crawling out, but I couldn't get J. J. to move. He was hurtin' pretty bad, I imagine. An aid man went in to put a tourniquet on his leg, and another mine went off. It sort of boogered up his face, knocked rocks and dirt into him and scratched his face up, but he wasn't hurt bad.

MORRIS

I put tourniquets on while I was lying there. It must have been a couple of hours. Basically, my left leg was blown off at the boot strap. It was just hanging by the muscle. I think I crawled some distance back toward where Rucker and the rest of the crew were. They say I fired my .45 [as a signal]. I don't remember doing that.

HUNDLEY
H Company

We advanced under smoke that day, supporting some rifle company [with our heavy machine guns]. Our squad got separated in the confusion. When the smoke lifted, this lieutenant [Rucker] called me to bring up the gun. I says, "Lieutenant, I've got the gun and the tripod, but the ammunition's somewheres else." So we didn't do any firing. We was out in that field all day, waiting for orders to move.

That night, this same lieutenant said he wanted me to volunteer to go in and get a fella out of a minefield. I never seen this officer before in my life. I thought of tellin' him to go to hell, but as a good soldier, it was an order from a superior, so I went.

It was pitch-dark. Me and this other fella went down on our hands and knees feeling for the mines. I was scared, but heck, I was scared every minute—no, every second—anyway that I was in combat. The guy I was workin' with, he'd feel in front of him and I'd feel in front of me, and we laid down toilet paper to mark the path. I didn't know him from Adam. Never did find out who he was.

The injured man was layin' on his side. If he'd rolled over on his back, he'd have rolled onto two of those shoe-box mines, and it would of killed him for sure.

"I don't want to look down," he says. He asked his buddy (he was a buddy of this other fella that went in with me) did he have the million-dollar wound. He knew his leg was damaged, but he didn't know his foot was about blowed off. It was hanging by a bit of skin just above his boot top.

His buddy told him, "You don't have to worry. You're going back to the States."

We felt around to where we could lay the litter down and rolled him onto it. Then we walked out on the path we'd marked. [Hundley completes his story in chapters 24 and 27.]

RUSSELL (RUSTY) RATH
mortarman[5]

It was blacker than hell that night. J. J. was out there yelling for help. His voice kept getting weaker and weaker. He was a very good friend, the head of our mortar squad. Somebody had to do something. I thought the world of him.

I went looking for the engineers to clear the minefield. No luck. Then I found a team of litter bearers and brought them back up to where we were in the field. While I was talking to Lieutenant Rucker, the medics deserted our situation, leaned the litter up against a tree and took off.

MORRIS

The way I heard it, they said, "We don't get paid for going into minefields." I really can't blame 'em an awful lot.

RATH

That's when I decided I had to go get him. I asked if there was anybody willing to go out with me. Roy England and another guy I don't know [Hundley] volunteered. I marked the trail through the minefield to where he was with V mail stationery and crackers out of a K ration. We went in exactly on the path I'd marked. There was a lot of praying going on, let me tell you. I shudder yet to think of it. We got him on the litter and carried him back to the aid station.

I was an ammunition bearer that day. The next day, I was a sergeant in charge of the mortar squad, the only one left who could take the job.

MORRIS

At the aid station, they snipped off what was left of my foot and threw me in an ambulance. I ended up in a field hospital. You talk about "M*A*S*H." That was a real "M*A*S*H." They had three operating rooms going at one time.

EPILOGUE

MORRIS

I was in the army hospital in Brigham City, Utah, till the following January [1946]. That's where I got my first leg. Did you know they wear out? I'm probably on my 10th or 12th one.

I play golf and racketball. I might limp once in a while, but the leg's been off twice as long as it was on, so I'm used to it. I've never had any feeling of resentment at what happened to me. Sooner or later, you're going to get it in combat. You can't roll the dice every day and not get waxed. And then when it happens, there's always somebody that's worse. People have a tendency to feel sorry for you, but it's old hat.

When I got out of the army, I got a law degree at St. Louis University and went into private practice with a firm there until 1972, when a friend suggested I apply for an appointment as an administrative law judge. I came to Denver to join the Federal Mine Safety and Health Review Commission, hearing mine safety cases.

I don't mind talking about the war. Matter of fact, my youngest came up to me a couple of months ago and said, "Dad, you never talk about the war. How come?" So I sat him down for about two hours. He finally got a little squirmy.

20

"I WAS BLIND."

Martin Duus (pronounced "Dew-is") was drafted at 18 in June 1943. Like many infantrymen, he wanted to be something else, in his case, a navy man, but he couldn't qualify. He was color-blind. Instead, he entered the army's ASTP program.

Duus and Cliff Ellis were roommates in ASTP at Texas A & M. When the program ended in the spring of 1944, they, like thousands of others from the cream of the wartime manpower pool, went to the infantry. By sheer chance, the two friends were both sent to the Second Platoon of G Company and went overseas together.

Today, Duus lives in suburban Philadelphia. Ellis lives in Emporia, Kansas. They have not seen each other since the war, but remain friends.

The war began for these men on 30 November 1944, near the Alsatian village of Nothalten. Duus was in a rifle squad. Ellis was the platoon messenger.

DUUS

That day was a complete disaster for our platoon. We were making breakfast when German machine guns started firing at us. We had thought they were quite a distance away. Captain Torrance gave the order to fix bayonets, our first experience with that order, and we started up a road. When we moved forward, they completely surprised us. They were only 20 yards away, dug in with rifles and machine guns, the whole bit.

Some of them threw up their hands to surrender, but then the firing started in earnest, and it got a little bit chaotic. I was carrying a [Springfield] '03 sniper rifle I'd been trained on back at Howze. The bar for the sniper site blocked the magazine, so you had to feed the bullets in one at a time. Going through the woods, I realized that was not the rifle for me. I ditched it as soon as I could pick up an M-1. There were a number of them around from the wounded.

We were pinned down in a real precarious position. A bullet went between my right arm and my pocket with sort of a stinging feeling. It was then I realized you could get hurt in this war. A fellow named Nolan [Pvt. William J. Nolan] two or three feet to my right screamed. I got his boot off and put sulfa and a pad on his foot. A sergeant got a wound that turned out to be self-inflicted. We heard later there were powder burns on his boot.

My squad leader, Sergeant Barker, was fatally wounded in the chest. [S. Sgt. William C. Barker died of his wounds 10 days later.] I did a bandage for him and got some sulfa on him, but he was obviously very seriously wounded. All this time, there was sniper fire going on. Sergeant Huskey [then a staff sergeant, later 2d Lt. Moe Huskey] told Al Marcinek and [Pvt. Darwin W.] Williams to go back and get the sniper. Half an hour later, Marcinek came back and said the sniper had killed Williams. I don't think they got the sniper.

ELLIS

I was in the lead as we were moving up on a machine gun nest. All I know is I got whopped. A sniper knocked me down. The first shot got me in the shoulder, then another one got me in the jaw. I took cover down behind a little embankment. Every now and then the machine gun would throw mud all over me. I was looking for a chance to get over the next ridge to get away from that gun. A couple of hours went by till I must have raised up too high. He got me in the head.

A medic came in and got the bleeding calmed down. My recollection is he didn't make it himself. The sniper got him.[1] I was totally blind. When it got dark, someone led me out of there till we hooked up with a jeep. It was full of wounded on the back, so the driver asked me if I was able to sit up front. I said, "Sure."

The Germans bounced a couple of bullets off the jeep on the way out. At the evac hospital, I felt this hand reach up and take hold of my head and someone say, "Jesus Christ, how did that man walk in here?" That's all I remember. I passed out.

DUUS

We were told the bullet removed some of the bone on the back of his head and exposed his brain.

ELLIS

All I could think about was I was blind. That was how it was till around Christmas, when I started getting glimpses of something red once in a while. Finally, I reached out for it. It was a nurse's hair, fiery red hair. I slowly progressed from there. On Christmas Day, when a fighter-bomber strafed the hospital, I could see the tracers flying around. Then, on a hospital train headed for Marseilles, I started seeing light bulbs. In two months, I was to where I could read. What came back had come back.

DUUS

November 30 was a terrible day. Our assistant squad leader, Frank Schmidt, was killed, and four or five others. It was all small arms, no artillery or mortars. Our left flank was exposed. The Germans must have waited till a whole group was out in the open and then opened fire. Virtually half the platoon was wiped out.

When the fighting subsided, Jack May was sitting in a hole when he saw a German silhouette pointing a pistol at him. He didn't have time to raise his rifle. He fired from the waist and killed the German. He showed us the pistol. [S. Sgt. Jack May was later wounded, on 15 March.]

We did some patrols after Nothalten. One I remember we went five miles into German territory looking for prisoners, but we never got any. Juel Gist was the squad leader and I was his assistant. We made a lot of noise with a roll of telephone wire we dragged along with us. There weren't any fancy nylon bearings in those days.

Gist was an excellent soldier, amiable, well liked. [See chapter 22.]

In January, we had that icy retreat from Niederbron to Rothbach. The French along the way would ask us, "Kraut kommen?" "Naw, naw," we'd say, but they knew better. When we crossed the bridges, the guards would ask, "You the last guys?"

One of my vivid memories of Rothbach was Sergeant Huskey walking along the parapet in front of our holes telling everybody what the situation was, to stay awake, and keep our eyes and ears open. [See chapter 26.] That's where they passed out white camouflage uniforms for everybody. I don't remember doing any shooting there. I must say I never really had a handle on where we were going, what direction we were going, or why we were where we were.

[But he has vivid memories of the events of 15 March, when the 7th Army and the 103d Division launched the final assault on Germany.]

I was running across an open field. Looking down, I saw four bullets strike alongside my shoe. I hit the ground in hopes that maybe they thought they hit me. When I got up again and moved, they never got back on me. I made it into the woods and jumped into a hole the Germans had dug.

While I was looking around, my legs cramped. I stood up to stretch and got hit in the neck with a bullet, just that fast. A stray bullet, I think. I don't think any German saw me. My initial reaction was that my arm had been blown off. I reached down to pick it up, but I couldn't lift it, it was so heavy. Which fortified my feeling that it was hanging by a thread. Actually, it was shock. My whole right arm was dead. I couldn't move it. I thought I'd lost it. I couldn't look.

There was water in the hole. I put my hand in the water and put it on my mouth. I guess it was the part of shock that has to do with dehydrating. I was conscious, and I knew I might bleed to death, but I don't think I panicked. I was damn glad I was hit and could get out of there. Absolutely. My fear was I'd get well enough to go back.

The bullet went in my neck and came out the back of my right shoulder. You know where the V is in your neck? Right there, then through my throat and through my lungs and my subclavian artery and what they called the spine of the scapula and out the back at the right shoulder.

The doctors wondered why I hadn't bled to death. I had what they called a hemothorax condition where the blood filled up part of my lung.

John Elkman and somebody else came by and found me. They sat me on a rifle and carried me back to the other wounded. John and I had been good friends for more than a year, in ASTP and then in the infantry. I think he found me because he had more mobility than the rest of us. He was the platoon runner.[2] [See chapter 22.]

A German medic was brought in to give first aid because our medics were either killed or wounded. They tell you not to drink water after you've been injured in the throat, but I was deadly thirsty, and I kept asking John for water. I think he brought me two canteens that night while I was lying there. It's all such a hazy situation. I lay on the ground all night with other wounded till they took us out about nine the next morning.

At the field hospital, our medics looked at the German's bandage and said everything looked okay. The thing that disturbed me most was being put with a roomful of people who had tracheotomies. I was listening to these people breathing through their throats and thinking, "I'm going to be next." But it wasn't necessary. In a couple of days, I was put on a train to a hospital outside of Marseilles, the Third General Hospital. There, they cut out a piece of my artery, so I have no arterial blood supply in my right arm.

When they tied off my artery, they had to break my collarbone, but they messed it up getting it back together again. They had to break it to get at an aneurysm and to see if they could find out what the nerve problem was. They were unsuccessful in that. I have permanent partial loss of the use of my right arm. I can't open my right hand at all. There's no collarbone on the right side.

EPILOGUE

Despite their terrible injuries—Duus prefers "injury" to "wound"—these men have led full and productive lives. Ellis went back to school at Emporia State University for his engineering degree, then worked for a gas company until he retired. He and his wife, Jean, have two children.

Duus went to law school at Temple University in Philadelphia and has been in practice in suburban Media, Pennsylvania, since 1953. He and his wife have three children. He has been active in the Kiwanis and Junior Chamber of Commerce, but never in veterans' organizations. "Sitting around spinning yarns and marching on Armistice Day, as we used to call it, didn't attract me."

DUUS

In June [1945] I came home by ship and was sent to England General Hospital in Atlantic City, a neurosurgical center. I was operated on there in November and again in March of '46. [Several other hospitals and rehabilitation centers followed.] In January '47, I transferred to Percy Jones General Hospital in Battle Creek, Michigan, and was discharged there that March.

They kept me for two years waiting for the nerves to come back. I was in physical therapy twice a day, trying to get more use of my arm. It was totally paralyzed at the beginning, but gradually came back. The second operation removed a bone callous that was pressing on the nerve. After that, I got quite a bit more movement.

The VA gave me 100 percent disability, but they reduced it later to 90 percent. That was in 1948, and that was the last contact I've had with the VA.

Military service was, no question, a highlight, a low highlight, or a high lowlight, of our lives. I don't remember very many pleasant experiences except the associations with other people. What stands out is a lot of privation, a lot of suffering, a lot of just plain inconvenience and dirt that made up our job.

I was fortunate to have survived, but I wouldn't call it luck. I don't think luck has a lot to do with anything. Or religion, either. Religion didn't enter the picture for me.

How much has my injury gotten in my way? A lot. I was right-handed, number one, and secondly, I was sort of a semi-professional trumpet player. It took me out of that completely. I tried to learn to play left-handed, but it wasn't the same. Switching from the side that's dominant is very, very difficult. I have learned to play golf, not well, but I play it. And we do a lot of traveling.

ELLIS

I came as near to dying in the hospital as I did in the field. The last week of January [1945] they put me to bed with laryngitis. The next day, I was transferred to isolation with scarlet fever, and the day after that, I was yellow as a Chinaman with jaundice. I couldn't see again because my eyes were swollen shut with bilateral conjunctivitis. The whole staff was swarming around me. They thought I had leukemia. But nine days later, I started making blood again, and I've been going ever since.

[His final hospital was Bushnell General Hospital in Brigham City, Utah, in June 1945.] That's where the doctors put the plate in my head. I was released from the army in August 1946. There wasn't anything more they could do.

I lost half my field of vision in both eyes permanently. More of the left eye is gone than the right. I have a plate over the hole in the back of my head that's three by two inches.

Telling you this is not the easiest thing to do. That's one reason I don't come to reunions.

JEAN ELLIS

He's been fantastic, but he doesn't like to talk about it. This is the first time in 45 years. When he got home, he told the story once and didn't want to talk about it again, and hasn't. He likes to talk more about the times at Camp Howze before you all went overseas.

I first found out about his wounding from a government telegram, and then a letter from his chaplain. I knew it was serious, but I was never told exactly what had happened to him. He got the Red Cross to write me a letter that told me he had hurt his arm, to explain why he couldn't write. Later, he sent me all the medical terms, but he didn't explain what they meant. Our family doctor is the one who told me he'd been blinded. It was quite a shock, but our doctor said it probably meant no sight on the left side of both eyes, and that's how it turned out.

ELLIS

I worked a full lifetime by finding something I could do.

JEAN ELLIS

We put the pieces back together, just like everyone else. It was long ago and far away, and it's just as well to leave it that way.

21

"MY HAND ONLY FOUND A STUMP."

When he enlisted in the army in 1942, A. J. (Jack) Reeder was assigned to the air corps, which was then part of the army. He qualified for West Point, but the air base where he was stationed did not get a West Point quota that year. Taking the next best thing available, he signed up for ASTP and spent two semesters at the University of Oklahoma as an engineering student. When ASTP was canceled, he went to G Company.

REEDER

I was smart enough to know that my chances of surviving World War II had just decreased substantially. We'd gotten the word that ASTP was canceled about five minutes before they marched us to the railroad station. When we got to Camp Howze, there were those tar-paper barracks under a pall of coal smoke. It was a foggy, cold March day, damp and cold, and probably as sad a day as I ever had in my life.

In the warehouse, they hung a "G 410" on me. I had no idea what it meant, but I soon found out. I went overseas as first scout in the Third Platoon, but later on I transferred to the Second Platoon as the messenger.

They picked me 'cause I was athletic and small and compact and could run like a rabbit. I had slugs bouncing around me several times, but it really wasn't that dangerous. I had been taught how to move, how to hit the ground and roll, and how not to get up in the same spot because there might be a bullet waiting. You can stay exposed for three seconds. It takes three-fourths of a second to realize there's a man up, then another second and a half for them to raise their weapons, and another half second to draw a bead. That's when your three seconds are up and you'd better get down.

We went on the line near St. Die, Alsace, in November 1944. My baptism of fire came a little later, when we were in a holding position and the 411th Infantry went through our lines to attack in the valley out to our front. They were absolutely chopped to bits. The Germans pinned them down with machine gun fire and then picked them off one at a time with mortar fire. I was in a hole with one of their squad leaders. He didn't have a man left. The wounded were being given treatment in that hole, and the water was draining out red. Oh, God, I was depressed and scared and frightened beyond any way I could describe.

Our company flanked St. Die, but it was liberated by the 103d. The townspeople have named their plaza "Place de 103d Division." I was back there in 1975 and mentioned to a shopkeeper that I had been a member of the 103d. From then on, the red carpet was rolled out.

Our first real fight in G Company was at a little place called Nothalten [on 30 November], where the Second Platoon took a lot of casualties. It was just about half wiped out before the Third Platoon ever was engaged in combat. As a consequence, a lot of people were transferred to the Second Platoon. That's when I became the Second Platoon runner.

About two months later, we got into a place called Rothbach [22 January 1945]. We had some scary days there, though I was personally in a very secure position. Three of us had a hole about five feet deep: Sergeant [Moe] Huskey, Sergeant [Joe] Bonacci, and me. Huskey [later commissioned a second lieutenant] was acting platoon leader. Ryerson [the platoon leader, 1st Lt. William H. Ryerson, Paterson, New Jersey] had been wounded by shell fragments.

This was just after Von Runstedt's failure in the Ardennes. Hitler needed something to show the people at home. This SS division [the Sixth German Mountain Division], supposedly under the personal command of Himmler, was going to chase the American army back to the Mediterranean Sea. He made a good start. We gave up several miles, miles it cost us dearly to get back in the spring. But we held them at Rothbach.

The biggest thing that happened to me was when I was guiding the FO up to the lines. A machine gun hidden in a barn opened up on us. Well, he opened up on the wrong people. The radio operator just pulled out his antenna, and the FO called in artillery. Within three minutes, he had shells landing all around that barn.

When I was back there in '75, you could see where the tile roofs in Rothbach had been patched from mortar and artillery damage. The new tile shingles weren't faded. I found the big hole I was telling you about too. Still there, up on kind of a lumber trail. We had logs about eight inches in diameter on top of that thing, and dirt on top of that. We were impregnable except from grenades at night, which was a constant fear that never materialized.

One night, I heard on the telephone that Jack LaVelle, the platoon sergeant of the Third Platoon, had been offered a battlefield commission. Captain [A. J.] Torrance wouldn't let him go because it required his absence for five or six days from the front. "I've got to have every man," Torrance said. Five minutes later, the phone whistled twice. That was the signal for the Second Platoon. I answered, and I had a pass to Paris. I couldn't believe it. I'd just heard the captain say he needed every man. What he really meant, I guess, was he needed every leader he had.

Fifteen minutes later, I had my pass to Paris. We were picked by lottery, 26 in the division [of 15,000 men]. I went, and I worried about my buddies all through the three days I was gone. When I got back, I found they had been pulled off the line the same night I left. I'd have enjoyed myself a whole lot more if I'd known that.

It was pretty quiet then for a month, gearing up for the spring offensive, we found out later. It was on the 13th of March, I believe, when Torrance assembled us in a courtyard in Obermodern to tell us the whats, the wheres, and the whens. That briefing was witnessed by French Alsatian civilians, some of whom were loyal to us and some of whom were loyal to the Germans. I had no doubt but that the Germans would know what was said minutes after we did.

All of my thoughts in the years since the war have centered around the 15th and 16th of March 1945. I saw more combat then than I saw the entire time put together.

On the morning of the 15th, we crossed the line of departure at 0630, to the best of my memory. Under cover of smoke, we crossed the Meurthe River. I was guiding an FO who was up there to direct artillery fire. I don't remember his name, but he was a good one.

A group of us got caught on top of a bare knoll. The Germans started laying in small arms and mortar fire. We ran for cover in a ditch by the road. The FO was right behind me, or I thought he was. But he couldn't keep up. I was a 10-second runner in high school. I jumped in the ditch. When he didn't show up, I crawled back to the top. He was lying out there with his right thigh laid wide open by a shell fragment. I went out on my knees, grabbed him under the shoulders, and dragged him into the ditch. He was still conscious. It wasn't any pleasure to him rolling down that embankment. I got him a couple of canteens of water and sprinkled his wound with sulfa powder. When I put the compress bandage on it, it went right down into the wound, it was that big. I got another compress from the platoon sergeant, Joe Bonnacci. He was carrying the medic's first aid kit, so he had an extra. The medic had been hit.

A. J. TORRANCE
company commander

I can't remember his name, but he was one hell of a good artillery observer. He lived, but I guess he was pretty badly crippled for the rest of his life. I helped bandage him and get him to the aid station.

REEDER

I didn't see him again, but nearly a year later, I was in a GI hangout near McCloskey General Hospital in Temple, Texas, when this lieutenant came bailing out of a booth and grabbed me like his long lost mother. It was the FO. He told me that had it not been for the battlefield first aid he received, he would have lost his leg and probably his life because it was several hours before he was evacuated.

When we advanced, G company went to the right, and F company went to the left, across an open field. The Germans were dug in along a tree line about 300 yards away. We started running and we never stopped. It was just fire from the hip and keep moving.[1] The only time we hesitated was to put another clip in that M-1 rifle. There was so much firepower we kept the Germans down pretty well and got across with a minimum of casualties.

The Germans at the edge of the woods surrendered. We sent them back and moved on till we ran into a dug-in position. They put up a pretty good little fight there. We lost Lt. [Theodore W.] Rustejkas, who was the First Platoon's leader. He yelled for a medic. As the medic bent over him, a bullet went through his helmet, and he dropped right onto the lieutenant.[2]

We cleaned that trench out in maybe 25 minutes in a hot exchange of small arms fire and took 57 prisoners. There weren't any wounded. If they were hit, they were hit in the head because that was all they were exposing.

[The next day, the attack resumed. Reeder was wounded severely. See chapter 22.] After I was hit, I used a walkie-talkie radio to direct mortar fire on those machine guns that were firing from the edge of town. I was up there alone, incapable of defending myself, doing everything I could to keep the krauts from launching a counterattack.[3]

Near dusk, Recon Smith—that's what we called him—he'd come from our reconnaissance troop—worked his way up to me. He gave me a quarter grain of morphine and made a sling for my arm. Then he had to move on. After dark, four litter bearers showed up to evacuate me. The dark was so thick you couldn't see your hand in front of your face. As they were packing me out, an artillery round came in. It killed all four people carrying me, amputated my right foot just above the ankle joint, and fractured my left leg four times.

I had shell fragments in my small intestines, my stomach, my liver, and my left lung.

I never lost consciousness. There wasn't any pain, just a tingling like your limbs feel when they go to sleep. I sat up and ran my good hand down my leg and found a stump. I started sounding off for help. I knew I wouldn't live through the night without it. Finally, the medics came. One of them said, "There's no use bothering with these." That's how I knew my litter bearers were dead.

There wasn't a lot of bleeding. Shell fragments are red hot. As they cut through my leg, they seared off the artery. By the time the medics found me, I had my belt on my leg for a tourniquet. I should have been more concerned about the other injuries. They were more serious, but I didn't know that. I knew the foot was gone, so that was where I concentrated my efforts.

Considerable infection developed later in my left leg, but no joint damage. I was fortunate. I have no fibula in that leg. It was in so many pieces the doctors just took it out and threw it away. The stubs come up from each end, but there's no connection in there.

It took me a number of years to figure out that the shell that hit us was one of ours, a short round. The Germans weren't going to waste ammunition on a litter crew. They were too short of ammo. I'm thankful I didn't figure it out sooner, or I might have been bitter. Patients who were bitter had no chance of recovery. Physically, maybe, but if their minds were twisted with rage, they had a hell of an adjustment to make.

I knew one guy from the 36th Division who had been wounded in the head. He woke up on the battlefield three or four days later with a burial tag on him. The temperature reached below freezing every night, and as a result, he lost all of his fingers except one, and his right thumb. Everything else was nubbed off at the joints.

We called him Nubby.

My God, he hated those medics who looked at him and called him dead. He was scheduled for burial and damn lucky he came to before it happened. I mean, the man was bitter.

[Evacuated to a field hospital in Saverne, France, Reeder underwent the first of many operations.]

The day after the surgery, a nurse held up a clip board and made me write a V letter to my parents. I asked her to do it, but she wouldn't. "I want this in your own handwriting." She knew what she was doing. I couldn't tell them much, not even that I had been wounded. All I said was, "The war for me is over. Don't worry about me. Love, Jack." My mother got that letter two days before she got the official telegram saying I'd been wounded. She knew it was my handwriting, so she knew my right arm was all right and my eyesight was all right, at least in one eye.

My father said that on the morning of the 16th of March, about seven o'clock Oklahoma time, my mother was awakened by what she thought was a gunshot. She had two sons in combat areas in Europe. She told my father that one of her boys was hurt, and she thought it was Jack. Seven o'clock in Oklahoma is two o'clock Paris time, which was about the time I was hit by that machine gun.

[His next stop on the way home was the 171st General Hospital, Nancy, France.]

I was scheduled for air evacuation to the States, but my leg just didn't feel right. I lifted up the sheet. The cast was blood-soaked from the foot halfway up to my knee. Infection had eaten a blood vessel in two. Somehow, though, I knew that if the doctor could save my leg, he would. I went out and didn't wake up till the middle of the next day, with the leg in traction. They kept me there till the bones had stretched out and the wound was healed enough so I could be put in a permanent cast.

I was having a degree of self-pity, but early in May, I was moved to the First Central Hospital in Paris. We were getting in POWs from the German prison camps and very soon learned to tell how long they'd been prisoners. The longer the bone is exposed, the blacker it gets. One that was white, he'd been a POW for a month. One that was gray, that was three or four months. One that was black, he'd been a prisoner for two or three years. Seeing that stopped my self-pity. I was alive, and I had never been a prisoner, and I could have been very easily.

But I never heard any ex-POW have anything but praise for the German medics. They were hospitalized with German troops in the same wards, and they got exactly the same medical treatment as the German soldier got. I never met a wounded American POW that was abused, and I met a bunch of them.

[Reeder was flown home on 26 May 1945. After a layover in the Azores, the plane started for Gander, Newfoundland.]

We were about 30 minutes out when the outside port engine caught fire. I thought, "My God, did I survive the war to drown in the ocean?" We turned around and headed back to the Azores. The flames were really jumping out of the cowling. Finally, when the engine pumped itself out of oil, the pilot fired the extinguishers and put that damn fire out, and we landed.

Within minutes, we were back in the air for Gander in another plane, and then on to New York. When we got to Mitchell Field Hospital in New York, they let us order anything we wanted. Most of us chose salads. We hadn't had anything fresh since we left the States.

[From there, he went to Bushnell General Hospital in Brigham, Utah, for long-term care.]

There was nothing there except arm and leg amputees, other orthopedics, and paraplegics. Nine-thousand patients. I was there a month when they decided to reamputate my leg. They rounded off the bone, made real fine stitching of it, what they called a fish mouth amputation. But I got serum hepatitis from blood transfusions. I came off that operating table a very sick young man. For three weeks, I was deathly ill. My weight dropped to 87 pounds, casts and all.

But by September [1945] I got to feeling pretty good. They wouldn't give me a furlough, so I took off. I had a little collapsible wheelchair that I'd bought with my own money. If you had both legs off, the army would furnish you a wheelchair, but if you were missing just one, you had to furnish your own. I packed a little bag with clean clothes, slung it over the handle of that wheelchair, and rolled it out to the highway to hitchhike to Salt Lake City.

I couldn't spend any money in that town. I was a war hero to them. Whatever I wanted, someone wanted to pay for. Once, I had my wheelchair stolen while I was in a bar. Thirty minutes later, the police found this drunk rolling it down the middle of the street and brought it back to me. I had a good time. Frankie Carl was playing at one club, and Nat King Cole at another, so I'd see the early show and the late show, night after night. As an old jazz fan, I really enjoyed that.

[When he returned from his Salt Lake City vacation, Reeder was transferred to McCloskey General Hospital in Temple, Texas.]

I had lost a very good friend out of the Third Platoon, a kid by the name of Meadows [William J. Meadows, wounded 24 January 1945, at Rothbach] from Vernon, Texas. His whole skull two or three inches above his eyes was laid open by a tree burst. I helped carry him off the mountain. I never had any hopes for him to be alive.

A couple of days before that, I lost another friend, a big Cherokee Indian named John Finley. He was supposedly killed when our outposts were overrun.[4]

But eight months later, I rolled my wheelchair into the auditorium at McCloskey and damn near ran over both Meadows and Finley. Finley's left arm had been shattered by a burst from a machine pistol. The bone damage was repaired, but part of the nerves were severed so that his hand drooped. He could close his fingers, but he couldn't extend them. Over the years, he got enough repair to the nerves that he could slowly but totally extend his fingers.

I was best man at John's wedding in Tulsa in June of 1950. I've since lost track of him. One time, I called every Finley in Tulsa. Nobody knew him.

Meadows never fully recovered. He died about 1947 or 1948.

[At McCloskey, Reeder was fitted with an artificial foot and discharged 14 March 1946, two days short of a year from the time he was wounded.]

I put my bags in the seat of my wheelchair and walked behind it the quarter mile to the cab stand. The wheelchair took most of my weight. Waiting for the cab, I discovered I'd left my cane hanging over the foot of my bed. I wasn't about to go back. From then on, I never walked regularly with a cane till three years ago, when one of my hip joints went bad. My walking was limited more by the muscle strength in my leg than the amputation.

But I had 35 excellent years. I worked in an office in Tulsa beside a man who didn't know I was a leg amputee until I came to work with an empty pants leg one day. It gave him such a shock he accused me of trying to assassinate him.

EPILOGUE

Reeder went home to his prewar civilian job with the Army Corps of Engineers for a short time, but shortly enrolled at the University of Oklahoma for an accounting degree. After an apprenticeship with the IRS, he went into practice as a certified public accountant. Reeder was interviewed in 1986. He died of cancer on 23 April 1992.

REEDER

I built a reputation regionally as well as locally as an income tax expert. I was good at it. Now, I'm semiretired. I sold my firm in 1982.

I've been attending reunions since 1949, when it was just G Company. Several of us were sitting around talking one time when Bob Allen [Robert F. Allen, also wounded on 16 March] said to A. J. [Torrance], "I rode an ambulance back the night of the 16th of March with one of your boys. I don't know who he was. That poor son of a bitch was blown to bits. There's no way he could have survived. Do you know who he was?"

Torrance said, "Why don't you reach across the table and shake hands with that son of a bitch? He did survive."

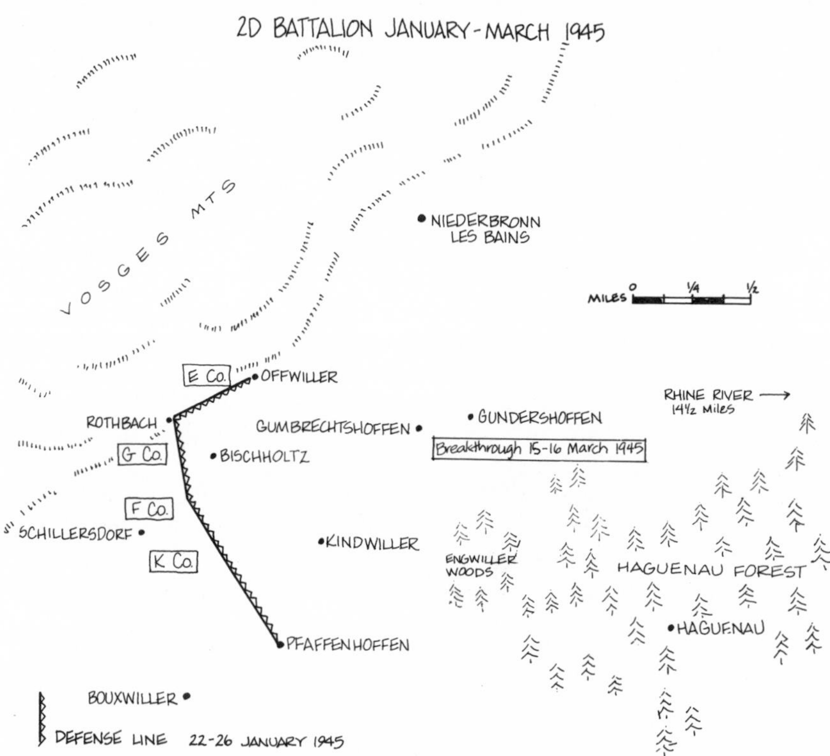

Pfaffenhoffen-Rothbach-Offwiller winter defense line and bitterly contested ground around Gundershoffen.
Map by Karen Schober

22

MARCH 16

It was a beautiful early spring on the edge of the French Alsatian plain that morning of 16 March 1945.

The Second Battalion had spent the night hiding in a woods overlooking the village of Gundershoffen. Between the woods and the town was a mile of newly ploughed field bisected by a two-lane road. There had been hard fighting and heavy casualties the day before as the battalion pushed out of its static Vosges Mountains bases in the great Seventh Army attack into the German heartland. Only 14½ miles to the east lay the Rhine River and Germany.

The battalion's goal was a bridge in Gundershoffen needed by the tanks that would pass through the infantry to seize a bridgehead on the Rhine. On the outskirts of the village, the Germans waited with their "harvesters of men," 20 machine guns that fired fifteen hundred rounds a minute, three times the speed of the American guns.

The foot soldiers were supposed to have had the bridge by 9 A.M. the day before. Now 24 hours behind schedule, the pressure was on. They were tired and nervous. G Company had lost 4 men killed and 22 wounded the day before. The other companies' casualties were not as severe, but everyone had taken a beating, then spent a sleepless night waiting for a counterattack that never came. Capt. A. J. Torrance, G Company commander, looked out over the flat, open ground and recommended a night attack.

TORRANCE

I was dismayed. I could see through the glasses that dirt had been newly turned over at the edge of town, so there had to be many weapons in those holes. I said to the battalion commander, "I wish we could get a night attack. It's going to be murder going across in daylight." He agreed, but he told me, "We've got to go as fast as we can get organized."

BOB SCHROEDER

private, first class, Torrance's messenger

General McAuliffe [Anthony McAuliffe, division commander] said, "Attack at all costs." I haven't had any respect for McAuliffe since.

TORRANCE

That was the order, so we took off in a column of platoons, G Company in the lead with F Company behind us to the right. We hadn't gone 50 yards when automatic fire broke out from in front of the town, and the Second Platoon, which was in the lead, began to get cut up pretty good. I sent them to the left of the road and told Lt. Paul Carlino [platoon leader] to try to move the platoon up in the old, classic fire-and-movement maneuver to see if they couldn't get under those gun emplacements.

A squad would get up and run 10 or 15 yards, hit the ground and fire, and a little later another squad would get up and go through them. But they didn't get very far. It was like attacking over a pool table. The fire was awfully heavy. The Second Platoon was almost wiped out in an hour. We had thirtysome men when we started. By a little after noon, we had 15 still able to fire. They were trying to get up, but they reached a point where it was impossible.

The battalion commander moved E Company in on the right side of the road, figuring they might draw enough fire away to let us move our platoons up. Well, they made a terrific effort, but they ran into the same thing we did. I sent my runner, John Elkman, out to Lieutenant Carlino and [T. Sgt.] Joe Bonacci and anybody else he could reach to tell them, "Fire and movement. Fire and movement. They've got to move."

"Captain," Elkman said, "they can't move. They're pinned down."

Carrying those messages took a superhuman effort on Elkman's part. He was up and running the whole day, a prime target, and three or four times I saw the dust puff up around his feet. He did every single thing I told him, he got every message out and got every message back, and he lived. I put him in for the Silver Star. A fine, brave young man. I do believe that somebody was looking after certain people, and he was one of them.[1]

JACK REEDER

private, first class, Second Platoon

I was in the attack point as the runner for Carlino. We kept closing on our scouts, who were supposed to be a hundred yards ahead of us, at least. Joe Bonnaci turned around and said, "Reeder, this is our day. This is it." Over and over he said it. We had no cover, no concealment. We were out there like ducks on a pond.

But we were under orders, and we went. It never occurred to me not to. You didn't do things that way then. Five minutes later, Bonnaci was dead, killed by the opening machine gun burst from the edge of the town. He and all three squad leaders. Lieutenant Carlino was wounded in the heel, probably after he hit the ground, because he didn't lay his feet flat. Standing on his toes, so to speak, lying flat on his belly with his heels still sticking up, he got a bullet through one heel and died from shock or loss of blood, one or the other—or both. He lived quite a while, but nobody could get to him.

Bonnaci and the rest of them were just riddled. Sgt. Juel Gist was down behind a little bush. He had concealment but no cover. He was there for three hours before they finally got him.

I got a slug in my elbow. BANG! Just like that. I scrambled into a ditch. It was my only hope. Very soon after that, Gist and I were the only ones alive up there, and Gist didn't last too long.

When they got me back to Battalion Aid that night, Father Kleffman [Capt. William C. Kleffman, the battalion's Catholic chaplain] kneeled over me, and I told him about the terrible day that the Second Platoon of G Company had suffered. [See chapter 21 for the rest of his story.]

TORRANCE

We finally got some artillery fire on those machine guns, and about dark we were able to get into the town. I took the reserve platoon, the first, into town and crossed the bridge, which was still intact. We had secured our objective. Unfortunately, we were 35 hours late and the battalion was decimated. The strength of the Second Platoon was down to 12 men. [Normal complement was 40.]

The next day, I went back to look over the ground. Sergeant Bonacci and Lieutenant Carlino were furthest out in front, on a little knoll under a tree. Both dead, with six or seven dead behind them. They were almost up to those machine gun emplacements and apparently were still putting some fire in there when they were hit.

Carlino was only with the company two or three days. He had been the GRO.

DICK STANNARD
private, Second Platoon

Halfway across the field, a machine gun opened up on us. The first burst killed Lieutenant Carlino,[2] who had only joined us a couple of nights before. The story went around at the time that he wasn't doing his job as graves registration officer, so Regiment sent him down to lead a rifle platoon, a death sentence, as it turned out. Until then, he had had a job as safe as a clerk's in Paris, at least from a rifleman's point of view.

TORRANCE

Carlino was a straightforward young man, athletic, seemed intelligent. It was just that he had not been under fire much. Battalion sent him down and told me to loan Huskey [2d Lt. Moe Huskey, the regular leader of the Second Platoon] to F Company for a day or so. They were short of officers and needed someone with frontline experience. Well, it was six of one and a half dozen of the other. Both officers were going on the attack. Would one assignment be safer than the other? No.

I told Carlino what he'd better do, and told Bonacci, our veteran platoon sergeant, "He's your platoon leader. You know the guys and he doesn't, so stay with him and help him out." In my opinion, he wasn't killed because he didn't know what to do. He was out front where he was supposed to be.

1ST LT. JOE MEADOWS
G Company executive officer

Carlino must have had a premonition he wouldn't live through the attack. The night before, he gave me his wife's address and asked me to write to her. I told her I had known him only briefly and liked him very much, that he was a fine person. I never had an answer from her.

SCHROEDER

We were halfway to the town when they opened up on us. I made a heck of a dive into a grove of evergreens, but I looked out, and our two radio carriers were lying in the middle of the road, face down. I thought they were hit. I didn't think anybody would lay down in the middle of the road and still be alive.

When the firing died down a little bit, I went out, and here those guys were. They didn't have sense enough to flop into the ditch. So I got 'em back under cover and got 'em hooked together. You had to plug the battery pack that one man carried into the radio that the other one had. The forward [artillery] observer asked me where he ought to fire, and I said, "Well, fire along the edge of town and take the pressure offa those guys from the Second Platoon." But he was just out of artillery school, and the artillery manual says, "Thou shalt not fire artillery within 75 yards of your own troops." It was too close for him. He wouldn't shoot.

The FO we had before would put fire wherever we needed it, right on our own troops when he had to. But he got wounded the day before [See chapter 21]. This new guy started firing at what he thought was a tank, but it was just a pile of wood with a log stickin' up.

A German construction crew must have used that grove of trees for a bathroom. There was a hundred piles of crap in there. I was crawlin' around in the trees and stuck my hand in some, just about the time a couple of our airplanes started strafing right over us. This poor sucker, this artillery observer, was tryin' to read his map that was all covered with crap and call on the radio to get the planes stopped, and at the same time dig a hole with that little trenching tool. I don't think anybody could dig faster with a backhoe. It was his first day at the front.

H Company had some 81 mortars off to our left. I ran down there to get 'em to fire on the German machine guns. Usually when you wanted mortars, they didn't have any ammunition, or they had ammunition and the mortars weren't there. But this time, they had a gun and some rounds, and they fired.

When it was dark, we came out of the bushes and walked into town. The Germans evidently had pulled out. I followed Torrance to an officers' meeting. I heard him tell the battalion commander, "I never want to see that son of a bitch again as long as I'm alive." We never saw that forward observer again.

2d LT. BOB LAWLER

First Platoon leader, F Company

As we approached these twin towns [Gumbrechtshoffen and Gundershoffen], we were caught out in the open. In the smoke and confusion, our air force strafed and bombed us. It was probably 5 or 10 minutes, but it seemed like hours. We lost a few men from that bombing. A bullet or piece of shrapnel went through my gas mask.

JOHN KAISER
staff sergeant, F Company

I never saw Gundershoffen. One of our smoke shells hit very close and burned the man next to me. We were up and down, taking cover, trying to get into the shelter of a house on the edge of the field. A German officer in the house shot me with his pistol. When the other people in my squad got into the house, he surrendered. The bullet went in below my left hip, passed through, and went into my right leg. It hit the meat, not the bones, but even today I can't lift my right leg as high as the left.

The medics came through with a jeep that night, but I didn't feel like I was as badly wounded as some of the others, so I stayed in the house till morning.

2d LT. JOHN S. CLARK
Third Platoon leader, F Company

Me and my little platoon messenger, we started out and it was hit and move a few feet, hit and stay a minute or two and move a few more feet this way and hit, roll over and hit, crawl a little farther, roll over to the next furrow. Little short jumps and jerks. I could hear the bullets pass. Sounded like bees. Several of the men seemed to think I'd been hit two or three times, but I wasn't.

Me and some of my men made it to the edge of town. Then I got a man inside. That started quite a movement forward. Some more got in, and I was right behind them. Torrance was right behind me. The Germans had machine guns in a house. One of my men, I don't know who now, got upstairs and took command of one of those machine guns. I don't know how he did it.

G. GARDNER WILLIAMS
private, first class, F Company

There was a lot of plowed ground and a bunch of German machine guns. Four of us volunteered to go up and knock one out. We climbed and crawled across this field. I was the only one who made it. The others were hit on the way. When I got up to where they could see me, the Germans started running, and their own men killed them. I got into their foxhole. It was just full of canisters. I turned the gun around and fired it all day long.

An hour after I got in the hole, machine gun fire tore up my shoulder. I was wearing a fur liner in my battle jacket that stopped the bleeding, so I didn't get weak or anything. I kept on firing with one hand.

I guess I was 200 or 300 yards in front of the rest of our troops. At dusk, the line moved up and passed me. I did a lot of yelling to make sure they knew it was me and not a German. I got out and started walking back to find help. On the way, I picked up one of the fellas that had been with me. He was hit in the ankle.

CARL NICHOLS

second lieutenant, Fourth Platoon leader, F Company

The attack had to cross maybe one thousand yards of open field. They mowed us down just like wheat. Perhaps not that bad, but in my mind that's the way it was. I got about to the midpoint when I realized the crowd had got thinned out. I dived into a German foxhole at the same time a sergeant dived in. There was another kid who wanted in too, but there just wasn't room. We had squatter's rights. "Give us a chance," I told this kid. "We'll make room for you just as quick as we can." He jumped up to make a run for it. BANG! Dead as a doornail.

I don't know who he was. I didn't know the sergeant either, but we were good friends for a short while. He was a good soldier, and he really knew how to dig. He should have been a geologist. First he'd dig and I'd shoot, then I'd dig and he'd shoot.

HAROLD MOTENKO

private, first class, F Company

I was first rifleman, I think we called it [actually *first scout*], in Lieutenant Clark's platoon. That field must have been a mile or two wide. Clark couldn't get anybody to go out. He or Captain Gibbs, one or the other, yelled, "Goddamnit, if you don't get started, I'll shoot you."

It was suicide. A completely open field, no cover. There were no volunteers, but I was first rifleman, so I started out and they followed. I could hear the officers threatening some of the men behind me: "Come on, get out there, or I'm gonna shove a bayonet up your ass."

I kept hitting the ground and getting up and running and hitting the ground and getting up and running till finally I was so tired I couldn't hit the ground anymore. I stayed up and kept running and then something nicked my wrist. I dived forward and got hit by a machine gun bullet. There was a tremendous burning sensation. The bullet caught me as I was diving for the ground. It went in on top and came out the bottom. It just missed my spinal cord and lungs.

I could feel the blood congealing on my stomach. I was moving around, trying to get my pack off, when I heard a voice from far off yell, "Motenko, keep your goddamn head down, or I'll knock it down." It was John Clark. He came running across that field, zigzagging toward me, to ask how I was. If I didn't keep my fanny and my head down, he said he'd knock me out. Then he got up and continued on.

I started yelling "medic," but nobody came. It must have been an hour or more. Finally, I ran back toward our old lines. I hopped a fence, and on the other side I found the medics. They were too scared to come out. But listen, this is the best part: I still had to walk to the aid station, where they took one look at the wound and got me on a stretcher.

John Clark saved my life. If it weren't for him, I don't think I'd have made it. He was Old Army and believed in the book. If you followed the book, you had a chance.

JIM McCARTHY

private, F Company machine gunner

That morning, we started across a big field toward the town. Did I hear talk about it being a suicide mission? Naw, the officers didn't confide in me. We went down into a bog and then out into the field. At that point, I'm hearing bullets fly a little bit.

There was two huge shell craters. Lieutenant Lawler and me and some of his men, we're in one, and Captain Gibbs and the other machine gun was in the other. Our gunners had got wounded, so my buddy, Bill Mahoney, and I are on the gun now. We'd been ammunition bearers, so we're moving up in life.

Mahoney gets on our gun, and I'm laying alongside him feedin' in the belt when a German machine gun fires point blank into us, knocking the gun out of our hands. Mahoney put his arm up and caught a ricochet in his wrist. One glanced off my helmet, but it didn't even rattle my brains. I didn't have any.

I took the bullet out of Mahoney and threw it away. Well, you wanta see a crazy man? "What the hell you do that for?" he says. He wanted it for a souvenir.

The gun would only fire one shot at a time. Somebody said, "The other section [machine gun team] is down." They were out in the open. I started out there to get their gun. Lieutenant Clark says, "Where the hell are you goin'?" When he realized what I was doin', he says, "Go git it and be right back." If he'd thought I was goin' the wrong way, he'd of shot me dead, believe me.

I was puffin' like hell besides bein' a little on the, uh, crazy side. What am I doin' up here? I'm gettin' shot at. I rested maybe a minute and ran out to the other gun crew. They're all hit but two guys. I says, "Grab your ammunition and follow me." I got up but this one guy stayed down. I'm standing there, under fire. I went down again. I says, "When I get up, you get up." He still hesitated. I told him, "Get up or I'll kick your goddamn guts out." He finally got up. We ran back to the crater.

I set the gun up, but it got quiet then. We were basking in the noonday sun when here comes our air support. Bombing *us*. The medic that was there and me, we started diggin' in. I broke my trenching tool and grabbed Mahoney's. His broke too. Usually you could chop wood with those damn things. I managed to scrape out a pretty good hole when here comes our planes again, strafing and bombing. We pushed Mahoney into the hole and covered his body with ours. It was a foolish gesture. If you're hit with one of those slugs, you're gonna be 50 feet in the ground.

NICHOLS

Seven of our P-47s peeled off and bombed and strafed our position. This sergeant and me started diggin' sideways, back into the wall. It was a fearsome few minutes. P-47s had eight machine guns. When they fired, they literally plowed the ground.

Not long after this happened, I got a little R & R down at Nancy. This young major saw my patch and asked me if I knew anything about a unit in the 103d that got bombed by mistake. He was afraid they'd annihilated us. He felt so bad about it he paid for my drink. He claimed it wasn't their fault. The air corps bombed according to colored smoke rounds from our artillery, which was so inacccurate they dropped marker rounds right amongst us.

Incidentally, I met Marlene Dietrich while I was down in Nancy. She was on a morale tour. Had breakfast with her one morning. I thought she was an old lady, but gosh, she wasn't but about 40 then.

McCARTHY

Lieutenant Clark yelled over at Lieutenant Lawler, "How the hell long are we gonna screw around here?" He's swearin' and gettin' mad. Lawler says, "Why the hell don't *you* move out? I don't see you gittin' your ass off the ground." So Clark got mad again. Clark is out in the open, down behind a little roll of a hill. Captain Gibbs gets up on the edge of his hole, looking at the town. It was quiet. He thought maybe they'd pulled out. "What the hell are we doin' here?" he says. That's when Clark got up and started to push into the town.

Lawler was next. "When I say 'Go,' we go," he says. But one of my team wouldn't move.

"You hear me, McCarthy?" says Lawler.

"What am I gonna do, carry him?"

I jumped back down in the hole. Lawler says, "If he don't move this time, either you shoot him or I shoot him." The man got up, but he wanted to hit the ground every 10 yards even though it wasn't that bad. Clark's men were in the town ahead of us.

NICHOLS

We were stuck out there till Clark and that bunch got into the town up a ditch they used for cover. They shot a few krauts and ran 'em out. That's when we came out of our hole and started goin'.

McCARTHY

I didn't wanta leave Mahoney. He was like my own brother. So I says, "Can you carry ammo? Grab a can." It was maybe the length of a football field to the edge of town.

NICHOLS

Gibbs sent word to Lawler and me to take the bridge that was the mission of the whole dang battalion. The idea was to hold it and let the 411th Infantry go through and head for the Siegfried Line. So we started fightin' down those streets toward the bridge.

McCARTHY

Mahoney was gettin' feverish and real shocky. We come around the edge of a building, and a German soldier steps out and opens up with his burp gun. We hit the ground. Nichols stepped on Mahoney's arm, and he passed out. I carried him toward the rear and ran back to the gun. On the way back, I passed a German. I didn't have a damn thing with me, rifle or nothin', cause I had to carry Mahoney. The German didn't want me, and I didn't have nothin' to want him with. We both got the hell outa there.

LAWLER

It was slow moving in the town, fighting house to house. I lost one of my men, a guy that shouldn't have been with us, really. He was much too old to be in the infantry.

McCARTHY

We heard a burp gun open up ahead. A guy comes running back and tells Lieutenant Lawler, "Schnabel [Pfc. Arthur Schnabel] is down." He was an older man, Lawler's runner, and Lawler liked him a lot.

LESTER (DOC) DUCKETT

medic, F Company

Schnabel and two or three other men in Lawler's platoon were on a patrol a little further out to see what was happening. He spoke German, but not good enough to satisfy the Germans. He got killed.

McCARTHY

Three of us volunteered to go up and get him. He was lying in the street. I picked him up and put him on my back. He bled down my neck. I think he died on the way because there was a change in the weight.

CLARK

The company commander told Lawler to get on through to the bridge and set up the machine guns. Those Germans shot one of his boys right between the eyes. Lawler come back and said he couldn't make it, so I said I'd try. We worked our machine guns up around the bridge and stayed in a little house. The next morning, we could pick out Germans in their foxholes, but by then they was ready to give up.

McCARTHY

Lieutenant Nichols talked [in a memoir he wrote after the war] about the murderous fire we faced. That's bullshit. There might of been one more incident, if that. We got to the bridge and set up in the basement of a house. We were so damn tired we couldn't keep our eyes open.

NICHOLS

We went on to the bridge, McCarthy and me and one other person. The Germans had blown it. It was early evening. Here we were, and we don't know whether there's anybody else or not. That's an awfully lonesome feeling, you know? We set up the gun in a house. I was the lieutenant, so I said I'd take the first watch.

There wasn't any shootin' goin' on, and that's scary as hell. If there's shootin', at least you know where they are. It behooves you to stay awake. But I was so sleepy I was about to die. We hadn't slept in two days. I shook McCarthy and told him, "You have to take the gun. I can't stay awake any longer." He looked at his watch and said, "Lieutenant, it hasn't been but 20 minutes." But he got on the gun. When I woke up, there were streaks of daylight showing, and everyone was asleep. We'd all slept through the whole dadgum night. We came crawlin' out kind of sheepishly. There wasn't anybody around much to see us, a few guys creepin' around with their rifles like they weren't sure, so we told 'em, "Don't worry. You're safe." It wasn't two hours before tanks were going through with infantry riding on top.

We moved up to the Siegfried Line behind them. It was a lot of 12-foot-thick concrete bunkers interlaced with communications trenches. By now, Gibbs had given me Fussell's platoon, the Second [Fussell was wounded on 15 March] and told me to go clean up the area. We made a sweep, but there was nothing out there but dead Germans.

Mortarmen enter Gundershoffen, 17 March 1945, after its capture the day before.
Courtesy of the National Archives

MEADOWS

A day or so after we took Gundershoffen, I went back to the battlefield to register the dead. Men from our own artillery were filching stuff off the bodies of our men. [See “Interlude: A Painful Part.”]

STANNARD

The days after Gundershoffen are pretty much of a blur, constant movement along with the endless tension and watching. The squad was resting one time when the company exec, Lieutenant Meadows, came by and stopped for a minute. “You still alive?” he asked me. I think he was kidding.

EPILOGUE

Vivian Byars of Duncan, Oklahoma, was married to two of the men who fought that day at Gundershoffen. She was widowed by the battlefield death of Juel Gist. After the war, she married Jack Reeder.

VIVIAN GIST REEDER BYARS

I found out about Buddy's [Juel Gist's] death while I was at work. The telegram—you know, "We regret to inform you . . ."—they just handed it to me. That shot everything. He was a real special young man: on the football and basketball teams, salutatorian of his class, just a happy, smiling sort of guy.

I met Jack in 1946. He'd written to Buddy's parents, and they asked me to see if Jack had any more details about Buddy's death. I was back in college at Ada by then, and that's where Jack lived. We got acquainted, and in 1947, August 3, we were married. Buddy's parents were very nice about it. They told me I had my whole life ahead of me.

Jack and I were married 32 years, till 1979. I think he got bored. You know how it is. In midlife, men think life has passed them by. But we have three children, and grandchildren, in common, and we still live in the same town [Duncan, Oklahoma]. I remarried in 1982.

REEDER

I think that what happened to me may have had a negative effect on my marriage. My injuries limited my physical activity, of course. I could not hike or camp out with the boys.

VIVIAN BYARS

I remember thinking Jack looked older when I first met him than he did years later. He was pretty well worn out recovering. As far as our life together was concerned, his injuries were not especially troublesome. There were things he could do and things he couldn't do, but it was not a heavy thing with our family. He handled it pretty well.

Jack and I visited France in 1975. He was able to point out the little slope where Buddy was killed. Buddy's buried in the military cemetery at St. Avold, France. It's a beautiful place in a beautiful valley, the same valley where my uncle was killed in World War I. It seems like it was all kind of useless. Just what good did it all do? Especially for Buddy or my uncle.

Buddy's younger sister, Mary Belle Davison, is making up a memorial to him.

MARY BELLE DAVISON

Buddy's 50th high school class reunion is in 1992. We want to have the memorial ready when they all come to town. I have a picture of him when he was 10 or 12 in his baseball uniform, and Vivian is going to contribute his medals. [Gist received the Bronze Star, Purple Heart, and Combat Infantry Badge.]

I was a senior in high school when Buddy was killed. He was my older brother, born April 2, 1924. A very dear relative came and took me out of class one day and took me home. He didn't tell me what had happened, but I well knew. All the family was gathered. The adults already knew, but they wanted to tell me and my younger brother, Harold.

My dad, Irvin Gist, never got over Buddy's death. He died two or three years later, just grieved himself to death. He didn't want the body brought back from France 'cause he didn't want to go through all the sad memories again.

For myself, I have never felt Buddy's was an unnecessary sacrifice. Lots of people do, I know, but I feel like we need to stand up for what we think is right.

*

John Kaiser lives in the Baltimore suburb of Towson, but he spent most of his life in Ohio. A ceramic engineer, he is now retired.

G. Gardner Williams was a 100-pound, unathletic, deskbound accountant, a self-described "little skinny guy," when he volunteered for the army in 1942. He was in ASTP at the University of Oklahoma for a year, till the program ended and he was sent to the 103d at Camp Howze.

KAISER

In the hospital, they closed the rectal wounds where the bullet went through. Then I came down with yellow jaundice. I had the best of treatment. Because of the jaundice, I had a private nurse around the clock. I must have been there about six weeks when I was released to a repple depple. That's where my right wrist started bothering me. I'd fallen on it before I went overseas. They found it had been broken all that time, so I went back to the hospital, for bone grafts that time. I came home on a hospital ship. Till November, I was in a military hospital in Ohio. I was discharged in February 1946.

The army was a great experience, but I rank my career first. I really enjoyed making glass.

WILLIAMS

It was quite a shock. I didn't believe in killing. I always tried to take prisoners. But just before I was hit, I did shoot someone. It was a reflex action. He came around the corner with his rifle pointed at me, and I shot from the hip.

That caused me a lot of trouble after the war. I guess it was what they called war fatigue. It was something I knew I shouldn't have done. For about a year, I had problems breathing. I'm sure it was a guilt complex. After that, I was okay.

I must have gotten a charge out of combat. I never had any fear. When it was over, I actually missed it. I never thought I was brave. More like foolhardy. As time went on, I got the feeling there wasn't a shell or a bullet for me. A short round landed right at my feet once and didn't go off. That made me think I was never going to get hit, and I guess that's what got me hit.

But I didn't care for army life at all. I told 'em when they handed me a rifle I would never shoot anyone. I didn't believe in it. I'd always gone to church, the Methodist Church. When I was in combat, it bothered me to see a lot of foxhole religion, people who were very religious under fire but then would go out and carouse and be drunk when it was over. I always wondered whether my religion was that type or not. Never did figure it out, but I don't think so.

There are some good memories. Stuff like the time I sang German songs all night with a family in Alsace. The fella had hidden a pig, so we had pig heart and red wine. The old man had been in the kaiser's army in World War I.

Another vivid memory is Lieutenant Murphy [1st Lt. Warren Murphy of Vanderpool, Texas, executive officer of F Company]. A real born leader. We were down behind a railroad crossing. He says, "I wonder if the Germans are on the other side." He walked to the top of the track, and they fired a few rounds at him. "Yup," he says, "they're over there." He never took his hands out of his pockets. A great guy, just an ol' country boy.

Then there was the time we took a bunch of refugees out of a cave. On the way back to our lines, someone tripped a flare. We were afraid we were going to lose a few, but they had all gotten down in the snow. There was complete silence.

I went back to help a little old lady with a big bundle of stuff she was carrying. When she heard me sniffling, she pulled out a handkerchief, held it to my nose, and said "Blow" in German.

When my feet were frozen [See chapter 14], I didn't think there could be anything worse, but that German machine gun tore up my left shoulder pretty good on March 16. It took three different operations, but they put it back together. I don't have any trouble using it.

I was in Marseilles recuperating and doing statistical work for a colonel when I got word my mother was very ill. The colonel gave me permission to hitchhike home. I rode a B-25 in its little Plexiglas nose part way and got to New York the day after a B-25 flew into the Empire State Building.

I stayed home in Dallas till my discharge that September. I got a couple of degrees at Southern Methodist and worked at many jobs till I was almost 40, when I began teaching economics at Texas Wesleyan. I just retired last month [in May 1987. Since then, he has become a popular actor in the Dallas-Ft. Worth area.]

23

"YOU HAD TO PROTECT YOUR MEN."

Clyde Rucker was one of the few professional soldiers from the prewar army who served in the 103d Division. G Company, Third Platoon, was his outfit from day one.

When he arrived at Camp Claiborne, Louisiana, in the fall of 1942 to start whipping the recruits into shape, he was the platoon sergeant. Overseas, he won a battlefield commission to second lieutenant and became the platoon's commander, the job he held until the end of the war. There was always a hard core of professionals like Rucker. In training, they were viewed with a mixture of hatred, awe, fear, and contempt ("Who'd pick the army as a career in peacetime?"). But in combat, these old timers came to be treasured and admired by their youthful charges. They were often the only ones who knew what they were doing. The comments of the late James Teague, who came under Rucker's wing from the ASTP, are typical.[1]

TEAGUE

He was a hard-nose, but I'm alive because he was hard. He knew the infantry; he knew infantry tactics. Some people can and some people can't do that kind of work. If he started with a group of men, he would do his best to get them where they were supposed to be going. He would tell his superior officers that "it can't be done," and they would accept his judgment. Rucker had 12 years in the infantry. He knew what would work and what wouldn't work. When he told his scouts to get in front [of the platoon], by gosh, they stayed in front, without question.

He was rough, but it was a rough business.

RUCKER

You had to speak up to protect your men. The whole platoon went on a raid one time across the Saar, and this major from Battalion tagged along. He was a bit of a boozer, and he made all kinds of racket. I had to say something to him [Rucker was still a sergeant]. I don't remember exactly what.

God, it was cold. We got several prisoners. Battalion was always hollering for prisoners [for interrogation]. I told Torrance we ought to just keep 'em in the basement. Then we'd have one available whenever they asked, and it would save us all these trips across the river. He wouldn't buy that. [He laughs.]

It wasn't too long after that that we retreated to Rothbach. Some of the machine guns were frozen. Digging in, we had to go down a ways to find dirt that wasn't froze. The night the Germans hit us, we were in houses down in Rothbach. Petrie [1st Lt. Sidney A. Petrie, the platoon leader] had just got his liquor ration. [Officers were issued liquor once a month.] We were gonna have a big feed with some eggs we got from the local people, but when the Germans hit, we had to get up the mountain into our holes. Petrie left his liquor settin' there on the table. He threatened to go back down there, but he never did.

We were in those holes quite a few days. A tank would drive up and down the valley every afternoon spraying our positions. Petrie decided he was gonna take a bazooka down the mountain and try to knock it out. He was that kind of a guy, always wanted to see what was over the next hill in front of him. Well, he got pretty close, I guess, but they spotted him and shot him. I think he was just a little too inquisitive. He was wasted, I'll say that.[2]

It wasn't too long after that I was sent to the division rear to get commissioned. They gave me a little interview and a physical. That was all there was to it. I remember the regimental commander pinning the bars on my shoulder. I was only off the line for two days. Torrance had me take over the Third and Fourth platoons, both.

[The next major event was the massive Seventh Army attack of 15 March 1945. The village of Gundershoffen was the objective.]

I felt pretty good that morning. We were the last platoon in the battalion. I liked having a lot of people in front of me. But there was all this smoke, and the rest of the battalion got lost. When the smoke cleared, God, there was Germans running all over the place. They were as surprised as we were. They were in back of us, in front, all around us. A whole lot of 'em surrendered.[3]

There was firing back and forth. One guy lost his arm when he was hit by a phosphorous shell. I think he might of got killed. There were quite a few casualties, then and that night. The next day, the 16th, we moved on toward Gundershoffen. We could see the Second Platoon out in the field. They really got it. [See chapter 22.] Torrance was gonna send my platoon in there after 'em, but I sort of talked him out of it, I think. "If you send us in there, we're gonna be in the same mess they are," I told him. He finally changed his mind. The company moved across that field and got into town. Lieutenant Clark [F Company]—he had a battlefield appointment too—is the one got 'em in there. My platoon had no trouble. We followed whoever was in front of us.

[The Third Platoon, relatively unscathed in the two-day fight to capture Gundershoffen, thus drew the job on the third day, 17 March, of assaulting the Siegfried Line fortifications.]

We attacked up a hill that afternoon. I told Teague and several more of 'em, "I want to hear a lot of racket," and boy, they did. There was supposed to be a BAR in each squad. Well, I had two in each squad, six altogether. It sounded like an army going up there with them, and the machine gunners firing over our heads. There was some dead Americans along the way from a previous attack, but we never suffered any casualties. What Germans was up there hung out white flags. I think they were ready to quit anyhow. Just trying to slow us down a little bit.

I never had a problem getting the men to carry BARs. I just picked out the ones I figured could handle it and told 'em, "You take it."

[Rucker's last combat occurred a month later. See chapter 24.]

EPILOGUE

Rucker lives in retirement in Rancho Cordova, near Sacramento. His wife died in 1987.

RUCKER

After the war, I came back to the States with the 45th Division. I went back to master sergeant when I was assigned to Ft. Lewis, Washington, worked for a while with the National Guard, and then went back to Germany in 1950. I took a warrant [officer's commission], worked around several places in Germany, and came home and retired in 1959 at Ft. Lewis. I had 25 years of service. When I moved to Sacramento, I worked for Aerojet for 10 years and for the state for 6 more. But I'm really retired now. I haven't worked in 12 years.

You can see I've been in a lot of outfits, but that deal with the 410th and G Company was the most important experience I ever had.

24

ERKENBRECHTSWEILER

On 22 April 1945, the men of the Second Battalion knew the war was almost over. Since the breakthrough to the Rhine more than a month earlier, they had cruised through a defeated Germany without a shot fired.

The American foot soldiers were riding at last, on every conveyance the supply people could muster: kitchen trucks, tanks, six-by-sixes, jeeps. Smashed German tanks and armored personnel cars, wagons, refugees, dead Germans, dead horses, and thousands of prisoners were everywhere along the roads. It was a different war from the one they had known. They headed south through the Rheinland and then Württemberg in southwestern Germany, bound for Hitler's redoubt at Berchtesgaden (not defended, as it turned out) and Austria. Then the column arrived at Unter Lenningen, one of the beautiful old villages on the approach to the Alps. One thousand feet above on a plateau was another postcard, the village of Erkenbrechtsweiler.

As the troops lolled around Unter Lenningen that afternoon, the ominous word came down that Erkenbrechtsweiler was full of German soldiers. G Company was ordered to climb the mountain, seize the town, and then defend it. A very unwelcome piece of news. Nobody had been expecting trouble. Uppermost in every man's mind was the fear he would be killed in the last days of the war.

This order placed a heavy responsibility on 1st Lt. Joseph W. Meadows, the new commander of G Company. Meadows had moved up from executive officer after A. J. Torrance was promoted to executive officer of the battalion. Erkenbrechtsweiler was Meadows's first real test as a combat leader.

G Company, backed by the heavy machine guns of H Company, struggled up the steep trail in late afternoon through a tangled jungle of fallen trees that the Germans had blasted with plastic explosives. At the crest, 200 yards from the edge of the village, the battle began.

2D LT. CLYDE RUCKER
Third Platoon leader

A German scout car came right at us. We fired, and it rolled over my messenger, Murphy. He thought he was killed and started hollering for the medics, but he wasn't hurt at all. It creased his helmet a little bit. One fella got out of the car and ran behind a building. One of my men killed him.

MEADOWS

When we got into town and realized we weren't alone, we organized defensive positions. Unfortunately, we were spread out a little bit more than was desirable. It was a long time before we got any artillery support. It never occurred to me, which was foolish on my part, not to call for 81-millimeter mortar support [from H Company]. I was wrong there. We were within their range. I was thinking more about searching artillery fire.

All through the night, they hit us with those 120-millimeter mortars of theirs. They weren't very accurate, but God, they sent a lot of those damn things in. WHOOSH, WHOOSH, WHOOSH. It was pretty exciting. We put the prisoners in the basement. One of those guys spit in my face. Schroeder knocked him down.

BOB SCHROEDER
private, first class, G Company messenger

There was a German soldier laying upstairs in our headquarters house who'd been wounded on the Russian front. When the barrage started, we all headed for the basement, but we left him there. It didn't faze him. The Russian front must of been a good conditioner.

MEADOWS

We finally got artillery support the next day after the rest of the battalion came up to relieve us.

[From an official report Meadows cowrote after the battle:] "Throughout the night, the enemy succeeded in infiltrating into town and harassed communications and defenses. . . . There was about four hundred yards separating the two [platoon] defense groups. . . . [The Germans] completely cut off one rifle and one LMG squad. . . . This group was continuously attacked until they were forced to surrender. The company did not know this unit had been cut off until one of its patrols attempted to contact them and was driven off by heavy automatic and bazooka fire.

"Around 0600 23 April 1945, F Company entered the town [and was assigned] to fill the gap between Company G's two separate defense sectors. . . . At 0900 Company E attempted to enter Erkenbrechtsweiler, but the enemy, attempting to surround the town and cut off the route through which our troops had entered town, pinned elements of the company down with heavy MG and automatic fire from the woods."

LORIN LEPLEY

G Company staff sergeant, machine gunner

We were on an outpost in the last house in town, my machine gun squad and some riflemen from the First Platoon. There was a little shooting through the night. Before daylight, one of our fellows tossed a grenade that wounded a German coming up the street. In the morning, they made a determined effort to get to us. We were out of ammunition by that time, so we surrendered. Nobody was killed. We had a couple of minor wounds. One fella was shot in the instep; the Germans sent him to their medical facilities.

We had no contact with Joe Meadows or anyone, didn't know what was happening anywhere except we could hear others firing. There was some discussion with the other two sergeants [about surrendering]. It's pretty hazy. It was a tense time.

We hung a white rag out the window toward the street 'cause they were getting fairly close. One of 'em yelled, "Come out," so we went out with our hands over our heads. They shook us down for weapons there in the street and marched us off a short ways.

I was the senior noncom, so they sent me back to deliver the message to Joe [Meadows] that they wanted him to surrender the town. I knew Joe wasn't going to go for that deal, but I didn't have much choice but to give him the message. They sent a guard with me. Walking through our lines was the first I knew that everybody else was all right.

RAY MILLEK
second lieutenant, E Company platoon leader

We came in the morning of April 23 to help relieve G Company. For maybe a couple of hours, we waited for a counterattack, when here came a German under a white flag. He had a GI with him.

ROBERT MEREDITH
staff sergeant, E Company

The American come in town with a white flag on the end of a stick, see, with some Germans. We was gonna get those Germans, blow 'em up, but our boy told us, "Don't make a move. If you do anything to us, it's gonna be bad for everybody." So we sent 'em on back. I don't know what ever happened to those boys that was captured.

MILLEK

This German officer said he wanted to talk to the ranking officer. Someone pointed me out, and I asked the kraut what he wanted. "We want you to surrender this town. Otherwise, we will annihilate everybody in it." There was no mistaking what he said. He spoke good English. I said, "Do you realize you've got a lot of civilians in here? You're going to annihilate your own people?"

"It makes no difference," he says. "If they're unfortunate enough to be caught here, then that's the way it is."

I said, "I'm keeping our boy."

"Well, do that," says the German. "That's up to you. We have 12 more back there with orders to shoot them if I don't get back at a certain time."[1] I looked at the GI and I asked him, "Is that true?" He was just a baby-faced kid. "Yeeesssss," he tells me, very scared. I felt so sorry for him. But I said, "Kid, you've got to go back. I'm sorry." But then I said, "Wait a minute. I'm only a second lieutenant." I didn't want this stuff on me, you know. "I'll get somebody with higher rank." So I sent them on, and we finally found Meadows.

Meadows listened. "Blow it out your ass," he said. I'll never forget it. The guy saluted him and took off, with the prisoner.

"You dumb son of a bitch," I says. "Why did you say it that way? They're going to be tougher on those guys. You could of said, 'No, we don't surrender.' "

MEADOWS

I don't remember what I said exactly, but I didn't say "Nuts," I can tell you that. I hated McAuliffe.[2] I was standing outside the CP when I saw this German walking down the street. He had one of our men with him as a prisoner, with a white flag on the end of his rifle. He spoke perfect English. "You are surrounded, and we want you to surrender." "Hell, no," I said. "Are you going to leave this man here?" And he said, "No. What chance do I have of getting back?" So I had to let the man go back for fear they might kill the other prisoners.

I wasn't about to surrender. We were surrounded, but not totally enveloped. We still had the gully where friendly troops could get to us. I never had a doubt there were enough troops down below [in Unter Lenningen] to come up and support us. It was a matter of time.

But that was one of the times that it was no fun to be the guy that makes the decisions.

JOHN S. CLARK

second lieutenant, acting F Company commander

Ol' Whitey [Joe Meadows] was runnin' G Company by that time, and they got cut off in a little town. (Never could find that bloomin' place after the war. I looked several times.) The battalion commander tells me, "Gibbs has got sick. I want you to take F Company up there."

Well, I took off and got into town about nine o'clock in the morning. I found Whitey and asked him how many houses he had. He says, "Two or three." I says, "You're kiddin' me, Boy," but he wasn't. The Germans had the rest of it. Whitey didn't have any radio communication, couldn't call in artillery or nothin'.

And then here comes one of our soldiers with a white handkerchief on the end of his gun. "Whatcha got there?" I hollered to him. "Hell, I ain't got nothin'," he says. "They got me."

JIM McCARTHY

F Company machine gunner

Pitch-dark, we're goin' up this steep hill in strict silence, silent as you can be with all that stuff to carry. I heard an ammunition bearer behind me throwin' his cans away. I waited for him to catch up. "[. . .], where's your ammo?" He told me it fell off his pack. "When we get to the top," I told him, "if you don't have your ammo, I'll kill you." He went back and picked it up.

We got into town with some pretty good shootin'. Right in the middle of it, this drunk GI got a motorcycle somewhere and was ridin' around. We seen a sniper rifle come up, so we dumped about half a belt into the guy and got the GI off his motorcycle. He wasn't hurt.

Clark told us to set up in a house out on the point, the same place where a team of G Company machine gunners was captured the night before. I went back and told Clark we needed at least a squad of riflemen around our perimeter or the same thing could happen to us. Clark agreed, but he says, "Who do I give you? I ain't got nobody." I says, "Well, if you ain't got nobody, you ain't got us." More or less. Not that we told him to go to hell. You couldn't talk to Clark that way. But he agreed to get us some help.

Pretty soon, up comes this guy, musta weighed 300 pounds, with another kid who was an ex-cook that had screwed up and got sent to the line. Whatever damn misfits from every squad is who was sent us. I put the cook in the attic and told the others to dig in outside, but the fat guy comes in and says it's too rocky. He started to cry. I sent him down to the cellar. I told one of my machine gunners I was gonna catch an hour's sleep and warned him to wake me easy 'cause I'd have a .45 in my hand.

He shook me too hard when he woke me up, and I fired. Missed him, luckily. Naturally, he wasn't too happy, but I'd warned him.

CLARK

I told Whitey I was goin' down the street and camp out in a couple more houses, me and the radio operator and a staff sergeant. Pretty soon, just like ol' Whitey said, we was battling for every inch we could get hold of.

RUCKER

My whole platoon was holed up in a house, firing all night. There was a wounded German outside, hollering he wanted somebody to come out. We thought it might of been a trick, but I guess he really was wounded and trying to surrender. He was still out there, alive, the next morning.

GARY HAVEMAN

sergeant, H Company machine gunner

I was outside with Johnny Low when a German threw a hand grenade that hit a chicken wire fence. Otherwise, we'd have been killed. Johnny shot him in the hip. We could hear him all night praying in German.

RUCKER

Our only contact with Meadows or the rest of G Company was through Ivan Fagre, one of the company messengers. He was continually running back and forth, letting us know what was going on.

MEADOWS

Fagre was hit in the heart by a bullet. I remember him with a great deal of affection. He was a bright, interesting young person, one of those we got from ASTP.

JAMES TEAGUE

sergeant, G Company

While we were loafing around earlier that day, I told Ivan, who was a real good buddy, "I'll bet you five dollars we don't go back into action." "I'll just call that," he said, and it couldn't have been 10 minutes when somebody said, "Rack 'em up. We're moving out." Fagre was shot in the heart that night or the next day. The main reason he survived was I've owed him compound interest for 41 years at five percent.

SCHROEDER

We were checking out houses. Fagre was two steps up the stairs of this place when a bullet hit him in the back. It might of been a stray bullet—could have been one of ours, even—'cause when I turned around, there was nobody to shoot at. Fagre laid there all night. Then F Company fought their way in to us around ten o'clock the next morning, and we got him out.

MEADOWS

I thought he was dead. When I got home to San Francisco, I was at the Shrine East-West Game in January of '46, and there was Ivan Fagre. He was on leave from the hospital, with that bullet still lodged in his heart. But he was out there mountain climbing, skiing, and all the rest of that stuff.[3]

CLARK

Those Germans was fightin' tooth and toenail. My radio man got shot, broke his leg. I asked for artillery, but the colonel said he didn't have any, but then he remembered some 155s he could get ahold of. My radio man says, "How you gonna fire that big stuff in here with us in here?" My idea was to start out on the edge of town and draw the fire in as close as we had to. But it's a whole lot easier to get artillery started than to get it stopped. When two or three rounds landed within 50 yards of the colonel, he says, "Don't throw any more of that damn stuff."

Meanwhile, E Company, what was left of 'em, got into town too, and we began branchin' out a little more, gettin' another house, maybe another house, and another one.

MILLEK

E Company went up a draw to where G Company was surrounded. We were told we were going to have to fight our way through to help them. On our right, there was a house overlooking the edge of town. The captain says to me, "Millek, you lead the attack, and you, Phegley, look at that house." I was leading the Third Platoon at the time and getting all the bad jobs. Lead this, lead that, lead the attack, 'cause I was the oldest lieutenant.

I rebelled. We'd recently got two new officers. One of them, [2d Lt. Burton W.] Phegley, was real good. "Just a minute," I says. "I'm always getting the dirty jobs." And Phegley, being an honest fellow, says, "He's right. Let's flip a coin." So we flipped, and Phegley won. He went to clean the house out, and I had to go attack the town. As fate would have it, he got killed going into that house, and we didn't have a man hit.[4]

[Phegley was awarded the Silver Star posthumously. The citation says in part: "On 23 April, 1945, Lieutenant Phegley led a combat patrol to secure and hold high ground . . . so that the rest of Company "E", 410th Infantry, could join two surrounded rifle companies in the town. Although halted by small arms and artillery fire several times, he continually reorganized his group and aggressively led the men against the enemy positions until mortally wounded by sniper fire."]

SAM NATTA

E Company mortarman

I was just back from the hospital, and my arm wound was nowhere near healed. I was nervous, I was scared, I wasn't ready to be back up there. The trail ran up a hill through trees the Germans had cut down for roadblocks, and I thought, "Oh, God, what a place to put a machine gun." A shell burst, nowhere near me, and I took off and got in the rocks. Millek came after me and talked to me. It wasn't a chewing out, more of a counseling session.

Right after that, Tom Kelly got hit in the foot. When I saw him jump in the air, I think I forgot my own mental state. I went out and helped him hobble back down the mountain. I haven't seen him since the door closed on the ambulance, but I always think about him. After I got him out, I stayed down at the bottom of the mountain. I'd heard our company had broke through to G Company, so I didn't see any point in going back up there.

TOM KELLY

private, E Company

We walked into a hornet's nest on that hill. A machine gun got me in the lower right leg and foot. Sam Natta helped me to the ambulance. The ambulance got shot up on the way out. Red crosses made excellent targets.

CLARK

The colonel told E Company's commander to go out to the edge of town and capture some pillboxes. As we were walking back to our companies, I told him he'd better talk the old man out of that idea. "Hell, you can't get out there. No way in the world." I guess he must have talked to the colonel again 'cause they called off that operation. He'd of never made it.

It was the artillery that finally cleared the town. The Germans pulled out after the barrage.

ROBERT LOYD

rifle squad leader, G Company

I had the first house as you came into town. Lieutenant Rucker was across the street with one or two of my men. The Germans were trying their damnedest to get in there, and I thought there for a while they were *gonna* get in. Up on the side of the mountain, it was just alive with Germans.

I was new at being a squad leader. I didn't want the job, but the platoon sergeant says, "You want to take orders from a replacement that's never been in combat?" I says, "No," and he says, "Well, you better get to work then," and that was that. I hated giving orders that might get somebody killed.

During the night, the Germans set fire to one of the beds that had a feather tick. Hell's fire, you couldn't hardly put that son of a bitch out. But we never left the house all night. But Rucker left his, come over to see if we were all right. That took guts. He was the best soldier I ever saw in my life.

DICK STANNARD

private, G Company

The house was pitch-dark except for the yellow muzzle blasts of the M-1s. Coming down the stairs to go outside, I saw a soldier carefully taking his rifle apart. The parts were all over a table in the dining room. He was a young, kind of gentle guy.

LOYD

Was you in the same damn house I was? I heard Plowboy Goodrich say, "[. . .], what are you doin'?" [. . .] said, "I'm cleanin' my rifle." "Well, Jesus Christ," Plowboy says, "this is a hell of a time to clean your rifle." This fella claimed it jammed on him. You wondered where in the hell he was at, but I never said anything about it afterwards.

OSCAR HUNDLEY
machine gun squad leader, H Company

The Germans surrounded the house we were in, but we didn't know it till someone failed to cup a cigarette. That lit up the whole cotton-pickin' situation, and all hell broke loose. We had our machine gun set up outside the house. It was dark, see, but I could hear someone running. I didn't know who, so I laid down on the floor and turned my rifle on the door. I was gonna shoot whoever came through, but then I recognized the voice of one of our men. He and the second gunner had run off and left the gun and all the ammunition within 30 yards of the Germans.

So here we were, standin' in the doorway trying to figure out what to do, when Higley just walks out there, drags the gun back into the house, and then goes out again and gets the ammunition. By himself, with no help whatsoever. He didn't show any fear. He might of had it inside, but it didn't show outside.

DAN HIGLEY
machine gunner, H Company[5]

"We moved the machine gun back into the doorway to give us more protection. . . . The attack came sooner than we expected, at about 0200. We had no way of knowing the enemy strength. . . . Our big concern was how to defend ourselves against the hail of lead the krauts were pouring our way and how to keep them from breaking through our position. The enemy was firing with machine guns, small arms, and bazookas, but fortunately for us, no artillery or mortars. . . . The only thing we could do was fire in front of us, trying to tell from the flash of the enemy machine guns just where they were located. About 20 minutes after the attack started, Hundley was painfully wounded." [See chapter 27.]

There were about seven or eight G Company riflemen firing from the upstairs windows. "With the machine gun, we had enough firepower to let the enemy know we were not going to quit." A little later, one of the G Company men with us, a bazooka man, was mortally wounded through the chest. The aid man did what he could to help him, but the man died several hours later. Two other G Company men were wounded."

We really lit up the night. "The noise of our gun and the flash from firing made our position stick out like a sore thumb. . . . When daylight came, we discovered our machine gun had two or three direct hits and the doorway was riddled."

A man, maybe a German soldier in civilian clothes, tried to set fire to hay in the barn next to our house. Some of our people wanted to shoot him on

Oscar Hundley was carrying his wife's picture in his wallet when the bullet struck him. The bullet also damaged the picture of Hundley.
Courtesy of Oscar Hundley

the spot, but finally decided not to. "We were in no mood for having someone set our house on fire. . . . We thought he got off easy with being thrown down the stairs and allowed to stay in the cellar until morning, when he was turned over to G Company."

In the house next door, a sniper bullet "grazed [Charles J.] Bornstein in the face and then struck [Charles L.] Wollery in the eye. Woolery's house was under such deadly sniper fire that it was impossible for him to be evacuated for nearly twelve hours while he was bleeding and in great pain. Woolery finally pulled through but he lost the sight of his eye. . . . He had just returned from the hospital a few days before after recovering from a shrapnel wound on March 15."

CHARLES BORNSTEIN

machine gunner, H Company

We were on a machine gun in the second floor when a bullet went through Woolery's left eye, out the temple, and hit me in the face. It split my cheek wide open. I didn't realize how badly I'd been hit. One other person [Ray Tava] and I went out the back window to get help for Woolery. I slipped off the roof and hurt my knee when I hit the ground. I wasn't able to go anyplace after that.

RAY TAVA

machine gun section leader, H Company

I thought Woolery was a goner. There was blood all over the floor, and he was turning blue. I and another guy [Bornstein] went out an upstairs window to get a medic. This was daylight by now, after things had quieted down some, but when I crossed the street, a sniper put a red furrow right across my butt.

I made it to G Company and got ahold of our medic, Doc Latham [Alonzo T. Latham, then of Sparkill, New York]. He brought some blood plasma, and we got it into Woolery. After a while, another company broke through and relieved us, and we were able to get him to the aid station.

CHARLES L. WOOLERY

machine gun squad leader, H Company

I don't know what happened. I heard a pop or a crack and woke up in the hospital.

EPILOGUE

The defense of Erkenbrechtsweiler was successful. The American cost was one killed and five wounded in E Company; two killed, seven wounded, and twelve captured in G Company; and four wounded in H Company. The following day, 24 April, the 409th Infantry drove the Germans out of the surrounding woods, and the race to Innsbruck resumed.

MEADOWS

Going through the Alps, we'd see all these crosses along the trail. It surprised me that people still believed in God under the Hitler regime.

*

Burton Phegley, the E Company officer who was killed, left behind a wife and a 23-month-old son, Michael.

BETTY PHEGLEY CONNER

Burton Phegley's widow

He was overseas hardly any time at all. I wasn't notified of his death till after VE-day. There was no hint anything was wrong. . . . They told me he was killed instantly by a sniper on a patrol. We were devastated. Burt was a very special person, a wonderful person. A real gentleman.

We were married January 24, 1942. He was still a civilian at that time, singing, playing piano and bass with a group that played cocktail music in St. Louis and Springfield. In 1942—September, I think—he was drafted and went to OCS.

MICHAEL PHEGLEY

I have always missed him. I have no memory of him, but he is part of my life. I visit his grave often. His Silver Star and Purple Heart hang in my family room. I feel no bitterness, but I feel regret. Growing up, I was close to his parents, my grandparents. They talked a lot about him. Grandma didn't ever get over it.

My father came from the small community of Modoc, Illinois. I remember when his body was brought back for the funeral in 1948. He was buried with his parents and several generations of Phegleys in the family plot.

ADRIAN PHEGLEY

Burton Phegley's older brother

It was such a shock to me, I couldn't believe it for a long time. I can remember so well waiting for the mail, hoping there would be a rebuttal, telling us there had been a mistake. I was outraged. It was so close to the end of the war. Everybody knew the war was over, but they just kept pouring the boys into situations that were not at all necessary. On the day of the funeral, there was a second lieutenant, the military escort, I guess, who came and stood with us. He was bored with his job. I asked him if he'd like to be relieved. He said yes, so he left. That's the only time we had a visit from the military. I've never had anything to do with the military since then.

*

Lorin Lepley and his fellow captives all survived their captivity.

LEPLEY

The Germans moved us back through the woods. American artillery was coming in. The Germans were in a pocket 25 or 35 miles in diameter. All we did was walk from one end of that thing to the other. They were trying to find a point where they could get through.

On the second day, they had us in a barn with two guards. An American captain and his jeep driver had been added to our group. The guards gave us their rifles, and we took over the town. Everybody that had guns, we made 'em stack 'em in a pile in the barn. The townspeople were told to hang white sheets out their windows. We could hear artillery. We didn't want our people to shoot up the town.

It wasn't too long before we heard equipment coming around the bend, but it was an SS outfit. We got recaptured real quick. Immediately, they made us run a gauntlet and took swats at us with potato mashers [hand grenades]. They took us into the woods outside of the town, lined us up against a woodpile, and searched us for valuables. I lost a Parker pen on that deal that had been my father's.

A Russian civilian who'd been helping us was in the group. The SS officer shot him down with a burp gun. It was a shock. I thought we were all going to get it, but the only one he killed was the Russian. It was like the German went off his rocker for a minute.

From there, we were taken in a convoy to another town and put in a basement overnight. A guy who was guarding us kept us there the next day instead of putting us back with the convoy. We worked out an understanding with him that if he was captured by the Russians, he'd be in civilian clothes, and we'd get him to the Americans. As it turned out, it was a French armored outfit that took the town. They released us to the [U.S.] 10th Armored Division.

The armored guys processed us through a repple depple in Innsbruck. Those guys didn't make any effort to get us back to our outfit 'cause we were pulling their guard duty. It must have gone a week and a half like that when one day I saw Joe Meadows go by in a jeep. I got him stopped and said, "For Christ's sake, get us out of here." The next day, we were back with G Company.

When the 103d was breaking up, I was one point short of enough to get out, so I was sent to the 45th Division and came home with them.

I wouldn't ever want to have to do what we did again, but there is hardly anything I would take for the experience and the memories and the associations.

I was discharged in November 1945. In 1946, I went to Ohio State on the GI Bill and got a degree in industrial management. That led me to a job with Ohio Fuel Gas for the next 34 years, when I retired.

*

Members of H Company think a single bullet wounded both Woolery and Bornstein. Woolery lost his eye. Bornstein was evacuated to Paris, underwent surgery there, and rejoined his unit in Innsbruck. He stays in touch with Woolery and Hundley, but has not seen them since the war.

WOOLERY

I was in the hospital till February of '46. They had to make me a new eye. I guess I'm lucky. I went to work as a machinist after the war. You lose your depth perception with only one eye, but I've made it okay.

TOM KELLY

My leg healed okay, but it's permanently stiff. I have to wear a hearing aid from the mine explosion.

25

"GOD HAD PLANS FOR ME."

Joseph W. Meadows spent most of his combat time as the self-described "ass kicker" of G Company. Officially, he was the executive officer and second in command until the last battle, when he was company commander.

A Bostonian who moved to San Francisco, he was drafted before the war started, in March 1941, to serve one year. With the attack on Pearl Harbor, he was denied discharge and did not get out until December 1945.

Commissioned after OCS, Meadows spent a year training troops at Camp Roberts, California, and lobbying his superiors for a combat assignment. Then he married Margaret in the spring of 1944 and lost all interest in going overseas. Six months later, he was at the front.

MARGARET MEADOWS

I was working for a department store in San Francisco when I met Joe.

MEADOWS

After two dates, I asked her to marry me. I was at Camp Roberts[1] trying to get assigned overseas, but after that, I wasn't interested in going overseas anymore. We were married April 19, 1944.

MARGARET MEADOWS

I spent 10 days with him at Camp Roberts. That was our honeymoon. I went back to my job till June, and then I took off for Texas when he was transferred to the 103d Division. It was quite an experience. I'd been told the trains often ran out of food, so my mother packed an enormous basket of fried chicken and sandwiches. I was very popular at lunchtime.

It took four days and three nights, but it seemed like forever. We were sidetracked all the time. I sat up most of the way. I ran out of food. Going to the diner, the soldiers would go, "Yay hoo," and pat you on the butt. It was terrible. It was fun, but it was terrible. Exciting and scary all at one time.

In Gainesville, we got a room, beautifully wallpapered with newspapers, with kitchen privileges. We shared the house with three adults and two kids, one bathroom for the seven of us. I had to clean the kitchen every time we wanted a meal, they were such slobs. And expensive! Forty-five dollars a month. After the war, we got an apartment in the Marina district of San Francisco for 42.

It was five or six miles to town, and we walked it to get to the grocery store and the one show. I always had to be on the left side so he could salute. Joe's arm would start going up and down, and the hand holding mine would get all drippy. He'd say, "Those sonsabitches," but he'd smile and salute. They loved it.

MEADOWS

I'd see 'em coming [enlisted men]. They'd line up a few paces apart to make me salute over and over.

MARGARET MEADOWS

When the word got out that the 103d was going overseas, I went to New York. It was only a rumor, but it sounded pretty firm, so I took a chance. It was only two or three days, and here he was. His aunt arranged a room for us at the Westbury in Manhattan, real nice, and with martinis to put us out of our pain. At four o'clock the next morning, he had to get up and get back to camp, and that's the last time I saw him till the war ended.

I spent that Christmas in Boston with Joe's family. That's where he was from, and I thought I should be there. I did a lot of crying that Christmas. That was during the Battle of the Bulge, and it was terrible. I hadn't heard from him in a long time, and they were singing "White Christmas," and oh, God, I'd stand there and weep. I was such a long way from home.

In February, I decided to chuck the whole thing. I went down to the train people and pleaded my case. Told them all kinds of lies about my mother being sick and my father dying, anything to get on the train and get back to California.

MEADOWS

So many of the things I remember are single happenings. One of my jobs was to make sure everybody moved. Early in the fighting, attacking across a field, I found this person just lying there. I told him, "Get up, goddamn it, it's time to be going." He still didn't move, and the reason he didn't was he was dead. I figured it was time for me to get out of there. This was serious business.

Another time, going through a woods, a soldier thrust his BAR into my hands and said, "Here, Joe, I've had enough." I slapped his face and told him to get back in there. He took his weapon, and 10 minutes later he was dead. That made me feel real good, yeah.

BOB SCHROEDER

private, first class, company messenger

Meadows was the nicest guy in the world, most of the time. But there was one time I captured some prisoners that were carrying booze. I got myself so drunk I could hardly walk. I had one of the prisoners carrying my rifle. Meadows took me behind the barn and kind of straightened me out. After that, I never once took a drink of anything while we were up on the front.

MARGARET MEADOWS

The war had its highs and lows, its scary moments, and some miserable times, but it was fun, and it's fun to look back on. The scariest time was when I got Joe's Purple Heart and his Bronze Star in the mail. I didn't know he'd been near a shot.

MEADOWS

The Purple Heart was from March 15. I heard a pop, and I thought I'd lost my ear. I put my hand up. It was a relief to find I still had an ear. Then I felt something warm. The bullet had grazed my shoulder. I was never in the hospital, but it was worth five points.[2]

EPILOGUE

Meadows is the only man interviewed who served in both World War II and the Korean War, the latter with great reluctance.

MARGARET MEADOWS

When Joe came home from Europe, I had this nice apartment waiting, and I took care of him for a while. He had a terrible time finding a job. Thirty years old, with no college. Nobody was interested.

MEADOWS

I finally took a job clerking in a drug store.

MARGARET MEADOWS

Then Nate Dodge asked Joe to go to work for him.[3] He did, and he stayed with the company all those years from 1946 till 1981, manufacturing fire hoses, conveyor belts, and ship's hoses.

In 1948, I got pregnant and quit my job. We bought a little house and were trying to become a family, and then Joe was called back for the Korean War. It was devastating.

MEADOWS

Life was just turning real good for me. I was bitter. They were going to have me take over a rifle company, but on the boat over, a rule was passed that anyone 34 or older should be returned home. I was on my way, though, so they kept me there, but they made me a communications officer instead of a company commander. And my tour was shortened, to 17 months instead of 18.

I was never hurt there. I think God had plans for me. Over the years I've helped a lot of people with emotional problems and business problems. And my daughter's algebra problems.

*

The Meadows lived in the San Francisco Bay Area until his retirement. They now live in Bothell, Washington, a suburb of Seattle.

26

BRAVE, NOT FOOLISH

Was it luck, or skill, or prayer, or training, or something else that caused some men to die and others to emerge unscathed in combat?

Moe Huskey, who led the Second Platoon of G Company through some of its roughest days, made it all the way without a scratch.

Huskey was one of the "originals" of the 103d Division. He had two years of intensive infantry training before he went overseas, but so did many other originals who were killed or wounded. Drafted in 1942, he was sent to Camp Claiborne, Louisiana, and assigned to the Second Platoon. Except for two hair-raising days with F Company, he stayed there until after the war ended.

A sergeant when the division went into combat, he received a battlefield commission to second lieutenant three months later and became leader of the platoon he had joined as a buck private.

Why was he never injured?

HUSKEY

One reason is I'm brave, but I'm not foolish. Another is that I was extremely lucky. A friend of mine wasn't two feet away when he got killed at Nothalten, and a couple of other guys were hit by the same machine gun cross fire.

Did that experience give you the feeling that you were somehow to be spared?

HUSKEY

Well, I'm not a deeply religious person, but my wife was home making novenas.

KAYE HUSKEY

I'm a Catholic. Moe is not, but I prayed that he would come through, and he did. I'm a strong believer in prayer.

HUSKEY

We had 58 casualties in the platoon out of the 42 men we started with. The men who were not hit had to be extremely lucky.

The first major problem we had was at Nothalten on November 30. We lost about 12 men. We were advancing through an area of low weeds and brush. The krauts had us zeroed in with crisscross machine gun fire. By some miracle, most of us got across two or three hundred yards to a little road, but that's where my buddy [S. Sgt. William C. Barker] took one in the shoulder. The bullet went through both lungs and broke his ribs in the back. You could see his field jacket going up and down as he breathed.

I gave him all his sulfa pills, but he had to lay there like two hours, till it got dark, before we could move him. He died in England. The doctors couldn't save him.[1]

[Huskey evacuated seven wounded men at Nothalten. For that, and for leading his men through heavy enemy fire, he received the Bronze Star.]

Remember Rothbach a few months later? [January 1945.] I had a feeling we were going to be up on that mountain for a while, so we dug our hole nice and deep, big enough for three guys. We found some bridge timbers down at the edge of town and drug them up there for the roof, shoveled about a foot of dirt on top, and lined the bottom with straw and leaves. We were set, and it paid off. I think we were there [in subfreezing weather] for about three weeks, and we were fairly comfortable.

DICK STANNARD
private in Huskey's platoon

I shared a hole on that hill with a guy I only knew as Blackie, a replacement.[2] I don't think I'd ever seen him before. I don't know who dug it, but it had a roof, and all we did was move in and start shooting at German soldiers we could see across the valley. We were lying on top of our sleeping bags against the cold.

The hole was only about a foot deep in front, dug straight back into the hill so that the back was about four feet high. We had grenades lined up on the edge of the hole. A machine gun picked us up. The guy was really good.

He must have been hundreds of yards away, but he was shooting right into our hole. The bullets caved in the back and buried our feet in frozen dirt, sawed off the top of the parapet under the grenades, and shot our rifles to pieces.

We threw the sleeping bags out onto the snow to get a little deeper, and the gunner shot them to pieces too. Blackie got his hand up too high and had several fingers shot off. I got a flesh wound in the arm. We lay for hours, too scared to move. Neither of us seemed to bleed much.

Finally, Blackie said, "The hell with this. I'm getting out of here," and took off, with me right behind him, running from tree to tree. It was still daylight. The machine gunner picked us up again, but the only further damage he did was kick up a clod of frozen dirt that hit me in the hip.

HUSKEY

Your squad leader should have booted you into making your hole deeper.

CLYDE RUCKER
platoon sergeant, Third Platoon

Me and [Roy] Hinshaw had a hole together. We hadn't dug as deep as we should have. We were laying there firing at anything we could see across the valley that afternoon when they opened up with a machine gun right into the hole. We were down low enough where they couldn't hit us. I told Hinshaw, "Soon as they let up, we're gonna go deeper." We started throwin' that red dirt out, God, we went down about another foot. That night, the snow camouflaged all that fresh mud.

HUSKEY

We did a lot of night patrolling through the kraut lines during that winter period. I was platoon sergeant by that time, and it was standard operating procedure for platoon sergeants to lead patrols. Then they sent me to the rear for three days of indoctrination and gave me a commission. I came back to the company, and they soon announced that lieutenants would now lead the patrols. We never lost a man.

I remember one slender, young fellow volunteered to go on one. I finally told him okay, but when we got down to the spot [where] we were going to kick off, he got so excited he started vomiting. I always thought that might of been you. You remember anything like that?

STANNARD

I can't imagine I ever volunteered for a patrol.

[As the battalion prepared to launch its biggest attack, Huskey was loaned to F Company for two days. On the first day of the attack, he served as F Company's executive officer. In the hierarchy of hazard in the infantry, executive officer was a safe job compared to rifle platoon leader. Meanwhile, an officer with no combat experience, 2d Lt. Paul Carlino, was assigned to take Huskey's place as leader of the Second Platoon of G Company. See chapter 22.]

HUSKEY

It was a bad deal that a new officer was assigned to the platoon just before an attack. Unfair to him and unfair to his men. I never met Carlino. The way I heard it, he got in trouble politically with the leadership at Regiment, where he was the GRO, so they decided to put him in a rifle platoon and give him a little baptism of fire. Get him oriented to the war, I guess.

No one is sure that his inexperience caused any problems, but many of the people that were there thought that if someone with more experience had been leading the platoon, they wouldn't have lost as many people.[3] [Carlino survived his first day on the job, but he and five of his men were killed by machine gun fire on the second day.][4]

But I would not say anything against him. I wasn't there. He made a judgment on what to do. For all I know, I'm alive because I was pulled out and Carlino was substituted for me.

That first day in F Company, they didn't want to give me a platoon, not knowing the people, so I followed along behind the company commander like the executive officer does, supposedly to take over if he's killed or wounded. I'm sure if that had happened I'd have given the job to some other officer, but it didn't. But F Company lost its Second Platoon leader on the 15th [see chapter 11], and I was assigned to his platoon.

It was an awkward situation. They didn't know me, and I didn't know them, but in a war, you get your loyalties together in a big hurry.

That second day, we succeeded in getting into town first,[5] crawling along the furrows two or three hundred yards to the first house. The Germans could see our packs, but they couldn't get their fire low enough to hit us. One of our scouts was a little Mexican kid. He wore me out trying to keep in contact with him. He and the other scout busted into that first house, and two Germans surrendered. Suddenly, there was no more resistance. We didn't lose a man.

EPILOGUE

Luck played one more winning hand for Huskey. He was on leave in Paris when his company was cut off and surrounded by diehard German troops in Erkenbrechtsweiler, Germany, 12 days before the end of the war.

Like many members of the division, he was headed for Japan when the atom bomb ended the war. He stayed in Europe in the army of occupation until June 1946, when he came home to Detroit and resumed his career with Sears.

KAYE HUSKEY

I felt cheated. So many got home ahead of Moe. But we had a big homecoming. My boss got us a room at the Statler when rooms were hard to get, and later we had a cottage on a lake and spent a week out there alone.

HUSKEY

It was cold, and there was nothing much to do but stoke the fire.

KAYE HUSKEY

I stayed with Sears through the war and seven more years, but then I stepped out of the picture. Sears at that time wasn't too happy to have husbands and wives working together. Moe kept climbing up the ladder and did real well.

HUSKEY

The war was a tough time. I'll tell you how I rank the whole experience. If I had had a son when the Vietnam War was going on, I'd have sent him to

Canada. I did my duty, but I wouldn't want my son to go through all that misery.

That's a hard thing to say.

INTERLUDE: A PAINFUL PART

Misconduct, and worse, makes up a painful part of the Second Battalion's history. Here are the stories, unvarnished by any of the explanations or excuses that could be offered.

Killing or Abusing Prisoners

RAY MILLEK
second lieutenant, E Company

[16 March 1945, near Gundershoffen] We had a buck sergeant, I forget his name, walked over to [a wounded German] and said, "Hey, this guy's got a GI watch on him."[1] He put his .45 right to his head and pulled the trigger. Brains splattered all over.

CARL NICHOLS
second lieutenant, F Company

[22 January Rothbach] They came at us with bayonets, but we stopped them before they got into our positions. The next morning, the guys began to ease out to where the German dead were lying. Snow was melting on one of them. [. . .] went up to him. The German raised his head. He was badly wounded. [. . .] put his .45 pistol up to his head and pulled the trigger. He wasn't prepared for what happened. The man's head just exploded and splattered everything. [. . .] told that story many times. I don't think he ever got over it. He'd laugh about it, but it weighed on his mind.

JIM McCARTHY
private, F Company

Nichols wasn't there. I wasn't either. It happened before both of us got to the company. It was a carbine, not a .45. I heard him talk about it many times. The German was layin' in the snow, and when [. . .] went up to him, he moved, and [. . .] blew his head off. He was as good as dead anyway, I guess. [. . .] used to have nightmares. We'd hear him mumbling in his sleep, "I killed him. I got the Luger." When he was awake, he maintained his image of tough guy.

*

Some German soldiers were killed in the act of surrendering.

RAY OFFERMAN
staff sergeant, F Company

[10 December 1944, Vosges Mountains] After I was hit, the fellas that were with me saw the sniper. When he saw them, he put up his hands. They shot him.

BOB SCHROEDER
private, first class, G Company

I never saw it, but I had reason to think it might have been true, from the person who told me. When the Germans stood up to surrender, our guys would shoot 'em. I don't know if you'd call that misconduct, though. I heard they did it first to us.

During the winter, on a raid, we found a dugout full of civilians. How they survived, I don't know, it stank so bad. The guy that seemed to be their leader, a civilian, was trying to take care of them. We talked nice to him, him being a civilian. The next day, the damn fool comes out of that dugout in daylight, I guess on the strength that we'd been nice to him, and one of our guys shoots him. He must have thought he was safe.

DICK STANNARD
private, G Company

[late March and 23 April] I saw needless shootings twice. The first was when we were in occupation duty near the Rhine, guarding a German military hospital. The company had taken heavy casualties at Gundershoffen a few days earlier, and several replacements came in. One was a sergeant, from the MPs, as I remember, who'd never been in combat. He got drunk on guard duty, and without provocation suddenly fired his M-1 at the hospital. We were told several nurses, doctors, and prisoners were killed or wounded.

The second time was a month later, at Erkenbrechtsweiler, Germany. The company had been surrounded all night. After the siege was lifted, three or four of us were ordered to escort a half dozen prisoners down the mountain to bring up ammunition and food. Halfway through the woods, a German machine gun opened fire. We hit the ground and the prisoners scattered. Some of the guards opened fire. Several prisoners were killed or wounded. I'm certain they were only trying to run back to the safety of our lines. I'm ashamed to say I don't know what happened to them.

BOB LOYD
sergeant, G Company

I remember that first incident. German women would come up to the hospital fence, and they weren't supposed to do that. Trying to talk to the prisoners, and other things. Know what I mean? That might of been what teed the sergeant off, but I wouldn't shoot a man for that, would you?

MARTIN DUUS
private, G Company

[30 November, Nothalten] There were many Germans shot with their hands in the air, which is one of the unfortunate circumstances of war, I guess. They were in their holes. As we got up to advance, they stood up and yelled, "Kamerad." I would guess that more than half a dozen were shot. It was inexperience, I guess, our first face-to-face confrontation with German soldiers.

It happened later, too, on March 15. We had strict orders that, to the extent we had people we could spare, we could send them back with the prisoners, but only if we could spare them. [There was no specific order to shoot prisoners if necessary], but I don't know what other . . . you could interpret it that way. I think it *was* interpreted that way.

I was running across a field with one of the replacements. Two Germans were coming up to surrender. They had their arms in the air, and before I realized what he was doing, this fellow shot both of them. [On reflection, Duus added], I wouldn't say they were prisoners as such at that point. They weren't under the control of anybody yet. They were still loose in the field, shall we say.

HAROLD MOTENKO

private, F Company

[16 March, near Gundershoffen] I don't want to talk about it. People do crazy things in time of war. Our people kept yelling to these German medics, "Drop the bags." The medics were holding their [first aid] bags over their heads. The Red Cross was right there. Well, they couldn't understand what the hell we were saying, and our people shot them.

NICHOLS

[15 March near Gundershoffen] Germans came streaming out of a dugout. Those Germans would fight like tigers up to the last minute, then when it's over, it's over. So this guy had his hands up, but he made the mistake of dropping them to unsnap his belt. A guy with a BAR cut him in two. That made me sick. Here's this boy, fought maybe on the Russian front, and his mother lost her son because of a little silly thing like that.

McCARTHY

[23 April at Erkenbrechtsweiler] We had this kid, a screwup, they sent to me. At daybreak, a German officer and a sergeant walked up to surrender. This kid fired from 50 feet away. Then he yelled "Halt." He comes runnin' down the stairs yellin', "The Luger's mine, the Luger's mine." All a man's life was worth to that bum was a Luger. But he didn't want to go out in the street. "He might still be alive," he says. "All the better," I says, hoping this German might shoot him. But he was dead. The kid got the pistol. We let the sergeant get away. Why the hell would you kill a man who wants to surrender?

MELVIN SEILER

staff sergeant, E Company

[November 1944] There was no more fighting, just one German out in the field, and he wanted to surrender. He had his hands over his head. [. . .] hollered at him a couple of times, but I think the German was afraid to come. He kinda turned and ran. Then [. . .] shot him. I think he liked to shoot people.

MILLEK

[15 March, Gundershoffen] Now, you're gonna take prisoners [when you're on the attack], which we did. Behind us, the lines could have been filled in again after we drove through. Where are you gonna send 'em? We had one tough guy in the company. We'd say, "Take 'em back," and (wink) he'd know what to do. He'd shoot 'em. I can think of one incident, three or four prisoners. It was just that one time. I don't think it was an atrocity. I think it was saving our own troops, to prevent the Germans from picking up their rifles again. We did it. Everybody did it.

McCARTHY

[15 or 16 March, Gundershoffen] You know what it meant to tell a man to take a prisoner back and be back in 10 minutes? I heard a rifleman told that. He left with the prisoner. We heard "BANG, BANG," and here comes the rifleman. We said, "So you took your man back?" He says, "They told me to be back in 10 minutes." He either shot him or let him go, one or the other, and we heard the shots.

[But on the other hand on 15 March], this German got a few of our men, but he burned out the barrel on his machine gun. We could hear him yelling, with his hands comin' up. He got up, but [2d Lt. John] Clark knocked him down so we wouldn't shoot him. He saved that German's life. If it hadn't of been for Clark, he would have bought the ticket.

We had one incident near the end of the war that didn't look good, but that was the exception. We were goin' through a German village. There was no combat, but there wasn't no white flags either. Those people were well versed that they either got the hell out of the way or they went and hid in the cellar. I'm goin' down one side of the street, and this other guy is goin' down the other side. We're watchin' for anything that moves. A woman opened a window in front of me. My partner snapped off a shot and killed her. It was not deliberate.

BOB BRENNAN
sergeant, E Company

[November and December in the Vosges Mountains, and toward the end of the war] Some prisoners were led back, but it was stupid to take a surrender after they killed or wounded a few of your men and then ran out of ammunition. You're gonna observe the Geneva Convention with them? I never personally shot a prisoner, but I know there was a lot of Germans shot because they initiated the firefight, and then tried to surrender.

I'll tell you something else. We had this one little sucker, a medic, who would hasten the departure of the Germans if you didn't watch him. The wounded would be hollering, "Wasser, wasser." He'd say, "You want water, you son of a bitch? I'll give you water." That was the worst thing you could give a guy with an internal wound.

ED FITZGIBBONS
E Company mortarman

[15 March] Our medic hit a prisoner in the mouth with a .45. Even after the war, some of our guards were pretty rough on prisoners—beat them, kicked them. I never abused anybody. Things like that had an effect on me.

A. J. TORRANCE
commanding officer, G Company

There were some things that happened where injured prisoners might have been shot. Maybe somebody considered them potentially dangerous. Who knows? A man on the ground with a gun is still dangerous. I wouldn't be surprised if some of those things happened. But I figured if you got a prisoner, he was out of action.

*

A tragic episode that occurred on the winter defense line was mentioned by several people, but details are hazy. It apparently involved a tank destroyer unit that was sometimes attached to the 410th Infantry. The divisional history, "Report After Action," says that the Second Battalion "discovered . . . a huge cave where several thousand French had built an 'underground city' . . . for fear of Allied bombings. . . . 103d Military Government officers evacuated 3,800 persons to a camp safely behind the front. . . . Several times, however, the Germans brutally sent shells crashing into the line of civilians and killed and wounded more than a score."[2]

The following statements only hint at the confusion that must have surrounded this operation.

RAY MYSLIWIEC
sergeant, E Company

On New Year's Eve, some boys got trigger happy and fired on civilians who were hiding in a cave. It wasn't our boys, though. This was right after the Battle of the Bulge, and everybody was nervous. We didn't know whether they were going to come at us or not. We were all on our toes, frightened, scared. Somehow, they shot up these civilians. There should have been an investigation.

NICHOLS

[From a wartime memoir he wrote.] "That was quite a night when those Frogs tried to walk through our lines. We must have killed fifteen of them. Some TDs thought we were krauts and started shooting at us. It was quite a war till one of our boys crawled around and stopped 'em."

JOHN CROW
second lieutenant, H Company

This TD outfit got shot up one night, and they, in turn, shot up a whole bunch of people coming out of a cave. They thought they were Germans.

We carried civilians out all night long. They really caught 'em good. But I would say it was a legitimate mistake. Whatever was moving was going to get shot, especially when they answered in German. [German is the principal language of the Alsatian French.]

*

Only two German atrocity stories emerged from the interviews: SS soldiers killed a Russian civilian who was helping a group of American prisoners (see chapter 24). And, in the recapture of Schillersdorf, an American soldier was found dead and frozen in the snow. The Reverend William Kleffman, the battalion's Catholic chaplain, said it appeared the man was begging for his life when he was shot.

German troops of the Sixth Mountain Division showed astonishing discipline on the night of 22 January 1945. Attacking E Company's outpost in pitch-darkness, they leaped into the defenders' ditch and took them all prisoner without shooting a man. (See chapter 4.)

Desecration of the Dead

JOE MEADOWS
G Company

[17 March, at Gundershoffen] One of my jobs as company executive officer was graves registration. There were six or seven [dead] there. I found men from our own artillery filching stuff off the bodies of our men. One man removed a watch. I shot at him. I missed. I just wanted his attention. I got the watch back. I just couldn't believe what I was seeing, robbing our own bodies. Apparently it was something that had happened before. They were all over our bodies. I ate the battery commander's butt out. He said it wouldn't happen again. Shocking. Disgusting.

MOTENKO

[Late January, Rothbach] We were surrounded for three days. Then we counterattacked. On the way back to our positions—it's terrible to think about—I saw Americans chop fingers off to get rings off dead soldiers.

NICHOLS

[Apparently the same incident] We made a sweep. There were nothing but dead Germans. This guy—God, I don't know if you ought to put this in the book or not—we'd pass those Germans, and he'd look at their hands to see if they had rings on. You know how he got the rings off? He'd cut off their fingers and just drop the fingers in his pocket. He had a pocketful of rings, watches, anything that glittered. He would pick up like a vacuum cleaner. Mean as a yard dog.

CROW

We had a guy who was quite a sis who would go out at night and get rings off the fingers of the dead by cutting off their fingers.

McCARTHY

[17 March near the Siegfried Line] The cooks brought up our first hot chow in quite a few days. One of 'em spots this tigerman [nickname for German tank crewman] that was cookin' in the sun, dead for about a week. He sees a beautiful ring on the man, so he runs over to beat everybody to the door prize, grabs the finger, and rips skin and everything right off. We weren't hungry anymore.

Desertion, Fleeing from the Enemy

CROW

[11 November near St. Die] We were going up to relieve the Third Division when we passed by a pile of American corpses. These two officers in our company were quite taken aback.

FRANK KANIA
private, H Company

There were quite a few bodies on the path. These two lieutenants turned white. The next day, they disappeared. We heard they were found in Paris later.

CROW

They claimed they were captured, escaped, and went into Switzerland. Later I looked one of them up in Paris. He was in a motor pool. I never heard any more about the other one.[3]

*

The most serious charge of dereliction, against the commander of E Company, was never proven. The company commander was accused by his men of abandoning them on 22 January 1945. (See chapter 4.)

E Company also had a platoon leader who failed repeatedly in his combat role. He eventually left the company as a nonbattle casualty.

MILLEK

His platoon was supposed to attack a hill. I found him in a ditch, sobbing. "I can't get up, I can't get up." He wasn't hit; he just wouldn't go. After that, I didn't have much use for the man.

BRENNAN

A malingerer, a son of a gun. He's the one that asked 1st Sgt. John Rhye why the men didn't like him. "Because you're no good," Rhye told him.

SPILMAN GIBBS
F Company commander

[25 January near Schillersdorf; he blames the German breakthrough on the commander of the company from another battalion that was holding the line to F Company's right.] I found out the company commander panicked and pulled out, leaving my flank wide open. He was asleep in a house; wasn't even on the line. [See chapter 14.]

JOHN CLARK

[15 March, Gundershoffen] That was the only time in my life I saw American soldiers run. They turned around and started haulin', the second and third platoons [of F Company]. We was in a woods, gittin' tree bursts from a tank. I run just as hard as I could out in front of 'em, maybe a couple hundred yards, and I got 'em all stopped. Everybody was tryin' to get out of that tank fire. It was amazing, the number of men that was killed.

SCHROEDER

[15 March, Gundershoffen; this is not the incident described by Clark.] We were out in an open field. One of the G Company platoons—I honestly don't remember which one—about 15 or 20 people, got demoralized by the bombardment and started running toward the rear to get out of the drop area. Things were so difficult I don't blame 'em a lot. Torrance told me to go after them. I got 'em turned around. I kinda knew who to talk to. There was no more said about it.

DUUS

Second Platoon

[The] 88s were coming in very heavily. [Stanley] Niciporek was hit head-on and disintegrated. A replacement who was hit was crying and yelling. Then somebody started to go to the rear. I don't know whether it was our company alone or other companies, but some of the fellows started moving back. Captain Torrance at the top of his lungs gave an order to "stop and turn around. Let's go."

It almost turned into a rout. The problem was we were sitting in this exposed situation and getting mortars and 88s, and nothing was happening. A shell would hit and somebody would get hit, then Niciporek got blasted, other people were getting hit, and nothing was happening. I think some panic developed.

Maybe a dozen or so started to walk to the rear, not running, but not crawling either. It was more wanting to get away from what was hitting in the area than a desertion kind of thing. But I think Torrance sized up the situation as maybe getting serious and yelled, and they turned around and came back.

TORRANCE

[23 January, Rothbach] Yes, I had people flee. I didn't see them. Some of our Fourth Platoon fled back to the First Battalion reserve. The colonel called me up and said, "Some of your mortarmen were so confused in this night fight that they lost their lines." Well, mortarmen aren't riflemen. I wasn't there to give them direction, so they fell back a couple of hundred yards. I think it was orderly, but they did fall back. I told the colonel, "Well, get their asses back up here. I'll get them back in position." And I did.

JOSEPH SKOCZ

staff sergeant, E Company

[November or December, Vosges Mountains] We were forced to walk over a rope and plank bridge in neck deep water [in freezing weather] when there was a vehicle bridge right nearby [that would have kept us dry.] The guys grumbled very badly about that. It was almost like the whole company felt like they didn't want to go any further. Not mutiny, they just wanted a break to wring out a sock or two.

MEADOWS

It was my job to make sure there were no deserters. We had a problem with two people who were assigned to the unit just before we went overseas from the detention barracks at Fort Leavenworth. They should have been shot, but they never were.

SCHROEDER

There was this nice guy, Tennessee type of person, a goofy kind of guy who cheated at cards and stuff like that. One night, we were doomed to walk all night in the rain. He says, "I've had enough of this shit." He walked away, and nobody ever heard a word about him again.

Self-Inflicted Wounds

MYSLIWIEC

[Looking at casualty list] [. . .]! I remember him. He shot his toe off. Couldn't take it anymore. That's why they got him down as wounded.

CLYDE RUCKER

second lieutenant, G Company

I had a guy that was shot in the foot, I think deliberately. We had another guy shoot himself in the arm.

TORRANCE

I remember those cases. Both denied the wounds were self-inflicted. One occurred before we had seen any real action.

CROW

We had two or three people do that over the course of six months.

High Level Outrage

The most outrageous misconduct was only peripherally part of the battalion's history: Gen. George S. Patton's attempt to rescue his son-in-law from a prisoner of war camp.

At least two E Company prisoners were among the thousands put at risk by Patton's irresponsible order. (See chapter 4.) A task force from the Fourth Armored Division went 60 miles behind German lines to a prison camp at Hammelburg. Of the 294 men who set out, 9 were killed, 32 were wounded, and 16 were never accounted for, presumably killed. The entire task force was taken prisoner, and all of its 53 tanks and armored personnel carriers destroyed. Patton's son-in-law, Lt. Col. John K. Waters, was badly wounded in the American attack on the compound and remained a prisoner.[4]

FOUR

H Company

27

"THE KRAUTS USED OUR MORTARS"

Oscar Hundley of Greensboro, North Carolina, was one of only a handful of men who served in both the Pacific and European theaters of war. He started his military career as a ski trooper with the 10th Mountain Division's 87th Infantry at Camp Hale, Colorado ("we spelled it a little different") in 1942. "I'd never seen a pair of skis in my life except in a magazine."

On 15 August 1943, the 87th Infantry invaded Kiska in the Aleutian Islands, fully expecting the kind of bloody fight that had been waged three months earlier to recapture Attu. "We just walked up the beach. There was no one there, but the Japanese left us a note in English saying they'd be back to get us."

Hundley saw his first casualty that winter of 1943–44 on Kiska, a soldier killed by a booby trap. That spring, he returned to Colorado and volunteered as a replacement, hoping to get in on the D-day invasion of Europe. Instead, he was sent to the 103d and joined Dan Higley's squad as a heavy machine gunner in H Company.

Daniel P. Higley of Wilmington, Delaware, never expected to be in the infantry. Drafted in 1943, he was in ASTP, training to be an engineer, until the program was canceled. When he arrived at Camp Howze, he had had no infantry training. "I never did learn to strip or assemble the gun. We had plenty of training to set up and fire, but that was all."

He started as an ammunition bearer, but worked his way up to gunner as casualties mounted. And in between, he carried the 53-pound tripod and the 40-pound gun many a weary mile through the Vosges Mountains of France and the plains of Germany.

HIGLEY

Carrying the gun caused the only injury I attribute to the war, some hip problems in later life. You couldn't balance the weight.

That first month in the Vosges, terrain and the weather were more of an enemy than the Germans. We had a jeep, but we hand-carried our gear 80 percent of the time.

In January, when we retreated from Niederbron to Rothbach, it was a contest to see who could stay on their feet, it was so icy. The cold was never worse than that night.

We spent all the next day digging our gun position. The ground was frozen down about four inches. That night, the cooks brought up hot chow. I was just finishing my meal when we heard that the krauts had taken the town above us [Offwiller] and captured E Company's outpost. "For some reason, the warning wasn't heeded immediately, and it wasn't until the krauts were firing burp guns at the other end of town that we realized our danger. Everyone grabbed their packs and equipment and dashed madly to get out to the gun position. The kitchen lost thirty messkits, and some men lost their equipment."[1]

A guy we called Rastus had the narrowest escape. He'd been drinking schnapps all afternoon and was sleeping it off when the krauts hit us. He sobered up in a hurry.

HUNDLEY

I'd just got my mess kit filled with pork chops and mashed potatoes when they come in, shootin' like a bunch of cowboys. I dropped everything and run in the house to get my equipment. There was this guy layin' on the bed, passed out. I shook him a couple of times and told him the krauts were here. He used profanity on me till the Germans hit the corner of the house with a burp gun. I turned around, and he was gone.

I went running out and asked Sgt. Sam Henderson, "Did you see Rastus?" Yep, he'd come runnin' out barefooted through the snow and disappeared into a foxhole.[2]

Henderson and I loaded up a baby carriage with extra ammunition. We was gonna take it out to the gun, but they were firing point-blank at us. We just left it and run out to the foxhole. There was 10 of us in that hole where there was only room for 4.

Henderson was a cool one. A few days earlier, when I'd just joined the company, he was explaining how our machine guns fired much slower but were much more accurate than the Germans' [500 versus 2,500 rounds per minute]. Just then, a German gunner throwed mud in the sergeant's face. "See what I mean?" he says.

When times were quiet, he and I made coffee for the squad. I found a can that came in handy for brewing. When Sam saw it, he straightened me out. The guys had been using it for a urinal. One of the sergeants in another squad just loved our coffee, so I poured him a canteen out of that batch. After he drank it, I told him what the situation was. Didn't make any different to him. "Just pour me some more," he says.

HIGLEY

"Just at daybreak the next day [24 January 1945], we spotted a column of krauts coming out of Rothbach in a column of twos. They must have thought we'd made one of our 'strategic withdrawals' during the night. . . . The gunners . . . waited until most of the column was within their field of fire. . . . It was a gunner's dream."

HUNDLEY

We were gonna wait till they got in between, but one of the riflemen got trigger happy and opened fire too early, so we had to open fire too. One of our gunners split a German in two.

HIGLEY

"Although taken completely by surprise, the gray clad Jerries hit the ground almost instantly and soon took cover behind a slight embankment. . . . A few were killed. . . . Throughout the day we continued to fire, with little effect. That evening, they escaped under cover of darkness.

"[The next afternoon] we caught our worst mortar barrage of the war. . . .

It gives you a strange feeling to hear those shells screaming overhead, not knowing when one may be a direct hit on your foxhole. Nothing but the goodness of the Lord kept our whole squad from death . . . because the krauts were zeroed in. . . . One landed on the corner of our roof, but was a dud and didn't explode. The irony of it all was that the krauts were using our own 81-millimeter mortars . . . that fell to them two days previous when eight men from our mortar platoon were taken prisoner [on the E Company outpost line]."

[A month and a half of relative quiet followed the fighting at Rothbach. Then, on 15 March, the final assault on Germany began. Gundershoffen was the battalion's objective.]

HIGLEY

Our machine gun squads were assigned to support the various rifle companies. Mine was in support of the Second Platoon of F Company. Our platoon leader was 2d Lt. Ray Biedrzycki, who was killed later in the day. We could hear artillery and small arms off to our right as we moved up. "Loaded down with ammunition cans, raincoats, gas masks, entrenching shovels, and our weapons, it was the most grueling physical ordeal we ever had.

"About 10 A.M., a heavy artillery barrage caught us in an open field. One of our men had a shell land not more than a foot away. It lifted his leg in the air, but he wasn't hurt. It had hit in soft ground and spent itself."

HUNDLEY

We were catchin' fire right and left that morning. Higley never showed any fear. The rest of us were down behind a road embankment, but he was leaning up against a tree eating K rations, bullets just flyin' around him. Somebody had to reach up and pull him down. A rifle company guy was digging in beside me. "Sure glad to be near all that firepower," he says. I told him five seconds after we opened up, he was gonna wish he was the hell away from us. Our guns always drew fire.

HIGLEY

G-2 [divisional intelligence section] underestimated the enemy's strength. We were held up several hours till the riflemen of F Company advanced across an open field to the edge of the Engwiller Woods. The krauts in there had been dug in all winter. The riflemen suffered heavy casualties.

No sooner had they cleared the woods than a heavy barrage from a self-propelled 88 hit us. You could hear the muzzle blasts, the gun was so close. Thirty or forty of us dived into a huge underground emplacement the krauts had occupied during the winter. Lieutenant Biedrzycki[3] and several others who stayed outside were killed or wounded by tree bursts. [See chapter 11.]

"Only the Lord's protection kept the casualties from being much higher."

HUNDLEY

It must of been in those woods where this German tried to throw a potato masher into our gun position. He was just determined to throw that thing, runnin' at us with one arm blowed off while our gunner kept firing at him. He fell forward and sort of threw it into the ground. If he'd of been a normal person, he'd have throwed it right into our position.

[That night, Hundley helped pull a wounded G Company mortarman out of a minefield. See chapter 19. A month later, Hundley and Higley fought in the battalion's last battle, in Erkenbrechtsweiler, Germany. See chapter 24. Higley made it through unharmed, but Hundley suffered a crippling arm wound.]

HUNDLEY

(By now a squad leader) I had two men upstairs in the house we were defending [in Erkenbrechtsweiler]. When I didn't see any flashes comin' from their windows, I started upstairs to check. At the landing, a sniper bullet hit me in the left elbow and knocked me down. You know in the movies how they stagger around? It wasn't like that for me. I crashed.

It felt like my arm was sticking straight up. I reached up to pull it down, but I couldn't feel anything.

"Well," I thought, "did them so and so's shoot my arm off?"

A doctor told me later it was 'cause the nerves were straightened out that it felt like it was sticking up, even though it was dangling.

There was seven of us wounded or killed in that house that night.

HIGLEY

"We could hear him moaning in great pain and calling for someone to help him, but we couldn't leave the gun. Finally, . . . some other men did what they could to stop the bleeding. It was a medic, Pfc. Edgar Martin, that saved Hundley's life.[4] Running down the street through enemy fire, he succeeded in reaching us and giving first aid. He used up all his bandages in finally stopping the bleeding."

HUNDLEY

It was at the 256th Field Hospital, I think, where I was first operated on. The doctor says, "Sergeant, I don't know whether I'm going to cut this arm off or not." I says, "Well, you're the doctor, but save it if you can." I woke up in a body cast with my arm sticking out.

MRS. SUNSHINE HUNDLEY

I didn't know anything had happened till I got his Purple Heart in the mail.[5] That liked to of scared me to death. It was a week before I knew if he was dead or alive.

He wrote me a letter saying he'd be in the hospital for a few days. It wasn't till he got to Augusta that I found out how hurt he was. But I was thankful he still had an arm on him.

HUNDLEY

In Augusta, we called it Balone's Meat Market after one of the doctors, Captain Balone. The doctors there said the first man who worked on me back in France was the one who gave me all my maneuverability. I was sent to Daytona Beach to convalesce. The leg cases played softball against the arm cases, and if that wasn't a humdinger! It was there I started to get a little motion in my elbow, and they decided not to break the joint. They'd been talking about making it solid with a metal brace on each side.

EPILOGUE

Higley considers himself lucky not to have served at Anzio or Okinawa, or in a rifle company.

A deeply religious man, Higley filled his wartime diary with references to the power of prayer and to the Lord's protection. He did not say why prayer did not work as well for some of his German enemies or for some of his fellow Americans.

After his discharge in November 1945, Higley went back to college and got a master's degree in economic geography at the University of Chicago. He then became a banker in Wilmington, Delaware. He and his wife have two grown children.

HIGLEY

The type of duty I had was not nearly what others had to go through.

One of my sisters told me that at the very time of the fighting at Erkenbrechtsweiler, she had a particular burden to pray for me. I believe God put it in her heart to do so. I know that God was good to me.

SUNSHINE HUNDLEY

Oscar finally got out of the hospital in 1947, after two years. It seemed more like six. You wonder why he came back and other didn't. It goes back to the Bible verse that says, "A time to be born, and a time to die." It just wasn't his time.

HUNDLEY

In the first part of '46, I had a tendon transplant to fix my wrist drop. I can raise my hand up, but I can't hold anything heavy. I can bend my arm to a little more than a right angle. A few years back, it got so I couldn't feel anything in two fingers, so I had two more operations. That made 10 altogether. But those last ones didn't do any good. The doctors said the nerves are dying.

For 30 years, I carried the mail here in Greensboro. I could of transferred inside with my veteran's preference, but I didn't want any special treatment. I retired in 1977, and I've been taking it easy ever since. Since 1977, I've made $125.

I've got 43 years on the boys that's still layin' over there in Europe. I was very fortunate.

2d Lt. John Y. Crow, 1946.
Courtesy of John Y. Crow

28

"OUR OWN ARTILLERY HIT US"

Second lieutenants were known derisively as 90-day wonders for the time they spent at Officer Candidate School earning their gold bars.

John Crow of Baltimore was more of a 270-day wonder. "I was a little bit wild," he explained. "They kept turning me back." When he finally graduated, the new shavetail was assigned to H Company.

CROW

While I was at Howze, the division went through glider training. I was sure we were going to make a glider landing someplace, but so many gliders got shot up in Europe that summer and fall [of 1944] that they canceled the whole idea.

The platoon was having a little practice of some kind when I arrived. I asked for the platoon sergeant [Technical Sergeant Bernard Brast, now of Houston], and he said, "You come on up here." I decided I'd better see if I could exercise my authority right off the bat, so I told him, "You get down here. I want to talk to you."

I didn't know who he was, especially that he'd been a boxing champ. But after I challenged him, he took me under his wing, and I didn't have any trouble with anybody 'cause he set 'em straight.

Bennie and I fought like cats and dogs, but we became great friends. He was at least six years older than I was, a Regular Army man. When we got into combat, if he was my friend that day, I ate good. If he wasn't, I was lucky to get anything.

The man had good sense, though. We were on a winter line. The Free French said they had some houses we could stay in. We left our holes and went down into the town, but after an hour and a half, Bennie came to me and said, "Lieutenant, I don't like it. I think we ought to get our men out of here." It was awful cold, and a couple of the riflemen with us said they were going to stay. I took our guys back up to the foxholes, and it wasn't more than a few hours later the krauts ran everybody out of town.[1]

We got into combat near St. Die on November 11, but I didn't lose a man till the end of November.[2] I thought I'd never forget his name, but I have. A sniper got him.

It was more or less routine after that, sort of like a big football game except the stakes were a lot higher. Many a day, I thanked the good Lord that I had .30-caliber machine guns and 50 yards between me and the front line. I always marveled at how the riflemen could get up and cross those open fields. I don't think I'll ever understand how they did it. I'm not sure I could have, but they did, and it was just a marvelous thing.

During the big attack on March 15, Bennie Brast did an extraordinary thing. We were pinned down on one side of a road, and we had to get across. Sarge picked that machine gun off the tripod, cradled it in his arms, and went across the road firing like Rambo.

My machine guns were attached to E Company. That same day, we attacked into a wooded area. The fighting was as bad or worse there than any we had. A man next to me had his whole jaw shot off. He didn't have any face. The only thing you could do was point him to the rear. He died. That's where Bennie got hit too. Artillery was coming in like crazy, bursting in the trees. To hear him cry, you'd think he was killed, but it wasn't that bad, an arm wound or something.

I think it was the next day when I was with the colonel [Lt. Col. James Robison, battalion commander]. He called in artillery on an 88, but our people brought it down on us. You haven't lived till you've had your own artillery on you. The colonel called back to get the firing canceled. A major told him he couldn't stop it. I don't think Colonel Robbie needed a radio when he heard that. From then on, they overshot us, I'll tell you. Robbie was a great guy, but that major was a pain in the ass.

After those fights in March, everything started to deteriorate. One funny thing that happened: we were moving fast through Germany. My jeep driver and I got into a farmhouse and made the old guy there get us some eggs. We ate eggs all night long. The next morning, it was a thrill to look out the window and see the Germans retreating past us. We'd gotten out too far ahead of our column.

The war ended in Innsbruck. When we got there, the Germans hadn't closed their CP yet. They were still armed, and there we were, practically side by side, but we didn't shoot each other. That was the understanding. It was very strange and very scary.[3]

But pretty soon, the Germans were disarmed, and our biggest problem was to keep the men calmed down among all those beautiful women. There isn't any army that isn't going to do some cat-calling. All the barracks were the same. There were as many fräuleins in there as there were soldiers.

EPILOGUE

A career in the peacetime army was Crow's goal. He was transferred out of the 103d to another unit in Europe.

CROW

It was amazing the way the West Pointers came out by the bushel basket once the war was over. They made it unbearable.

This colonel said, "There's one officer here that thinks he has enough points to go home, and he wants to stay in the service. I'm going to see that he doesn't do either," referring to me. That was the end of my military career.

I thought of joining the national guard when I got home. The general in charge told me I could get a second lieutenant's commission if I passed the social board. To which I said, "General, I've wanted to tell this to a general for a long time. Why don't you go to hell?" And I got up and walked out.

I've been in sales ever since I got out. I don't intend to ever retire. I like what I'm doing.

My first wife died 12 years ago. I have three girls, and my present wife has three girls, all grown.

One of the strangest things about the war was that when you shot at a man, he wasn't human. But then when he's wounded, lying back at the aid station, he's no longer an animal; he's a human. You give him water, give him a cigarette, whatever he wants. Fascinating. I think the good Lord saw fit to make it that way. You couldn't have a war otherwise.

Sgt. John Smiertka in a playful mood shortly before his death.
Courtesy of John Y. Crow

Barn set on fire in Bayerniederhofen by H Company following Smiertka's death.
Courtesy of Oscar Hundley and Frank Kania

29

THE LAST

Tension was high as the Second Battalion sped toward Innsbruck on 1 May 1945. No one wanted to be the last man to die in the war.

A few days earlier, when they thought the war was all but over, the soldiers had fought a pitched battle in Erkenbrechtsweiler. Now they were alert for die-hard stragglers as their column raced through the lovely Alpine villages of southern Germany.

Part of the column was in Bayerniederhofen, 20 miles west of Oberammergau, when the order came to move out. At that moment, Sgt. John T. Smiertka of H Company was fatally wounded, the last man killed in the Second Battalion.

KENNETH BERGSTROM

H Company mail clerk

You know he shot himself, don't you? At first, we thought it was a sniper that did it. Everybody scattered. Smiertka was well liked in the company. [As a result of his death], we blew one house apart. It wasn't the whole village. We didn't want this brought up. We didn't want to hurt the family. I still don't.

GARY HAVEMAN

sergeant, H Company

Smiertka was one of my men. I saw him get killed. I was 30 or 40 feet away when he jumped out of the jeep and his gun went off. I don't think there was an investigation, but his rifle was checked. A round was fired, and there was an empty shell case. I'm sure that's the way it happened. Doc Latham, our medic [Alonzo T. Latham, then of Sparkill, New York] was right there to take care of him, but there wasn't much he could do. I thought there was only two of us who knew what really happened, me and John Low [platoon sergeant, now deceased].

RAY TAVA
sergeant, H Company

At first, I thought he was killed by a sniper, but later we figured out what had happened. There wasn't too many that knew, about three of us. We kept it under wraps. I think it was officially recorded as getting shot by a sniper.[1] I was only 5 or 10 feet from him. The bullet went in his chin and out the top. Blood just gushed out. There wasn't anything anybody could do.

HAVEMAN

This was the 1st of May, remember. It was practically all over, but the battalion commander had told Captain Dodge [Nathaniel Dodge, H Company commander] to watch for snipers. If there was any problem, we were to burn the town down.

Our people thought a sniper shot him. Civilians started running. Some of them climbed trees and were shot out of the trees. Two or three buildings were burned. [The townspeople] were brought into the town square. Some kids were laid out on the canvas covers of the jeeps. Dead. I would say maybe half a dozen. That's the last I saw of them. It was a mess. We moved on.

[The *Narrative of Operations, 410th Infantry*, reads thus, "At 1415 [2:15 P.M.], a sniper seriously wounded two men. . . . The sniper was riddled by American fire, and his body dragged into the main street, where civilians of the town were forced to view him. In addition, two houses in the vicinity of the sniper's location were burned."[2]

*

The German version of this tragedy differs substantially. Frau Waltraut Schilling, chronist (historian) of this region of Germany, researched what she calls "The Black Day of Bayerniederhofen" at my request. What follows is taken from her letter.

FRAU SCHILLING

"There was no shooting during the entry of the troops. The priest, Pfarrer Kummerle, and the Bürgermeister, Josef Schnitzer, awaited the US troops at the entry of Bayerniederhofen, carrying a white flag and thus surrendered the village. The people were in their houses. They had the order by their Bürgermeister to stay inside and hanged white flags from the windows.

"There was no sniper, but two men were shot during the chase of snipers. 25% of the houses of our village were burnt down because of non-existent snipers. Nobody had rifles. . . . The NAZI did not allow the population to have weapons at all—being very afraid of possible opponents!

"There was a 'man with a beard' running toward the steep slope behind the burning houses. Of course he was not allowed to do this; of course he was at once chased as the supposed sniper by the GIs; there was much shooting, Franz Christa, 67, and Engelbert Hutter, 16, were hit and killed. According to the town register, 'shot at 14 hour 1 Mai 1945.' [In] the Parish register, . . . the priest added: 'shot by Americans in the breast.'

"The 'man with beard' escaped to Berghof [a nearby village]. May I add: this 'man with beard' had been in a stable nearby to help a mare foal. As soon as he became aware of the uproar in the village, he panicked, ran toward the slope to reach his family at Berghof.

"The boy was said to be rather an idiot. He and the old man peeped down at the GIs from the very top of the slope. The old man is said to have told the boy to shout 'Heil Hitler' and raise his arm—for fun—to make the GIs angry. They were shot at once and payed for their silliness—and malice.

"Nobody was allowed [by the Americans] to run in the streets and to stand on the leite [hillside], [so] it was the law of the warrior to rifle the two men. C'est la guerre.

"As far as I could find out: Christa was no Nazi. The boy, Hutter, was said to have felt as 'big Nazi' and it may be possible that this simple-minded idiot indeed had shouted, 'Heil Hitler' . . . to make the Americans furious.

"The people were forced rather rudely to come to the [town] square, had to stand hands raised for ca. 3 hours and had to view the body of Christa and the boy Hutter. The people—most of them women and children—were forced to watch the storehouse and the three . . . houses burning down to ashes. May I add something about the weather: this 1 Mai was very cold, some snow falling. It was very hard for mothers and little children standing there for hours. Nobody was allowed to extinguish the fires; the GIs surrounding the people with rifles.

"After some 3 hours, the fires had ended. As soon as the troops had left the village, people were allowed to go home. It seems to me that the burning of the Etschmann houses had already been planned by the POWs before the

US troops had arrived. A Polish POW had warned the women of the house where he had to work: 'You are poor things, poor women, poor children: dreadful things will occur, I know.'

"Most of the women and children at Bayerniederhofen were evacuated people and bomb victims of München [Munich], Augsburg etc. One old woman told me, weeping: . . . 'This 1. Mai 45 was worse than the bombing; I wished I had never come to Bayerniederhofen; the Americans and the POWs raged, screamed, roared, threatened us with their rifles. . . . and when we came home after the Americans had departed, the houses had been plundered. . . . I lost the rest of my things which I had saved from the Munchen bombing.'

"Mr. Stannard, in my first letter to you, I wanted to be polite, having written, 'The GIs were very nervous,' instead of 'they were full of panic of snipers.' I did not want to 'wake sleeping dogs!' The longer time goes by: let sleep them, all that bad reminiscences.

"May I tell you that I myself in April 1945 met the US troops some 20 km south of Augsburg; too in a very little village. The tank-troop made quarters the same way as at Bayerniederhofen, but that commander had the better nerves; no chasing for snipers—no shooting! I saw a jeep rolling up the field nearby, the GI in the open jeep shouting toward the woods full of hidden German troops: 'Hello, Kamerad, komm raus!!' And thousands came out with white flags in order to surrender: no shooting, and absolutely no burning of houses.

". . . As to the few Bayerniederhofen people who remember that "Black Day": they can not for get—but they can forgive—: please tell this [to] the old GIs still living!"

TAVA

The platoon had been on outpost duty. German troops were up in the mountains, but they never fired down on us. We came back into town to regroup and get new orders. There were snipers. Some of our people thought they shot Smiertka. The building where we thought the shot came from was set on fire. I think a couple of Germans got killed. One was in a tree, shooting at a jeep.

FRANK KANIA
jeep driver

Our captain had the house surrounded and ordered everybody out. A woman came out, but nobody else, so the captain had the boys throw some gasoline on and set the house on fire.

PVT. DAN HIGLEY

[From his diary[3]] "It [Smiertka's shooting] gave everyone the jitters. If snipers had been responsible, we might expect a similar thing to happen again. . . . Some of the men in the rifle companies had become suspicious of the civilians, thinking SS troops were hiding in town disguised as civilians. That seemed logical in light of the recent shooting. Almost immediately, however, fear turned to anger and Captain Dodge decided to call all the civilians out of their houses to line up in the street for an investigation. All of them denied that they knew who was responsible. . . .

"When Colonel Robison [Lt. Col. James C. Robison], our battalion commander, arrived on the scene . . . he ordered a more thorough investigation. When that failed to produce results, he gave the order to have several—three or four—of the buildings nearest the scene of the shooting burned to the ground. This was for the purpose of driving out any sniper who might be hiding inside, and also to show the civilians we meant business. The first building was a warehouse containing some supplies of ammunition. As it went up in flames, there were loud explosions but no sign of anyone inside. The other buildings were mostly barns, and they didn't produce anyone either.

"By this time, nearly all of us were sure Smiertka had killed himself accidentally. Colonel Robison probably was too, but he was smart enough not to let the Germans know it. A little later, Colonel Robison decided to drop the matter for the present, and have us start on our motor march."

KANIA

Smiertka was sitting on my jeep as we were pulling out of town. A shot came from the side of a house and hit him right in the temple. A [U.S.] rifleman noticed a kid up in a tree with a rifle and shot him down. The kid fired the shot. He turned out to be 12 or 13 years of age. There was no one else around. It was a senseless thing, but what can you do?

Smiertka shot himself? Hell, no, he was shot by this kid. That's my version.

Kenneth Bergstrom, H Company mail clerk.
Courtesy of Kenneth Bergstrom

I was right there, sitting in the jeep. If he was not hit by that kid in the tree and the house burnt down needlessly, then it could have been an accidental discharge of his gun.

I wrote to his mother and told her my version of his death.

HAVEMAN

Just before this happened, Smiertka was really upset. I don't know if his wife wrote him and said she didn't want him anymore or what, but he said he was going to have his insurance changed to somebody else. He told me he did it because she left him.

KANIA

Smiertka wasn't too happy. His wife sent him a "Dear John" letter. I advised him to change his insurance to his mother, and he did that, two or three months before he died.

BERGSTROM

He was quite a gambler. While we were still in the States, he sent over eight thousand bucks home to his wife. At least that's what the boys who gambled with him said. As the mail clerk, I was always sending money orders home for him.

From what I was told, he got a letter that day that said his wife was divorcing him, and that she'd taken all his money. An officer told me to return his mail to sender. There wasn't any investigation.

HIGLEY

[From his diary] "[That night], we heard that Smiertka had died in the hospital without ever regaining consciousness. He lived only six hours after the shooting. The final conclusion that was reached was that he had accidentally shot himself with his own rifle."

EPILOGUE

Not much is known about Smiertka except that he was married, was drafted from Detroit, was a machine gunner, and was a good soldier.

Conclusion: The Atomic Bomb

Within a month of the end of the European war, the 103d Division was deactivated, and its "low-point" men began transferring to divisions scheduled to assault the Japanese home islands.

The bad news was sweetened with the promise of a 30-day leave at home before shipping out for what everyone expected would be a tougher war than the one they had just survived. The reaction was varied. I assumed I would be killed. All of 19 years old, I planned to find a bride during those 30 days of furlough and leave an heir planted behind.

Most of the 103d men went to the 45th Division. The troops were waiting in a staging area near Le Havre to begin the journey home when the first atomic bomb was dropped on 6 August 1945, followed by the second bomb on 9 August. Japan surrendered five days later.

The devastating power of these exotic new weapons was instantly apparent around the world, and nowhere was awareness higher than among the troops at Le Havre.

"A roar went up when we heard about the bomb," Hugh Chance of E Company recalled. "It saved a lot of lives all over the world. I was glad they used it. I'm still glad."

There was no soul-searching then about the ethics of this incredible new weapon among the GIs, and little now. The nearly universal attitude is the one expressed by Chance. The bombs were viewed as saviors by these veteran infantrymen whose division had already suffered 4,150 casualties, and who knew the Japanese were a far more dangerous foe than the Germans.

Paul Fussell, an F Company platoon leader, wrote an essay a few years ago called *Thank God for the Atom Bomb*.[1] Cuttingly, he singles out for special attack critics of the American nuclear strategy who were either unborn at the time or spent the war in safe noncombat assignments. "When the atom bombs were dropped . . . when we [combat infantrymen] learned to our astonishment that we would not be obliged in a few months to rush up the beaches near Tokyo assault-firing while being machine gunned, mortared, and shelled . . . we broke down and cried with relief and joy. We were going to live. We were going to grow to adulthood after all."

The Reverend William Kleffman, Catholic chaplain of the battalion, says if it hadn't been for the A-bomb, "there was going to be slaughter from the Japanese, being the type of fanatics [they were], kamikaze and what not." But it troubles him that the two cities singled out for attack "were both places evangelized by St. Francis Xavier way back in the 16th century. [Hiroshima and Nagasaki] were practically wiped off the map—Catholic settlements. Sometimes you wonder what it accomplished."

The Reverend W. Richard Steffen, a Methodist minister, was a private in F Company. He is one of the few who questions use of the bomb: "At the time, I thought it was a great idea. It saved my life. But now I believe we should never have dropped it. A lot of experts think Japan would have surrendered anyway, and we would never have had to invade.

"Back then, though, I was in favor of anything that would shorten the war. It was just another big bomb. We didn't know about fallout and radiation and so on. But if I had known then what I know now, I would have been opposed to using it. There had to be some way to negotiate a peace."

Mr. Steffen has become a pacifist in the years since the war. During the sixties and seventies, he was a leading opponent of the Vietnam War while serving as campus minister at the University of Wisconsin at Stevens Point.

"I think there is no excuse for war, and the only way you're going to avoid it is to have people say, 'I will not participate.' I would encourage people to avoid the draft now."

He and his wife are enthusiastic participants in battalion and division reunions. He sees no inconsistency in that.

"At our reunions, people don't always agree with me, of course, but I like to think that my presence influences some of them," he said. "I go because the people I served with are my friends, especially the ones who have the same life-style. We don't all go out drinking and rolling dice."

Mrs. Richard Pearson, wife of an F Company sergeant, said she remembered both horror and relief at the news of the bomb: "You felt terrible about it, but at the same time you hoped the end was in sight."

Dick Pearson, her husband, asked, "How many of us would have been killed going in there? I think it was great, not from the standpoint of destroying a city and killing people, but in terms of saving so many casualties."

Harold Motenko, F Company private, said he was determined never to go to the Pacific. Once he got back to the States with the 45th Division, he intended to do whatever he had to do to stay: "The bomb saved a tremendous amount of lives, and some good things have come from it, like our tremendous strides in medicine. And it has kept us from another war."

To which Adele Motenko added: "We hope."

Jim McCarthy, F Company private, has no doubt the bomb saved his life:

"I thought it was the greatest thing that ever happened. I was in the Ninth Division at the time. We were told we were gonna be the spearhead. I was beginning to think my luck had run out. How long can you go in combat?"

Melvin Seiler, E Company sergeant, thought to himself, "I'm glad to be in a division that's coming home, even if it means we're going to Japan. Maybe we hoped it would end in time. Everybody was glad when the bomb dropped. That assault business had no appeal for me. But I never considered *not* going. We thought we had to. I don't think young people today feel that way."

Ray Millek, a lieutenant in E Company, says dropping the bomb "was right then and it's right now. I've never had any second thoughts. I love this country."

For Syd Fierman, F Company private, the war turned him against all things military: "From the time I got out of the service until today, I have never handled a gun. I would never buy a toy gun for my child or anyone in my family. I've seen what guns can do firsthand. I don't believe I would ever handle one again.

"But when you ask about the atom bomb, asking today and asking in August of '45 is a lot different. In today's reality, I wish we had never had it. But I still believe we should have dropped it. Doing what we did saved thousands of lives. It took a lot of Japanese lives, but what the hell? They were the instigators."

"The greatest thing that happened was Truman deciding to drop the atomic bomb," said Bob Brennan, an E Company sergeant. "I'm sure he saved a lot of lives on both sides. It would have been a real bloodbath for both the Japanese and the Americans. I'd tell 'em to drop it again if it came to that."

Marvin Shelley was executive officer of E Company and expected to be in the same job in Japan. "When you see what a horrifying thing it was, you have second thoughts. But the idea was to end the war quickly, and I'm sure it saved my life. All I could think about was we had had no amphibious training. How would we make it?"

Lester (Doc) Duckett, F Company medic, said, "I don't know why they didn't drop it sooner."

Bob Loyd, G Company sergeant, has doubts: "Today, it may not seem like such a good idea, but it was great at the time. It saved a lot of lives, I'm sure. But why did we drop two of them?"

Clyde Rucker, G Company platoon leader, professional soldier: "I was not pleased to be going to Japan. When they announced Japan had quit, the whole camp [at Le Havre] erupted. There were three divisions there waiting to ship out, the 45th, 76th, and . . . I forget the other. People were hollering, throwing hats in the air, it was pandemonium.

"We had to drop it. It was a terrible thing to do, but it made Japan surrender."

Notes and References

Introduction

1. Regiments were named as follows: "410th Infantry." The word *regiment* was never included. But it was always included for the division: "103d Division."

2. It helped that the army by this time was vigorously propagandizing infantry service as glamorous. There was much talk in the press of the "Queen of Battles," for example, and Bing Crosby did his bit by making a huge hit of Frank Loesser's song *What Do You Do in the Infantry? (You March, You March, You March)*.

3. The army was already "going metric," but only part way. A caliber, the measure of a rifle bullet, is one-hundredth of an inch. Mortar and artillery sizes were stated in millimeters.

Chapter One

1. Three men were wounded in the mortar barrage: Pfc. Albert D. Schmidt, Jr., Elgin City, Illinois, who died in 1978; Sgt. James G. Hamilton, Rockwood, Tennessee; and Sgt. Elmer Muskopf, St. Louis. Schmidt was Kopko's foxhole mate.

Chapter Two

1. Pfc. James F. Bolyard and S. Sgt. Norbert J. Sliga were killed the night of 8 December 1944. Their deaths led to a battalion order prohibiting men on guard duty from zipping their bags closed. Of Sliga, former S. Sgt. E. Robert Brennan said, "There was a good man, very kind guy, one of the original cadre. He had a premonition of death. I heard him say, 'I'm not going to make it.' "

2. Three men were wounded the night of 9 December: Pfc. Robert L. Miller, Pfc. Bernard F. Grabowski, and Pvt. Laroy Ragan.

3. Actually, a retreat, part of a general withdrawal of the Seventh Army in the aftermath of the German attack to the north known as the Battle of the Bulge. Army propagandists called the withdrawal by the Seventh, which was not involved in the Bulge fighting, a "line straightening" operation.

4. The late John V. Rhye (1st sergeant) and Millek (technical sergeant), the ranking noncommissioned officers, were in charge of the Second Platoon riflemen and the machine gun/mortar platoon, respectively. Rhye's platoon leader, whose reputation had been destroyed when he cowered in a ditch during an attack, was evacuated as a nonbattle casualty just before the company headquarters was overrun.

5. It was the 410th's First Battalion.

6. Many people say they never missed a day writing a letter.

Chapter Three

1. The Reverend William C. Kleffman, the battalion's Catholic chaplain.

2. The late John V. Rhye of Omaha served for many years as altar boy for the memorial service that Father Kleffman conducts at each battalion reunion. Rhye died 29 January 1989.

Chapter Four

1. An American hand grenade would not explode as long as the pin (or in Shelley's case, his wristwatch band) held the handle in place.

2. The captain and his driver, Pfc. John W. Lucas of Chipley, Georgia, were caught in a German roadblock, according to the captain's statement to investigators after the war, and Lucas was killed. The army's inspector general concluded there were no grounds to court-martial the captain. Woodbeck, Shelley, the captain, and other former captives were interviewed by the IG.

3. On 17 December 1944, 86 members of Battery B, 285th Field Artillery Observation Battalion, were captured at Malmedy, Belgium, in the Battle of the Bulge. Their captors, the First SS Panzer Division, machine-gunned them to death. The incident was widely publicized by the Allies.

4. Pfc. Richard Gwisdala of Detroit and Sgt. Joe Reith of Glendale, California.

5. Shelley and other captives believe E Company's commander gave the map to the Germans.

6. It only seemed that way. The mortality rate was not high in the German POW camps.

7. Stalag XII-A.

8. Twin-fuselage American fighter plane.

9. Dr. Charles A. Stenger, Ph.D., author of a study of American POWs, said in a letter to me that there is no evidence the Germans murdered any Jewish American POWs, but that there were "cases where they were singled out as Jews [and] sent to POW camps adjoining Dachau, etc. I am not aware of any official reports that suggest otherwise."

10. Stalag XIII-C.

11. Forty men or eight horses, the standard French boxcar of World War I.

12. Col. Paul R. Goode retired from the army in 1952 and died in 1959.

13. Many telephone systems were not automated.

Chapter Five

1. The Alsatian village captured by the Germans on 25 January 1945.

2. When the war ended in Europe, the grand strategy was to send some divisions to the Pacific. Men in those units would first get 30-day furloughs in the U.S.

Chapter Six

1. Dennis Bellmore, Moorehead, Minnesota, was awarded the Silver Star posthumously. He was killed trying to hold off the Germans with a pistol. His story is told in the division's history, *Report After Action* (Innsbruck, 1945).

Chapter Seven

1. This opium-based medicine is now available only by prescription and is rarely used.

Chapter Nine

1. It may have been Edward J. Murphy, who joined G Company from ASTP. Efforts to locate him through former residences in Utica and Schenectady were unsuccessful.

2. Teague, of Lubbock, Texas, died 20 April 1989. He was interviewed 22 June 1986.

3. First sergeant of E Company and one of the "originals" of the division. H died 29 January 1989.

Chapter Ten

1. *WINFRED L. FONTENOT*

I don't know how that story got started. It wasn't a bayonet. I was wounde the left hand by a sniper bullet and in the right arm by shrapnel. The hand wa worst. The bullet took out my knuckle. I was in hospitals for six months and came back to the company. Clark was still first sergeant at the time. I never kn made lieutenant. I was platoon sergeant of the Third Platoon. Our officer was

man [2d Lt. Abe E. Goldman of Pittsburgh]. He was wounded just before I was. I had four or five guys on the ground at the same time. Hell was just breaking loose.

Chapter Eleven

1. See chapter 14.

2. Officers believed, probably rightly, that snipers preferred them over enlisted men as targets.

3. No other officer is listed in the F Company casualty records at that time. He might have been in K Company, where the defense line was broken.

Chapter Thirteen

1. As odd as that sounds, it was true. The army believed it could mold people with no preconceived beliefs better than those who fancied themselves weapons experts. The army may have missed some Sergeant Yorks that way, but it was an effective training system.

2. Medics also ran the same risks as infantrymen, and paid a heavy toll. Six in the 410th Regiment were killed, 17 were wounded, and 8 were declared missing in action. But it was not until near the end of the war that they received any special recognition. In March 1945, award of a Combat Medic Badge comparable to the Combat Infantry Badge began. After the war ended, on 1 September 1945, medics began receiving $10 extra per month in combat pay, the same amount infantrymen received, but it was not retroactive.

3. The wounded man was Pfc. Edward A. Luebke of Two Rivers, Wisconsin. Luebke recovered from his wound, returned to F Company, and was killed in a raid on Bischholtz, Alsace, on 3 February 1945.

Chapter Fourteen

1. A company from another battalion was holding the line to the right of Gibbs's F Company. Several members of F Company, including Gibbs, believe the other company's commander fled to the rear when the Germans attacked, and that many of his men then abandoned their positions. The Germans broke through the hole and overran 2d Battalion's CP in Schillersdorf, nearly capturing the battalion commander. Gibbs said he learned of the dereliction after the battle at a meeting called to "find out what the hell had happened." The regiment's Journal of Operations and Narrative of Operations have several entries which lend support to Gibbs's charge, but there was no investigation and the officer who allegedly fled stayed in command. This was the second incident in two days in which company commanders in the 410th Infantry are accused of failing in their duty. See chapter 4 regarding E Company's commander, who was investigated but not charged.

2. In Chapter 13, company medic Lester "Doc" Duckett described this same fight. He said he was a candidate for a medal for his role until it was found he was a non-combatant under the Geneva Convention. The American Army in World War II rigidly enforced the non-combat status of medical personnel.

3. Pfc. Robert P. Dombrowski died of his wounds on 27 January 1945.

Chapter Fifteen

1. One of the battalions in the all-Nisei 442d Regimental Combat Team, most decorated regiment in the army. The 442d at this time was part of the Seventh Army.

2. Nichols wrote a long memoir shortly after the war and made it available for this book. Extracts from the memoir are in quotes.

Chapter Sixteen

1. Several men interviewed for this book were drafted with serious physical handicaps, particularly their vision. For example, I had 20/200 in my left eye and 20/100 in my right. The army supplied corrective "gas mask glasses" that supposedly fit inside a gas mask.

2. The division's patch was a green saguaro cactus on a yellow field. It was known as the Cactus Division.

Chapter Seventeen

1. G Company lost 10 killed and 16 wounded at Nothalten, most of them in the Second Platoon. The day before, Sgt. Owen F. McIlearney of Detroit was killed leading a patrol, and an entire squad of 11 men was captured on another patrol. F Company had 2 killed and 12 wounded. All participants remember only one day of fighting at Nothalten, on 30 November, but the official record splits the casualties between 30 November and 1 December. Casualties were recorded on the day they reached the aid station, which was not always the day they occurred.

2. Four G Company enlisted men who were killed at Nothalten won Silver Stars, the army's third highest award for valor. They were Pvt. Wilbur E. Humble, Jr., New Orleans; Pfc. Arthur W. Belliveau, San Francisco; Pvt. William C. Weaver, Cleveland; and Sgt. Owen F. McIlearney, Detroit. Pfc. Gilbert A. Amendt received the Bronze Star for the same action.

3. A similar priority system operated in the military hospitals behind the lines. At the 36th General Hospital in Dijon when I was there in January 1945, the new miracle drug penicillin was reserved for the American wounded. The Germans were treated with sulfa.

4. Carbines, much lighter than M-1s, were issued to officers. Both weapons were .30-caliber, but the carbine fired a smaller, lower-velocity bullet. Many officers carried

the M-1 instead of their standard-issue weapon because it was deadlier and helped disguise them from snipers. Luckily for Brawe, Torrance was carrying a carbine. Brawe, who with his wife Dorothy acts as secretary for the annual reunions, declined to be interviewed. "I don't want to embarrass the captain," he explained.

5. Torrance was awarded the Silver Star for rescuing the machine gun crew from the house. "I didn't get it for shooting Elmer!" Schroeder received the lesser Bronze Star decoration. "I don't know why," Torrance said. "He did exactly the same thing I did." Schroeder says his Bronze Star "didn't mean much. The company clerk got one the same time I did, for 'meritorious service.' " After the war, the army further cheapened the medal by issuing it to anyone who requested it, if he had received the Combat Infantry Badge. For anyone interested in getting one, here's what you do: Write to the Adjutant General and request the Bronze Star under authority of paragraph 15.1e AR 600-45, change 12, dated 10 September 1947, based on General Orders No. 3, Headquarters 410th Infantry dated 4 January 1945. Include your company, battalion, regiment, and division, and your army serial number. I received my medal in 1989.

6. Germany's frontier fortification on the French border. It was not heavily defended. Torrance was awarded the Bronze Star there, "mostly for urging the men to keep moving and getting through those pillboxes."

Chapter Eighteen

1. Woodside's weapon was the .30-caliber light (air-cooled) machine gun. Every rifle company had at least two.

Chapter Nineteen

1. I identified Hundley as Morris's unknown rescuer after I had interviewed both men. A similar thing happened with two other veterans, but I wasn't the one who made the connection.

S. Robert Genovese, now a Los Angeles land developer, was listed on our battalion roster as a member of George Company. When I interviewed him, I found he was from a different battalion. In the bitter fighting near Sessenheim, Alsace, on 18 January 1945, Genovese, a lieutenant in Charlie Company, rescued a soldier who had been shot through the eye. He received the Silver Star for his action. The next day, he himself suffered nearly fatal wounds.

Genovese didn't know the soldier he had rescued, and he had never had any postwar contact with his fellow veterans, but the interview stirred his interest, and he attended the 1987 reunion of the 103d Division. He was standing alone, a stranger in the crowd, when a man who saw his name tag walked up and said, "Genovese? You're supposed to be dead." The man was former sergeant John Pointer of Semora, North Carolina, who Genovese led off the battlefield.

Pointer had visited Genovese in the hospital in France and was told Genovese would not survive. When he found out differently 42 years later, it was an emotional moment for both of them. Later, when Genovese told me of their meeting, I couldn't resist interviewing Pointer, even though he and Genovese are outside the scope of this book. Pointer, permanently blinded in his left eye, credits Genovese with saving his life.

2. Franklin A. Cook, a farmer of Crawford, Nebraska. He recovered from his head wound and rejoined the company in Innsbruck, Austria. He and Morris visit each other regularly.

3. No one interviewed has stayed in touch with Roy England, though all remember he was from Texas.

4. Sam Johnson, then of Silver Hill, Alabama. Efforts to find him for this book were not successful.

5. Rath, a retired rural mail carrier who lives in Harvard, Nebraska, received the Bronze Star and the Purple Heart. He and Morris are still friends.

Chapter Twenty

1. One medical aid man was killed at Nothalten: Technician, Fifth Grade, Joseph Oko. Two were wounded: Pvt. John C. Sheppard of San Diego and Technician, Fifth Grade, Joe L. Puente. Ellis does not know which one treated him.

2. *DUUS*

John sent me a copy of the division history from Austria after the war with a note that said, "To Duke. I wish you were around to order your own." I saw John only one more time. In 1948, he came down to Philadelphia from New York and filled me in on what happened after I was hit. He also gave me my wallet, which had fallen out of the corpse on the battlefield. There were pictures of my French girlfriends and some French occupation money. A very strange feeling.

Chapter Twenty-one

1. We were told to use "marching fire" in this attack, something I'd never heard of. The idea was to throw out so much indiscriminate fire that the enemy couldn't get his head up to shoot back. Torrance said it was a "relatively new" infantry tactic. Paul Fussell, the writer and F Company platoon leader, called it an archaic tactic from the Civil War. Whichever it was, it worked in this instance.

2. Casualty records show two medics killed during the fighting for Gundershoffen: Pvt. John W. Mannisto on 15 March and Pfc. Ned O. Wiedbrauk on 16 March. There were also five wounded. Rustejkas recovered. Reeder said he lived in southern Florida until his death in 1984.

3. Reeder was awarded the Bronze Star for this action.

4. Three G Company men, including Finley, were captured the night of 22 January in Rothbach.

Chapter Twenty-two

1. Efforts to locate Elkman were unsuccessful. His last known address was Munster, Indiana.

2. Carlino was from Albany, New York. He received the Silver Star for leading the attack in which he was killed.

Chapter Twenty-three

1. Jim Teague was in ASTP at the University of Oklahoma when the program was dissolved. Following the heavy casualties of 15–16 March, Rucker told Teague he wanted him to be a squad leader. Teague reported the conversation this way:

TEAGUE I don't want to be a squad leader.
RUCKER I don't give a damn what you want.

"And," said Teague, "that's how I became a sergeant."

After the war, Teague became a certified public accountant and practiced in Lubbock. He died 20 April 1989.

2. Petrie was killed 24 January 1945. He was from Portland, Oregon. Rucker said he was transferred to G Company from an anti-aircraft unit that had been demobilized. He was awarded the Silver Star.

3. Rucker received the Bronze Star for actions that day. The citation read, in part, "For heroic achievement. . . . When his platoon was at a critical point prior to the rest of the company, Lieutenant Rucker . . . [found] that a crossroad near his position . . . was heavily mined, and also discovered the presence of three hundred of the enemy, . . . [and] . . . sent out messengers to warn the battalion."

Chapter Twenty-four

1. According to a newspaper story of this episode, the other captives were Charles Atkinson, Cedar Rapids, Iowa; Carmen Rego, Baltimore; Antonio J. Magliocco, Willimantic, Connecticut; Gerald W. Redman, Alvord, Texas; George V. Mahoney, Daniel, Maryland; Joe A. Putzel, Aurora, Minnesota; Athol E. Bell, Highland Park, Illinois; Robert L. Lintz, Elmira, New York; and three unidentified soldiers. The clipping was provided by John H. LaVelle, Beloit, Wisconsin, leader of G Company's First Platoon.

2. A reference to division commander Anthony J. McAuliffe's famous rejection of a German surrender demand at Bastogne, Belgium, during the Battle of the Bulge. McAuliffe was assistant commander of the 101st Airborne Division, the unit cut off in Bastogne.

3. Fagre won the Silver Star at Erkenbrechtsweiler. Efforts to locate him for these interviews were unsuccessful.

4. The other two men killed at Erkenbrechtsweiler were members of G Company. They were Cpl. Robert E. Birkhofer of San Diego and Pfc. Donald E. Mertinke of Eleva, Wisconsin. Both were recent replacements. No one interviewed had any information about them.

5. Higley's story is a combination of his interview and of a diary he kept during the war. Diary extracts are in quotes.

Chapter Twenty-five

1. Infantry replacement training center near Paso Robles, California, known to many as "the asshole of the world."

2. Besides the Purple Heart, Meadows won three Bronze Stars. "The first one was for the work I did at Erkenbrechtsweiler. They gave me another one for something else, but I don't remember for what. In Korea, I got another one, not for valor, for doing a good job as communications officer."

3. Nathaniel Dodge of Healdsburg, California, H Company commander. Dodge and Meadows knew each other during the war.

Chapter Twenty-six

1. Barker died of his wounds 10 December 1944.

2. Arvel T. Miller, a private, wounded 23 January 1945.

3. Six men in the Second Platoon were killed on 16 March: Carlino, T. Sgt. Joseph F. Bonacci, Sgt. Juel L. Gist, Sgt. Carroll T. Pott, Sgt. John Rudolph, and S. Sgt. Wilbert E. Triplett.

4. Carlino was from Albany, New York. He received the Silver Star for leading the attack in which he was killed.

5. Gundershoffen, Alsace, the battalion objective.

Interlude

1. It was part of battlefield lore that a prisoner on either side caught with enemy equipment was subject to instant execution, but this is the only known instance in the battalion. Many men got rid of their Lugers, cameras, and other souvenirs before a patrol or a battle, in case they were captured.

2. Ralph Mueller and Jerry Turk, *Report After Action* (Innsbruck: 103d Infantry Division, 1945), 62.

3. The two officers were lieutenants in H Company. One was tried by general court-martial, fined $85, and given a reprimand. The other was not tried. Two enlisted men from the 13th Airborne Division who were with the officers for part of their desertion were tried by general court-martial. One was sentenced to 20 years at hard

labor, the other to 15 years. A third enlisted paratroop deserter apparently returned to duty. He was listed as missing in action at the end of the war.

In F Company, in a separate case, a young soldier with an exemplary record as an enlisted man won a battlefield commission, got drunk, and went absent without leave. He was tried by general court-martial, reprimanded, and fined $250.

John Clark, Second lieutenant, F Company, complained, "Last time I saw old [. . .], that rascal was a captain same as I was. That sort of got on my nerves." Spilman Gibbs, F Company commander, said the officer rose to the rank of lieutenant colonel.

4. Richard Baron, Maj. Richard Baum, and Richard Goldhurst, *Raid! The Untold Story of Patton's Secret Mission* (New York: G. P. Putnam's Sons, 1981).

Chapter Twenty-seven

1. Higley kept a remarkably detailed diary, which he made available to me. Diary extracts used in his narrative are in quotation marks.

2. The late James Teague of G Company described a similar incident at Rothbach. His platoon had been relieved and was heading to the rear when a head count showed one man missing. "Hell, I was going to just leave him there, but Rucker [Clyde Rucker, platoon leader] made me go back and get him. He was passed out drunk in a foxhole." In other instances, liquor caused disaster. Robert Schroeder, G Company, told of an incident, also at Rothbach, when a jeepload of soldiers looking for beer were killed when they stumbled into German territory.

3. Raymond Biedrzycki, Hamtramck, Michigan, was a sergeant who earned a battlefield commission. He was leading the machine gun section that day. Frank Kania reports, "I was a machine gunner, and they wanted me to be an officer. I said, 'Just get me off this gun.' Biedrzycki, being my buddy, got me assigned as a jeep driver. He was Polish, like me. He took the lieutenant job."

4. Efforts to locate Martin were not successful.

5. Margaret Meadows reported the identical snafu.

Chapter Twenty-eight

1. This was during the Rothbach-Schillersdorf fighting 22–25 January 1945.

2. H Company had two men killed and nine men wounded in the fighting at Nothalten. The dead were Pfc. Ansel C. Deeter and Pvt. Ruben J. Gardner.

3. There were many strange events as the 103d Division entered its peacetime occupation mode. Among them was the liberation of high-ranking allied soldiers and civilians who had been imprisoned by the Nazis. French premiers Edouard Deladier and Paul Reynaud, as well as members of the French high command of 1940 were in this group.

One of the strangest events was related by Frank Kania, a jeep driver in H Company.

KANIA

Three Polish POWs came up to my jeep one day and told me they'd hidden stuff in a cave for the superintendent of the Messerschmitt factory, then sealed it up. The captain told me to take two or three jeeps and check it out. We took the factory superintendent with us to the cave and made him break through the wall. There was furniture, paintings, silverware, all pretty good stuff, but the Poles said they'd worked on a bigger tunnel.

We made the superintendent break through another wall. Sure enough, there was a box in there, full of German marks. Right out of the bank, whole packages of them. There must have been 20 packages about two inches thick. It was the Messerschmitt payroll.

We dropped the money off at battalion headquarters. We didn't think it was worth anything. But I heard later on that those marks were still of value. We could have sold them in Paris. [Nazi Reichsmarks remained the valid German currency until 1948. In 1945, they were also the valid Austrian currency.]

Chapter Twenty-nine

1. Smiertka's death was officially classified as "died of wounds."

2. All eyewitnesses agree that only one American was shot.

3. Higley kept a diary throughout the combat period. It provides valuable eyewitness testimony to many events.

Conclusion

1. Paul Fussell, *Thank God for the Atom Bomb* (New York: Ballantine Books, 1988).

Persons Interviewed

Barry, Dr. Richard: Clifton, New Jersey
Bergstrom, Kenneth: Elgin, Nebraska
Besenbeck, Elizabeth: Whiting, New Jersey
Best, June: Glendale (Queens), New York
Bornstein, Charles: Roslyn Heights, New York
Brennan, Robert and Lorraine: Euclid, Ohio
Byars, Vivian (Gist Reeder): Duncan, Oklahoma
Chance, Hugh and Dorothy: Jonesville, Virginia
Clark, John S.: Lugoff, South Carolina (deceased)
Conner, Betty (Phegley): Prairie du Rocher, Illinois
Crow, John Y.: Baltimore
Davison, Mary Belle: Texhoma, Oklahoma
Duckett, Lester (Doc): Wayne, Michigan
Duus, Martin: Wallingford, Pennsylvania
Egan, Mike: West Allis, Wisconsin
Ellis, Clifford and Jean: Emporia, Kansas
Engle, Mike, Jr.: Vicksburg, Mississippi
Fierman, Syd: Malvern, Pennyslvania
Fitzgibbons, Ed: Boxford, Massachusetts
Fontenot, Winfred L.: Lake Charles, Louisiana
Fussell, Paul: Philadelphia
Genovese, Robert: Van Nuys, California
Gibbs, Spilman and Helen: Riverside, New Jersey
Haveman, Gary: Fremont, Michigan
Higley, Daniel: Wilmington, Delaware
Howard, Claudia (Coleman): Wilson, North Carolina
Hundley, Oscar and Sunshine: Greensboro, North Carolina

Huskey, Moe and Kaye: Allen Park, Michigan
Kaiser, John J.: Towson, Maryland
Kania, Frank: Beverly, Massachusetts
Kelly, Dr. Thomas: Coquille, Oregon
Kleffman, the Reverend William: Omaha
Kopko, Marion: Queens, New York
LaVelle, John H.: Beloit, Wisconsin
Lawler, Dr. Robert E.: Oxnard, California
Lepley, Lorin: Galion, Ohio
Lowenberger, Leo: Port Washington, New York
Loyd, Robert: Columbus Junction, Iowa
Lyons, G. Robert: Bellefonte, Pennsylvania
McCarthy, James: Verona, New Jersey
Meadows, Joseph and Margaret: Bothell, Washington
Meredith, Robert and Veda: Elizabethton, Tennessee (Veda Meredith is deceased.)
Millek, Ray: Sterling Heights, Michigan (deceased)
Morris, J. J.: Littleton, Colorado
Motenko, Harold and Adele: Mission Viejo, California
Mysliwiec, Ray: Elk Grove Village, Illinois
Natta, Sam: St. Louis
Nichols, Dr. Carl G. and Mary Jane: Leland, Mississippi
Offerman, Ray: Detroit
Pearson, Richard and Selma: Piqua, Ohio
Phegley, Adrian: Tucson
Phegley, Michael: Florrisant, Missouri
Pointer, John: Semora, North Carolina
Rath, Russell (Rusty): Harvard, Nebraska
Reeder, A. J. (Jack): Duncan, Oklahoma (deceased)
Rucker, Clyde: Rancho Cordova, California
Schilling, Waltraut: Bayerniederhofen, Germany
Schroeder, Robert: Hunter, North Dakota
Scott, Terry and Vivian: Duluth, Minnesota
Seiler, Melvin and Lucille: St. Louis
Seward, John and Matilda: Johnson City, Tennessee
Shelley, Marvin and Laura: Scottsdale, Arizona

Skocz, Joseph: Crystal Lake, Illinois (deceased)
Steffen, the Reverend Richard: Stevens Point, Wisconsin
Tava, Ray: Grand Rapids, Michigan
Teague, James: Lubbock, Texas (deceased)
Timmons, Ralph: London Mills, Illinois
Torrance, A. J. and Ann: Warsaw, Virginia
Williams, G. Gardner: Arlington, Texas
Woodbeck, Orland (Woody) and Edna: Withee, Wisconsin
Woolery, Charles: Sedalia, Missouri
Woodside, John and Frances: Parsons, Tennessee
Young, Thomas; Bridge View, Illinois

Glossary

88: 88-millimeter German artillery, self-propelled guns, mounted on tanks, used as anti-aircraft. Highly accurate, much feared by American infantry.

ASTP: Army Specialized Training Program. Colleges throughout the country trained enlisted men as engineers, translators, meteorologists, and other professionals. Few ever graduated. The program was canceled in the spring of 1944, and nearly all ASTP enrollees were sent to the infantry.

BAR: Browning Automatic Rifle, World War I weapon widely used by U.S. Infantry in World War II.

boche: Slang term, primarily British and French, for German soldier.

bouncing betty: German antipersonnel mine.

burp gun: German machine pistol.

cadre: permanent personnel who trained recruits.

CO: Commanding officer.

CP: Command post.

DP: Displaced person. After the war in Europe, there were many refugees and people released from German concentration camps.

Easy: Phonetic name for E Company.

FO: Artillery forward observer, attached to every rifle company to provide close fire support.

Fox: Phonetic name for F Company.

G-2: Intelligence.

George: Phonetic name for G Company.

grease gun: American .45-caliber machine pistol.

GRO: Graves Registration Organization.

HE: High explosive.

Howe: Phonetic name for H Company.

K ration: Three meals a day, individually packaged in waterproof containers, designed to be carried by infantry.

LMG: light machine gun.

Luger: German officer's automatic pistol. Another German automatic, the P-38, was a much more common souvenir, but was not mentioned by anyone interviewed.

MG: machinegun.

million-dollar wound: A wound that took the soldier out of combat without injuring him seriously.

MLR: Main line of resistance, principal defense line.

MOS: Military job classification number. A rifleman's was MOS 745. In the Separation Qualification Record given to discharged soldiers, my marketable skills were described as follows: "Fired rifles, light machine guns, and rocket launchers. Cleaned and maintained equipment."

OD: Olive drab, the sickly green-brown color of American wool uniforms.

OPL: Outpost line, located in front of the MLR.

OCS: Officer Candidate School. Ninety days of intensive training at Ft. Benning, Georgia, produced most of the infantry's second lieutenants.

point(s): The system devised at the end of the European war to make discharge/continued service decisions equitable.

potato masher: German hand grenade that looked like a baton.

repple depple: Replacement Depot, where replacements were held until assigned to combat divisions.

R & R: Rest and recreation.

RTO: Return to Organization.

snafu: Situation normal, all fucked up.

shoepacs: Insulated, quasi-waterproof winter boots with rubber bottoms and felt sole inner liners.

six-by-six: Widely used six-wheeled army truck with six wheel drive.

Springfield '03: Standard American infantry rifle until replaced by the M-1. The '03 remained in use as a sniper rifle.

stalag: German POW camp.

TD: Tank destroyer, highly mobile artillery.

tigerman: German tank crewman.

UNRRA: United Nations Relief and Rehabilitation Administration.

USO: United Services Organization, quasi-private organization that ran service clubs and scheduled entertainers all over the world.

V mail: Airmail letter forms issued to overseas troops.

VE-day: Victory in Europe Day, officially 8 May 1945.

ZI: Zone of the Interior, meaning the United States.

Bibliography

Bacque, James. *Other Losses*. Toronto: Stoddart Publishing Co., 1989.

Baron, Richard, Maj. Richard Baum, and Richard Goldhurst. *Raid! The Untold Story of Patton's Secret Mission*. New York: G. P. Putnam's Sons, 1981.

Churchill, Sir Winston. *The Story of the Malakand Field Force*. London: Longmans, Green, 1898.

Department of the Army, U.S. Army Judiciary, Falls Church, Virginia. Various court-martial transcripts, 1945.

Foy, David A. *For You the War Is Over*. New York: Stein and Day, 1984.

Fussell, Paul. *The Great War and Modern Memory*. New York: Oxford University Press, 1975.

———. *Thank God for the Atom Bomb*. New York: Ballantine Books, 1988.

———. *Wartime. Understanding and Behavior in the Second World War*. New York and Oxford: Oxford University Press, 1989.

Hart, B. H. Liddell. *History of the Second World War*. New York: G. P. Putnam's Sons, 1970.

———. *Strategy*. 2d rev. ed. New York and Washington: Frederick A. Praeger, 1967.

Kerr, E. Bartlett. *Surrender and Survival*. New York: William Morrow and Co., 1985.

Leinbaugh, Harold P., and John D. Campbell. *The Men of Company K*. New York: William Morrow and Co., 1985.

Loesser, Frank. "What Do You Do in the Infantry? (You March, You March, You March)." New York: Frank Music Corp., 1943.

Mauldin, Bill. *Up Front*. New York: H. Holt Co., 1945.

Meltesen, Clarence R. *Roads to Liberation*. San Francisco: Oflag 64 Press, 1990.

Mueller, Ralph, and Jerry Turk. *Report After Action*. Innsbruck: 103d Infantry Division, 1945.

Meadows, 1st Lt. Joseph W. *Account of action of Second Battalion, 410th Infantry in ERKENBRECHTSWEILER, Germany on 22 and 23 April 1945*. Headquarters Second Battalion, 1945.

National Archives and Records Administration, Suitland Reference Branch, Washington, D.C. Various Second Battalion records. Declassified 1973 and 1987.

National Personnel Records Center, Military Personnel Records, St. Louis. Morning reports of Second Battalion.

Stanton, Shelby. *U.S. Army Order of Battle, World War II.* Novato, California: Presidio Press, 1984.

Stenger, Charles A. *American Prisoners of War in WW I, WW II, Korea and Vietnam.* Veterans Administration. Washington, D.C.: Government Printing Office, 1988.

Torrance, Maj. A. J. *SUBJECT: Account of actions of Second Battalion, 410th Infantry on 15 and 16 March 1945.* Headquarters Second Battalion, 1945.

United States Army in World War II, Office of the Chief of Military History. *The Last Offensive.* Washington, D.C.: Government Printing Office, 1972.

Veterans Administration, Office of Planning and Program Evaluation, *POW: Study of Former Prisoners of War*, Washington, D.C., 3rd printing, June 1983.

Whiting, Charles. *Death of a Division.* New York: Stein and Day, 1980.

Index

The Author

Richard M. Stannard was a rifleman in the Second Battalion's G Company. After the war, thanks to the GI Bill, he earned a journalism degree at Stanford and was a newspaper reporter in California for 14 years. He then served as a senatorial press secretary in Washington, D.C., before becoming a civil servant. In that role, he worked as an investigator/writer for the antipoverty program in Washington and Seattle while helping to raise his four children. Now retired, he lives in Seattle with his wife, Elaine, and granddaughter, Amber.